Candlemaking

For Fun & Profit™

Michelle Espino

PRIMA PUBLISHING

Published by Prima Publishing, Roseville, California. Member of the Crown Publishing Group, a division of Random House, Inc.

Random House, Inc. New York, Toronto, London, Sydney, Auckland

FOR FUN & PROFIT is a trademark of Random House, Inc.
PRIMA PUBLISHING and colophon are trademarks of Random House, Inc., registered with the United States Patent and Trademark Office.

Interior illustrations by Laurie Baker McNeile

Prima Publishing and the author hope that you enjoy the projects discussed in this book. While we believe the projects to be safe and fun if proper safety precautions are followed, all such projects are done at the reader's sole risk. Prima Publishing and the author cannot accept any responsibility or liability for any damages, loss, or injury arising from use, misuse, or misconception of the information provided in this book. In addition, business and legal information provided in this book is for reference purposes only, and is not intended to be legal or business advice. You should always consult a legal professional regarding the laws that may apply to your business.

Library of Congress Cataloging-in-Publication Data

Espino, Michelle.
    Candlemaking for fun & profit / Michelle Espino.
        p. cm. – (For fun & profit series)
    Includes index.
    ISBN 0-7615-2040-6
    1. Candlemaking. 2. Home-based businesses. I. Title: Candlemaking for fun and profit. II. Title. III. Series
TT896.5 .E68   2000
745.593'32--dc21

00-057999
CIP

01 02 03 04 II 10 9 8 7 6 5 4 3 2
Printed in the United States of America
First Edition

Visit us online at www.primapublishing.com

Contents

The FOR FUN & PROFIT™ Series

Introduction

SEVERAL YEARS AGO, A FRIEND showed me how to make my first candle. When I pulled it out of its mold, I realized my love for candlemaking. I was amazed at how easy it was to make that pretty purple candle, and I was determined to make more. Soon after that revelation, I converted my tiny kitchen into my first candlemaking studio. (I was in college back then, and I really didn't know how to cook food very well, so I was happy to find a purpose for my kitchen.)

Using only the instructions that came with my new candle molds, I made one candle after another, experimenting with all the colors, scents, and ingredients I could find. I discovered I had a passion for the candlemaking process and devoured every piece of related information I could get my hands on. Now I love getting away from my tech career as an information systems analyst by making candles as often as I can.

A Brief History of Candlemaking

Candlemaking was once a necessity. Before the advent of gas and electricity, people needed light to do things after the sun went down. Primitive lights were easily made out of strips of wood or dried plant stems dipped into grease or pine tar and lit. Torches and fire baskets also provided light for the earliest civilizations. Most early candles were made from tallow, a white, solid animal fat derived from sheep, pigs, and cows.

Beeswax, a huge improvement over tallow, was introduced to candlemaking in the Middle Ages. In thirteenth century Paris, the first guild of *chandlers* (the early word for candlemakers) went from house to house making candles. The fifteenth century saw the introduction of a mold suitable for casting candles. Tallow was the commoner's candle wax. Tallow candles were stinky, smoky, and left a greasy residue. Beeswax, on the other hand, was a sweet-smelling, slow-burning luxury wax obtained from the combs of the honeybee. An expensive commodity, beeswax candles were reserved only for religious activities, ceremonial purposes, and the most affluent of families.

Around the world, different societies tried diverse (and some peculiar) ways to obtain light. Oily fish, even fatty birds on sticks, were utilized as crude candles in some northern parts of the world. The Japanese tried boiling insects to obtain wax. American colonists learned that the waxy fruit of the bayberry bush produced green, woodsy-sweet scented candles, but it took too long to extract the wax from the berries to make them practical.

Major changes in candlemaking occurred with the growth of the whaling industry in the eighteenth century. Spermaceti, a wax crystallized from the oil of the sperm whale, became a common additive to tallow. Spermaceti wax reduced the stench of the tallow candle and made it harder and longer lasting.

Everyday kitchen candles were made by dipping several wicks draped over a stick into a large vat of tallow. Candlemaking was a necessary home craft until it became one of the first trades to industrialize due to the continual need for light.

The nineteenth century brought a series of milestones that spurred the mass production of candles:

1823—Stearin, a white, crystalline substance found in most animal and vegetable fats was isolated from tallow. The addition of extra stearin to tallow produced a less smoky, harder candle.

1825—A Frenchman developed the braided wick, which greatly increased the burning quality of candles.

1827—Another Frenchman pioneered the match, which shortened the time and effort of lighting candles.

1834—Joseph Morgan invented a candlemaking machine that could make 1,500 candles per hour.

1836—Palmatine, a palm oil derivative similar to stearin, was patented as a wax alternative.

1850—A breakthrough in candlemaking materialized with the development of commercial paraffin, a wax by-product of petroleum distillation. Paraffin was brighter, cleaner, and more longer burning than tallow.

Quality, affordable candles were finally achieved and easily mass-produced with the combination of the braided wick, paraffin, and stearin. This new golden era of candlemaking was short lived, however, as the need for candles faded after the arrival of kerosene lamps in 1857 and the introduction of the light bulb in 1879.

Now, candles have become popular pieces of home decoration in any style of modern living, as well as therapeutic devices for today's fast-paced, high-tech world. According to the National Candle Association, candles are used in seven out of ten households today. People enjoy the relaxing benefits of the soft glow of candlelight after a hard day's work, and scented candles have always been a popular medium for home aromatherapy and fragrance.

How to Use This Book

Whether you want to learn candlemaking as a hobby or for a source of income, you will find everything you need in this book to develop your skills. The goal of the first half of the book is to teach you candlemaking from a structural perspective and encourage you to develop your own candlemaking style. Trying the different candlemaking methods I cover is the best way to learn a wide range of techniques. This will allow you to discover all the concoctions of ingredients possible for a candle recipe and to create any type of candle, limited only by your imagination. The second half of this book comprises what you need to know to profit from your new skills, including pricing your work, advertising your business, and learning the basics of crafting as a business.

Even if you already have candlemaking experience, you will find this book a handy information reference and a great source for inspiring ideas to raise your craft to higher levels of challenge. At the end of this book is an extensive resource section, listing books, periodicals, suppliers, associations, and Web sites for candlemakers at all levels of expertise. My goal in writing this book is to provide you with a creative, exploratory approach to candlemaking. I hope you will enjoy it enough to make it your favorite craft. Good luck!

Basic Tools for Candlemaking

1 Tape
2 Additives
3 Measuring cups
4 Scissors
5 Pot holders
6 Wick

7 Melting pitcher
8 Double boiler
9 Aluminum foil
10 Wax paper
11 Wax paper cups
12 Candle mold

13 Scents
14 Color
15 Wax beads
16 Thermometer
17 Knitting needles
(for stirring)

18 Wick rod
19 Cutting knife
20 Mold sealer

Part One

For Fun

The Joy of Candlemaking

▼▼

THE VALUE OF CANDLEMAKING as a hobby today is that people love candles, and love giving them as gifts to friends, family, and themselves. In this age of mass production, it is a special gift to receive a unique, handcrafted candle that conveys the quality of its ingredients and the personality of its maker.

What I love about candlemaking is that practically anyone can do it! With a method for every level of skill and ability, candlemaking is an activity for people of all ages, from kids to seniors. If you can complete the most basic cooking recipe, you can make candles.

Imagine making a gift for a friend, choosing her favorite color as well as a scent to complement her favorite room in her house. Or having some of your best friends over and teaching them your great hobby. Whether you are making candles alone or with friends, the skills you need are basic enough that you can relax and enjoy your craft time. If you do happen to mess up, you can always melt down the error and start again!

Something from Nothing

Candlemaking incorporates basic skills with creative components to achieve a personalized, handmade product. It's easy to get hooked transforming some bulk wax into a magical, glowing treasure. Making a candle can be a relaxing, satisfying experience—hovering over melting wax, inhaling aromatic scent oils, and capturing your imagination in a gleaming candle is a great way to unwind.

Candlemaking Is a Piece of Cake

Actually, candlemaking is easier than baking a cake. In fact, I don't know of a simpler, more satisfying craft. Once you get the materials together and master the basic directions, you will be able to make a wide variety of candles just by tweaking a basic recipe. Whatever kind you decide to make, your foremost goal is to have fun while creating an attractive candle that burns well.

Candlemaking Methods

The different ways of making candles fall into three general methods of production:

1. **Dipping**
   Making candles by dipping involves dipping a wick in molten wax multiple times until the desired thickness of the candle is reached.

2. **Rolling**
   Making candles by rolling involves rolling a sheet of wax around a wick until the desired thickness of the candle is reached.

Ten Great Reasons to Make Candles

1. It's easy!
2. The feeling you get when you light the first candle made by your own hands is a pleasure all its own.
3. Getting started is inexpensive, and you can find a lot of the stuff you'll need right in your home.
4. It's a fun activity that you and your friends or kids can do to hang out together.
5. Handmade candles are great gifts!
6. You love candles anyway, and you're burning candles so fast you need something to do with all those leftover candle nubs.
7. You can stretch your candle dollar by making candles instead of buying them.
8. You can cultivate new friendships through a mutual love of candlemaking.
9. You can never have too many candles!
10. No one gains weight from enjoying your candle cooking!

3. Molding
   Making candles by molding involves melting and pouring wax to form a candle into a particular shape or container.

All candlemaking involves a variation of one or more of these three methods. While the processes of dipping and rolling candles are easily described, much practice is necessary to obtain good results. Candlemaking by molding is the most complex of the three methods. Since it is the one of greatest interest to most home candlemakers, I emphasize this technique in the projects I outline in this book. Preparing a mold or container, melting and pouring the wax, and producing a quality candle for display is the challenge of molded candlemaking. The following chapters give you all the information you need to get started, set up your workshop, and learn the basics of molded candlemaking through knowledge and practice.

Candle Decorating

Decorating involves the many types of surface techniques applied to a finished candle to render a particular appearance for display purposes. It is done after the candle is made, so decorating is not considered a candlemaking method. You can decorate candles created by any of the three methods described. Candle decorating is also outlined in chapter 4.

What if I Make a Mistake?

When I first began to make candles, I was regularly enlightened (no pun intended) by my mistakes. As a number of variables can affect a project, I discovered the importance of keeping my focus when mastering a new technique. A common mistake is a minor oversight in measurement. Sometimes it all turns out for the best, though. I would never have discovered how to make some of my best candles if it weren't for those little blunders. Fortunately, supplies aren't expensive and, if you do make a mistake, you can melt it down and try again. As with any craft, it is important not to get too frustrated when you are a beginner. Practice, practice, practice!

Handy Hint

Rotate candles after each burning to prevent uneven burning in drafts.

So Many Candles, So Many Possibilities

With so many varieties of candles available nowadays, it's helpful to know "candle lingo." Here's a descriptive list of common names for today's popular candle styles, which fall into five descriptive categories:

Candles by Substance

These candles are labeled according to the main composition of the candle mass:

Beaded/Wax Sand Candles: Containers of small beads of wax or sandlike granules of wax are considered candles, although it is not necessary to melt and pour the wax into the container. Candlemaking of this type is popular as it only requires filling a container with a positioned wick; heat and melting the wax are not involved in the process. You can also use wax beads and wax sand to refill a poured candle that no longer burns.

Beeswax Candles: Beeswax is a yellowish, natural waxy substance that honeybees secrete to build their honeycomb. Candles made primarily of beeswax are smokeless and have a faint to strong smell of honey.

Gel Candles: Gel candles are not made of wax. Instead, the fuel is a combination of common mineral oil and a patented gel resin. Gel candles are usually produced in transparent glass. Due to the gel's ability to contain a higher concentration of scent oil than wax candles, highly scented gel containers have become widely popular as a medium for strong home fragrance.

Oil Candles: An oil candle (better referred to as an oil lamp) is a container with a wick for burning oil or alcohol, usually in a tube-shaped glass.

Paraffin Candles: Paraffin is used to make most candles today. In its basic form, paraffin is a white, waxy, odorless by-product of petroleum distillation.

Candles by Shape

These candles are labeled according to their form:

Candle Gel

Believe the hype about gel candles. It's true, and as a result they are growing in popularity. Gel candlemaking is similar to traditional container candlemaking in that you have to liquefy the gel and pour it into a container, but it only takes a few hours for the gel to cool and be ready to burn. Candle gel can hold more scent and burn five to eight times longer than paraffin waxes. It can also be mixed or used in projects with wax to produce interesting effects.

Candle gel is composed of about 5% gellant and 95% mineral oil. Different manufacturers provide different grades and types of gel. Penreco holds a patent on this technology and is the manufacturer of Versagel, which comes premixed in three different blends that vary in thickness and fragrance retention. All are very clear gels and their solid form has a thick, rubbery feel. The following are the three types of Versagel.

Versagel LP: A low polymer gel suitable for clear candles with a low fragrance content up to 3%.

Block/Pillar Candles: "Block" and "pillar" are the traditional terms for any symmetrically shaped molded candle, although there are many symmetrical candles that are neither "block" nor "pillar" in shape. Today, you'll find star pillars, square obliques, octagon spirals, diamond tapers . . . the possibilities are endless! Typically, these candles are wide candles usually referred to by their diameter followed by their height (that is, a 4 x 6 candle is 4 inches in diameter and 6 inches tall).

Cake Candles/Country Candles: Cake candles, a.k.a. country candles, are shaped like small round cakes and decorated with wax whipped to look like frosty cake icing. These candles are usually colored and scented to simulate yummy food cakes without the fat!

Versagel MP: A medium polymer gel suitable for clear candles and medium fragrance content up to 5%.

Versagel HP: A high polymer gel suitable for candles with decorative embedments and fragrance content up to 5%.

Other manufacturers offer candle gel premixed with mineral oil or you can buy the gellant separately and mix it yourself. Gels that are premixed by a distributor or retailer and not by the manufacturer of the gellant vary in thickness and oil content. If you buy a premixed gel, look for firm gel that is not oily and that you cannot easily poke with your finger. If you choose to buy only the gellant and mix it with mineral oil on your own, ask the manufacturer or retailer about the characteristics of a well-made gel and for recommendations on preparing the gel formula. Mineral oil also comes in different quality grades, so ask what type is best suited for a particular gel product.

Container/Canister Candles: A container candle is wax poured into a container and intended for burning inside that container. There are countless containers suitable for candles; container candlemaking is a popular project for beginners because it does not require a special mold. The most popular containers are made of glass, ceramics, and metal. Canister candles are container candles with lids to cover the candle and preserve its scent when it's not in use.

Novelty Candles: Novelty candles have various asymmetrical shapes, and in many cases give the appearance of being something other than a candle. They may be decorated on the surface to look like a particular object or cast from a mold to replicate an object, such as a cut glass vase or a human statue. You can use any or a combination of the three basic candlemaking methods to make novelty candles.

Taper Candles: Taper candles are typically long, slender candles made to fit in a holder. Tapers can be poured, dipped, or rolled, but may not always taper (tapers decrease in breadth and thickness toward the wick end of the candle).

Candles by Usage

These candles are labeled according to their usage:

Birthday Candles: A favorite among children, birthday candles are small candles placed on birthday cakes for "making a wish" and blowing them out. Birthday candles used to be just short, skinny tapers. Now you can find all kinds of novelty candles suitable for birthday cakes.

Church Candles: Church candles are traditionally round pillar candles of different sizes used in religious rituals and made with a high concentration of beeswax. Church-type candles are popular in the home as well because of their simple, natural look and smokeless quality.

Dinner Candles: Dinner candles are traditionally tapers, but today, votive candles, tea lights, and other kinds are used at dinnertime. They are usually unscented so as not to interfere with the aromas of a meal.

Floating Candles: Although most candles can float, floating candles are made in special shapes to minimize water contact with the wick and keep it aflame while floating.

Garden/Outdoor Candles: Garden candles are utilized for outdoor purposes. Originally, the only kind in this category was container candles (usually called patio or lantern candles), but today it includes other types such as flares (torches) and citronella candles.

Holiday/Seasonal Candles: Holiday and seasonal candles of all types are used to celebrate a holiday or certain time of the year.

Hurricane Candles: Hurricane candles are not really candles, but a wide wax shell usually embedded with objects such as coffee beans or seashells that surround a votive or a tea light, similar to a hurricane lamp (the wax shell simulates the glass chimney of a hurricane lamp). They can also be wide candles made with a hard exterior wax shell inside which a votive or tea light can be placed once the inner wax has burned away.

Peg Candles: Peg candles are pillar candles specially shaped at the bottom to fit smaller taper holders. They are utilized for a longer burning time than that of standard tapers.

Tea Light Candles: Tea light candles are small utility candles, usually ¾ inches tall and contained in a metal cup. In the past, people mainly used tea lights to heat potpourri and foods, but today many decorative candleholders and lanterns are designed for tea lights because of their popularity as easily disposable, inexpensive candlelight.

Unity Candles: A unity candle is used during a wedding ceremony to symbolize the union of marriage. Typically, two taper candles, representing the couple as individuals, are used to light a large pillar candle (the unity candle) as a visible symbol of their commitment to each other. Unity candles are often ornate, heirloom-quality, and expensive.

Utility Candles: Utility candles are used to provide illumination or heat, or to light other candles or lamps. They are usually small, white, and unscented. Votives, tea lights, and emergency pillar candles available in grocery stores are common utility candles.

Votive Candles: Although the term "votive" may be used to describe any candle used as a vigil light, the term "votive" is most often used to describe pillar candles 2 inches by 2 inches, and smaller. Like tea lights, votives have also become popular sources of everyday home candlelight because of their versatile small size—you can use many of them without spending a fortune—and ability to provide scent and light unobtrusively in small areas, such as around a bathtub.

Candles by Technique

These candles are labeled according to the method used to make them:

Dip and Carve Candles: A dip and carve candle, or "cut and curl" candle, is a molded core pillar candle, often a star shape, dipped repeatedly into different colors of wax that is then cut and partly peeled away to show the colorful layers underneath. When lit, the flame burns the core candle down and illuminates the carvings from within. Like hurricane candles, when the core is burned hollow, you can refill dip and carve candles, or place a tea light inside the cavity to illuminate the design.

Ice Candles: Ice candles, an early favorite kitchen craft, are made by placing a core candle in a mold, filling the mold with ice, and then pouring melted wax into the mold. The wax melts the ice and hardens quickly, leaving interesting cavities in the molded shape of the outer candle.

Layered/Striped Candles: Layered or striped candles can be made in a variety of ways, but are typically created by pouring successive layers of colored wax into a mold.

> ## Did you know???
>
> The first candle mold was made of wood in fifteenth century Paris.

Sand Candles: Sand candles are made by making an impression in wet sand to serve as a mold. When wax is poured in the sand mold, a hard crust of wax and sand forms the candle surface.

Stained Glass/Millefiori Candles: Stained glass or millefiori candles have an outer coating of colored wax in a complex pattern of color that resembles millefiori, a type of stained glass. As the candle burns down, the flame illuminates the colored surface. As this is an advanced technique, stained glass candles are most often made by commercial candle manufacturers.

Twisted/Braided Candles: Twisted or braided candles are typically tapers twisted and flattened into spiral shapes or wound or braided around one or more other tapers while the candles are warm and pliable.

Candles by Ingredient

These candles are labeled according to particular ingredients incorporated in the making of the candle:

Aromatherapy Candles: Aromatherapy candles are made with fragrant oils from herbs, flowers, and other plants, and the scent is inhaled for its supposed therapeutic effects. The term "aromatherapy" has been loosely used in candle labeling to describe a candle scented with any type of fragrance that may stimulate aromatic recollections that arouse positive feelings.

Chunk Candles: Chunk candles are molded candles consisting of wax poured over small cut-up blocks of usually colored wax. The result is a variegated candle, decorated in the candlemaking process, rather than a standard candle with decorative items applied.

Ideas for Inspiration

Browse for candles and candle accessories when you shop to keep tabs on the candle marketplace and to jump-start some creative candle thinking.

If you see a candle you'd like to try to create, make a note of it or save a picture of it in an idea scrapbook.

In a creative rut? Switch gears and try something new. Try a different supplier and buy some new supplies. Take an artistic class, or just get away from that technique you've been perfecting and broaden your skill by attempting a different one.

Browse a craft store for possibilities on how to decorate candles.

Go online or read a book to do some candlemaking research. There are many other good references on the Web and in bookstores or libraries that cover various production and decoration techniques. On the Internet you'll find both helpful Web sites and lots of fellow candlemakers eager to share ideas and know-how.

Scented Candles: Scented candles, available in an endless variety of aromas, are by far the most popular type of candle. Votives, floaters, and containers are the most popular kinds of scented candles. They can be used to eliminate odors or simply fill an area with a pleasant fragrance.

Treasure Candles: Treasure candles are typically block candles embedded with small objects such as charms, trinkets, or lucky stones. As the candle burns down, it reveals its "buried treasures," presenting a memento of the candle (or the gift giver).

A Word to the Wise

Although you may be tempted to jump to the candle projects in chapter 5, I strongly encourage you to read the preparatory chapters first to gain an understanding of the materials used in the projects and to take the necessary safety precautions.

Also note that the candlemaking procedures I outline in this book are the accumulation of knowledge I obtained through many years of practice, experimentation, and reading about the craft. Although the basic candlemaking concepts are the same, my methods may differ from those you encounter in other resources. Since there is no longer formal training in candlemaking, it is for the most part a self-learned craft; so different candlemakers make similar candles in different ways. For this reason, I encourage you to read as much as you can about the craft to gain a well-rounded knowledge of candlemaking. With this knowledge and a bit of practice and patience, you'll be a great candlemaker in no time. Now it's time to get started!

> ## Did you know???
>
> Long ago, women used to put beeswax on their faces as a cosmetic. Often times, they would sit too close to the fire and the wax would melt. From this came the expression, "Mind your beeswax."

Getting Started

▼▼

YOUR NEXT STEP IN UNDERSTANDING candlemaking is to learn about the elements that make up a candle and the tools and supplies you'll need to get started. This chapter provides this introduction, as well as a reference on how to buy and choose your materials. You'll find a lot of information here, but don't feel the need to remember all of it! This chapter is a useful reference for creating your own candle recipes, so relax and read for knowledge and inspiration. All the how-tos on using the materials described in this chapter are outlined in chapter 4, and resources on where to buy these materials (through the mail or on the Internet) can be found in the Resources section at the end of this book.

Buying Equipment and Supplies

You'll find that you have most candlemaking equipment and supplies already in your home. For the items you don't have, don't feel that you have to buy everything new. You can save a lot of money by buying used items at a thrift shop or secondhand store. Just make sure the items you buy are clean and not rusty. If you buy a used heat source, make sure it's in good working condition. Don't use your favorite cooking pot or baking sheet because your candlemaking equipment must be used for candlemaking only. Since candle decorating materials vary widely by technique, some materials are listed and described in chapter 4 under each workspace area, and some are listed in chapter 5 within each project.

- **Additives:** The project instructions will specify what type(s) of additive(s) you need.

- **Aluminum foil/wax paper:** Use this to cover the pouring area. It is easy to peel off hardened wax on these materials. Heavy-duty aluminum foil works best.

- **Baking pans:** Depending on the project you're creating, you may need this to make small pieces of wax (chunks). Pans should be shallow.

- **Baking soda:** Use this as a wax fire extinguisher (never use water to extinguish a wax fire—this only spreads the flame).

- **Candle molds:** The project instructions will specify what type you need (metal, plastic, flexible, or other).

- **Color:** When choosing color, dyes specifically for candlemaking work best because the quality of color and amount used can affect the burning quality of the candle. If you choose crayons, use Crayolas—do not use cheap crayons—and only use crayons in small amounts for pastel colors (only ⅛ crayon per pound at most).

- **Double boiler:** The best heating method for beginners; an alternative to the direct-heat method.

- **Exacto knife:** Any smooth-edged knife will work—this is for cleaning seam lines.

- **Griddle pan or pot:** Use this to level your candle off—make sure you use something small, flat, and easy to clean.

- **Heat source:** This will most likely be your stovetop burner. The burner you choose must be able to boil water well, with temperature control. If you're using a portable burner, keep it in a safe place where electrical cords are not in the way. Smooth-surface burners work better than heat coils because they're easier to clean.

- **Measuring spoons:** Use these to measure your additives. The most commonly used sizes are ½ teaspoon, 1 teaspoon, and 1 tablespoon.

- **Melting pitcher:** A stainless steel melting pitcher with a pouring lip and handle works best.

- **Mold sealer:** Use this to seal the wick hole in most molds. If you can't find an actual candle mold sealer, white poster putty works well (white won't discolor the wick).

- **Mold stands:** Depending on what you're working on, you may need this for your mold. The project instructions will specify whether or not you need this.

- **Pantyhose:** These work well for buffing to remove fingerprints and surface "imperfections."

- **Paper towels:** These are good to have on hand for cleaning up melted wax in pitchers quickly.

- **Potholders:** Necessary when handling hot pitchers of wax and when using the double boiler.

- **Scent:** This can be any oil-based fragrance (perfumes, natural or essential oils, potpourri refresher oils, or aromatherapy blends). Many oils not specifically made for candlemaking may have a strong scent when the candle is freshly made, but they tend to slowly lose their scent. Scents specifically made for candlemaking hold the scent best over time.

- **Scissors:** You definitely need these to cut your wick, but they may come in handy for other candlemaking tasks also.

- **Skewers:** Wooden skewers or metal knitting needles are used to stir and poke the well. (Heavy-duty skewers work best.)

- **Tape:** Use this to tape the wick to plastic molds.

- **Thermometer:** Choose a candy thermometer that reaches 400 degrees Fahrenheit. A thermometer is essential to good candlemaking, since pouring time is very dependent on temperature. These are available at supermarkets or where cooking supplies are sold.

- **Unserrated knife:** Use this to slice wax into chunks.

- **Water bath and mold weights:** Some candle projects require a water bath to cool a candle and produce a smooth, glossy finish. A water bath can be a pail, dipping can, garbage basket, or any tall can able to hold water up to the height of the candle. A weight (a brick, heavy rock, or any dense object) is sometimes needed to keep the mold in place.

- **Wax paper cups:** Pour extra wax into these cups to reserve for filling in holes, or to test your color shade before using it (Dixie cups or larger). They're also useful when storing unused colored/scented wax in small amounts for later use.

- **Wick:** The project instructions will specify what type you need; make sure it is primed (if required) and properly sized for the candle.

- **Wick rod:** Any small rod strong enough to hold the wick when the wick is tied to it in mold setups (pencils, small skewers, and strong wire rods are examples of improvised wick rods).

The Elements of a Candle

The basic elements of a candle are the fuel for the flame and a wick to burn the fuel. Candle fuels are either wax or gel substances. (See the sidebar, Candle Gel, on page 8 for more information about gel candles.) Other elements are scent, color, and wax additives that enhance a candle's appearance and burning qualities.

Wax

Wax is the most common substance used for candlemaking today, and there are many kinds of wax available. Different waxes have different burning properties, so it is essential to know these differences when choosing a wax for a project. Most waxes are not normally used in their pure form for candlemaking, but are blended with additives to render a particular effect to the candle, such as hardness, color, and scent. A term you will see often in reference to wax is "shrinkage." This phenomenon occurs as a hole or cavity after you pour a candle around the wick when the wax molecules cool from their heated, excited state and settle down to a more compact solid. You must refill these holes with successive wax pouring until the surface is level. As wax with shrinkage requires extra effort when pouring, candlemakers usually look for a wax with as little shrinkage as possible, especially when making container candles.

The following are different kinds of wax used in candlemaking.

Paraffin

Paraffin is a petroleum by-product. It comes in different grades classified by its melting point (MP), the temperature at which the wax changes from a solid to a liquid. Paraffin suitable for candlemaking is further classified into low MP, medium MP, and high MP grades.

Low MP Paraffin

Low MP paraffin has a melting point of 130 degrees Fahrenheit and lower. If the wax is not fully refined, it may be oily and will melt before it burns. It is a soft wax, so it does not mold well and is best suited for making container candles.

Medium MP Paraffin

Paraffin with a melting point between 130 and 145 degrees Fahrenheit is best suited for molded candles. It is a good general-purpose candlemaking wax and is the paraffin widely carried by craft stores that sell candlemaking supplies.

High MP Paraffin

Paraffin with a melting point of 145 to 150 degrees Fahrenheit is best suited for tapers, dip and carve candles, and hurricane shells. Because a lower MP wax would possibly make your candle drip, the higher MP wax results in a longer-lasting candle.

Soy Wax

Soy wax is a plant-derived natural wax made of a blend of botanical oils in a soybean base. It has very little shrinkage and is available in container, pillar/votive, and novelty blends. This wax is a great alternative to paraffin as an economical, all-natural source of quality wax. Generally, soy waxes cool faster than paraffin, require no additives, and are self-releasing. As soy is a botanical wax, it holds and accepts essential oils better than paraffin does. Soy waxes range in melting points from 120 to 180 degrees Fahrenheit, varying by manufacturer and wax blend. Soy wax is becoming more popular, but right now is not easy to find outside of wholesale stores. Until it becomes more popular and is more commonly sold by major candle-making suppliers, you may need to order it online or use an alternative. (The projects in chapter 5 offer alternatives to soy wax.)

Beeswax

Beeswax is a natural wax secreted by honeybees. It is popular because of its smokeless quality, sweet honey scent, and slow burn rate. Beeswax has very little shrinkage and, as an additive, helps in any amount to increase burning time. It is rather sticky and a pure beeswax candle does not release well from a mold. It can be bought unfiltered (a muddy, dark gold color), filtered (honey-yellow), and both filtered and bleached (white). Beeswax is available in bags of small beads, pound increments, and smooth or honeycombed sheet form for rolling. It has a melting point of about 150 degrees Fahrenheit and is quite expensive compared to paraffin and soy wax prices.

Did you know???

Though beeswax physically resembles other waxes, it is entirely different in its chemistry and molecular characteristics.

Bayberry Wax

Bayberry wax is obtained by boiling the berries of bayberry shrubs. It is sage green, has a woodsy-sweet scent, and smells better with age. It is rather brittle, and has a melting point of around 118 degrees Fahrenheit. Bayberry wax is even more expensive than beeswax due to the fact that it takes 15 pounds of berries to produce one pound of wax. It is sometimes used to make authentic, period-style candles.

Tallow

Tallow is an almost colorless and tasteless solid fat extracted from the natural fat of cattle, sheep, and pigs. A soft wax, it is best used for container candlemaking, if used at all. Depending on the tallow

▼▼

The Latest and Greatest Advance in Candlemaking: Vegetable-based Soy Wax

I think it is important to highlight the benefits of soy wax for candlemaking, since this wax is relatively new and few candlemakers know the advantage of using soy wax over petroleum-based wax. Many consumers today are looking for more socially responsible and safer candle products, and soy wax contributes immensely to this challenge to manufacturers. Special thanks goes to Nature's Gifts and Heartland Candleworks, the inventors and manufacturers of today's popular soy wax blends. These companies generously contributed to the soy wax information in this book (see Resources for contact information).

The Benefits of Soy Wax

- Soy wax burns cleaner than paraffin, with reduced carbon buildup and no petroleum soot emissions.

- While beeswax also burns cleanly, it can cost six to eight times as much as paraffin. Soy wax burns cleaner than beeswax, is cost competitive with paraffin, and can be used in any type of candlemaking.

- Soy wax is cost effective, requiring no additives except scent and color, if desired.

▲▲

source, tallow candles may burn smoky and stinky. Tallow is used to make authentic, period-style candles.

Other Vegetable Waxes

Many varieties of plants from all over the world contain waxy substances that can be extracted for candlemaking. While extraction costs may prohibit their use as the main source of fuel for a candle, they can be used as additives to improve the quality of a candle

- Soy wax burns longer than paraffin.

- Soy wax produces no bubbles when poured, requiring no mold tapping.

- Soy wax, with a thick, Chapstick-like consistency, is easy to work with and gentle on the hands, actually leaving them smooth and soft.

- Seam and base trimming, and carving with soy wax are smooth and gentle.

- Scents that can be used in soapmaking can also be used in soy waxes, allowing scent-matched candle and soap sets.

- Soy wax cools faster than paraffin, requiring less wait between candle batches.

- Soy wax is environmentally friendly. It is completely biodegradable and water soluble, allowing it to be easily extracted from glass, tin, and other material for recycling.

- Soy wax in its pure form is edible and can even be used to sauté vegetables.

- Use of soybean wax creates important economic growth for the farming industry in the United States, and promotes economic diversity by drawing raw materials from multiple, renewable sources.

- Soy wax candles made with all-natural wicks, scent, and color can meet vegan criteria.

recipe. Consult a candlemaking specialty merchant or look up "wax" in industry reference guides such as the Thomas Register of American Manufacturers. (See Resources for more information on how to obtain these waxes.) While these vegetable waxes originate as natural substances, they may be further refined by various processes necessary for other applications that may add impurities to the wax. Always explain the purpose for which you are going to use the wax and request a type and grade suitable for candlemaking.

Base Ingredients at a Glance

Paraffin: Most common candlemaking substance

Soy wax: An all-natural alternative to paraffin

Beeswax: Used for natural scent and color—used also as an additive

Bayberry wax: Natural wax for authentic, colonial period-style candles

Tallow: Wax used for authentic, period-style candles

Other vegetable waxes: Used to improve the quality of a candle recipe

Wax blends: Wax used for containers, pillars/votives, and mottling

Candle gel: Clear substance, good for strong scents

Carnauba Wax

Extracted from a Brazilian palm tree, this is a hard wax that can be used to raise a candle's melting point. Other waxes extracted from South American palms, such as ouricury wax, possess similar properties.

Wax Blends

Some wax sold in craft stores is actually a blend of different types of wax and sometimes wax additives, specially formulated for use in certain types of candle molds or for achieving a particular candle appearance. Common blends are container waxes, pillar/votive waxes, and mottling waxes.

Container Waxes

Container waxes are super-soft blends specifically suited for filling a container with as little shrinkage as possible. Some retailers sell "one-pour" container blends that have no shrinkage and under certain conditions do not require additional pourings. Container blends can hold more fragrance if formulated with a higher oil content.

Pillar/Votive Wax

Pillar/votive wax blends are usually paraffin mixed with stearic acid to increase hardness and vybar to increase its ability to hold fragrance (see sidebar, Additives at a Glance, on page 30). A common melting point for this blend is 145 degrees Fahrenheit.

Mottling Wax

Mottling wax is a paraffin blend with additives that render a marble, bubbly, or frothy look to the wax, depending on the manufacturer's definition of "mottling." It is sold in different blends suitable for container candles or molded candles.

Buying Wax

All of the waxes I discuss above can be purchased from specialty candlemaking suppliers via the Internet or mail order, while most local craft stores only carry a few types of wax. This is because to buy wax for resale at reasonable retail prices requires a large-quantity wholesale purchase, which can be very expensive to ship. As a result, many craft stores stock a general-purpose paraffin (MP around 140 degrees Fahrenheit) sold in 10- to 11-pound slabs, a votive/pillar wax blend, and/or beeswax (because of its general craft use).

Pure paraffin is available in bags of small beads, pound boxes, 10- to 11-pound slabs, and 55- to 60-pound cases. Beaded paraffin is easiest to use and measure. A 10-pound slab of wax may seem like a lot, but you'll use it quickly, especially if you're dipping tall candles.

Grocery store paraffin, sold in pound boxes, can be used for candlemaking, but it is a low MP paraffin with which hardening additives are necessary in order to use it for molded candlemaking.

If you're lucky, you may be able to find a petroleum oil distributor in your area who can order candlemaking quality paraffin for you. You will have to buy it in at least 55- to 60-pound cases, but it may be cheaper to do so since you can pick it up instead of paying for shipping.

Avoid waxes that are discolored, look really bubbly, or feel oily, even if they are really inexpensive. These scale waxes are not refined enough for candlemaking, and will not produce quality candles.

Wax Additives

How do you want your candle to look and burn? Additives can give a candle a particular appearance (such as making it glow) and improve its burning qualities, as well as help you in the candlemaking process.

Different additive manufacturers may have different names for the same additive. Likewise, the same name from different manufacturers may actually be different substances that render similar effects. Regardless of the additive name, always read the package to determine if the additive is what you need for your candle project. Look for the melting point of the additive. If you're making a container candle, for example, you don't want to add an additive with a higher melting point than your container wax, because you want as soft a wax as possible for container candles. Also, keep in mind that the melting point for each of the following common additives is approximate—it may vary by manufacturer.

Stearic Acid

This is used to make candles harder and prevent them from losing their shape in hot weather. Stearic acid does not raise the melting point of wax, but does make a candle harder and stronger and therefore longer burning. Stearic acid makes colors pastel and creamy, and gives wax a soapy feel. Stearic acid may also make colors fade more quickly, so a color fade inhibitor additive is recommended with its use. Recommended use for stearic acid ranges from 2 to 9 tablespoons per pound of wax. If you're conscious about using animal by-products in your candles, make sure the stearic acid you buy is of the vegetable kind, derived from palm oil instead of animal fats. Stearic acid has a melting point of 160 degrees Fahrenheit.

Translucent or Clear Additives

These additives don't make wax transparent, but they definitely aid in making candles such as hurricanes glow while they burn. This additive is also good for highlighting embedded objects in your candles. Due to its high melting point, it also makes wax hard and longer burning. Colors become more vivid and the wax glossy. Recommended usage is 1 teaspoon per pound of wax. These additives have a melting point of 215 degrees Fahrenheit (may vary slightly depending on manufacturer).

Luster Additives

Luster additives are similar to clear additives except that they make the wax opaque instead of clear; they produce good white candles. Both clear and luster additives are man-made microcrystalline (highly refined) waxes that thicken wax and produce a small flame and less smoke. Different luster additives affect color and opaqueness differently. Recommended usage is 1 to 2 teaspoons per pound of wax. Luster additives have a melting point of 200 to 215 degrees Fahrenheit.

> **Handy Hint**
>
> Don't use too much translucent or luster additive in your wax, or your candle flame will be too small because the wax is too thick.

Additives at a Glance

Stearic acid: Makes candles harder and stronger

Clear/translucent additives: Make candles more translucent and wax thicker

Luster additives: Make candles opaque and wax thicker

Hot melt glue sticks: Make colors vivid and wax stronger

Vybar: Increases the ability of wax to hold more scent

Ultraviolet (UV) light absorbers: Prevent fading in candles

Clear Hot Melt Glue Sticks

These sticks, a common item in craft stores, are another additive you can use, especially if you cannot find any of the aforementioned additives. Hot melt glue sticks are similar to luster additives in character and make a strong candle with vivid colors. Recommended usage is one part to ten parts wax. Melting point may vary.

Vybar

Vybar enhances color and increases the ability of wax to hold more oil. It comes in two varieties: one for containers, with a MP of 130 degrees Fahrenheit; and another for molded candles, with a MP of 160 degrees Fahrenheit. Recommended usage is 1 to 2 teaspoons per pound of wax when adding fragrance oils.

Ultraviolet (UV) Light Absorbers

UV light absorbers prevent fading in candles. These substances are highly concentrated and only ½ teaspoon of the additive is needed for 10 pounds of wax.

Candle Scents

A candle scent can be any oil-based fragrance as long as it is water and alcohol free, but the best scents to use are those specifically made for candlemaking. Try not to use scented oils that are added to a carrier base, such as scented massage oils. The additional oil brings unnecessary additives to your wax and affects the burning quality, although careful experimentation can result in an acceptable balance between good burning quality and an interesting candle appearance. You'll have to experiment to find the right scent and quantity of scent for your candle batches. Some scents, especially some non-artificial essential oils (pure natural oils derived from plants), can smell different, even unpleasant, when heated or overheated.

Scents for candlemaking come in oils, or preblended with a little wax as scent chips. Keep in mind when buying a scent that packaging it in a glass bottle is the best way to preserve the scent's quality over time; scent degradation occurs more quickly in plastic bottles. Fragrance can be the most expensive ingredient in a candle, so make practical decisions when purchasing a scent. Typical scent amounts for candlemaking range from ½ ounce to 1 ounce per pound of wax.

If you're a beginner and want to use essential oils, first try a single inexpensive oil or a simple blend to experiment with the proportion you should use in your candle recipe to obtain a satisfactory scent strength. When you're comfortable with the strength of the aroma, move on and try a more complex or pricier scent blend. Given the expense, I suggest shopping for essential oils carefully and buying as high a quality as you can afford.

> **Handy Hint**
>
> Some people have allergies to particular scents. Experiment with samples or small bottles of scent before buying in quantity.

Candle Color

It is best to use dyes specifically for candlemaking, as the type of color and the amount used can affect the burning quality of a candle. Dyes made specifically for candlemaking come in powder, liquid, and chip form, and color wax evenly throughout a candle. Fluorescent pigment dyes are also available for candle dipping. These are oil-soluble dyes. Any oil-soluble dye can be used to color candles, but exercise care when using any dye not specifically made for candlemaking because additives to the dye might not blend well with wax and can affect burning quality. If you're going to use non-candlemaking dyes, it is best to use them in minute amounts or as surface decorating materials. Use crayons, for example, only in small amounts (about an eighth of a crayon per pound of wax) for pastel colors or for tweaking a light color to get a particular shade.

Liquid and powder candlemaking dyes are extremely concentrated—a drop or a pinch of these dyes can color many pounds of wax at a time. Powder dyes can be messy and hard to measure. You can also use natural dyes as long as they are water soluble, and water and alcohol free.

Candle Wicking

There are five types of wicking specifically designed for candlemaking—flat braid, square braid, zinc core (metal core wick for containers), paper core (paper core wick for containers), and cotton core (natural core wick for containers). Each comes in different plies ("ply" specifies the number of threads) of small, medium, large, and extra large, but the sizes may vary by manufacturer. Wicks can also be bought primed (predipped in wax) or unprimed. A primed wick improves the burning quality of the wick and prevents air bubbles from sticking to it during pouring.

Flat Braid Wicks

Old-fashioned flat braid cotton wicks are good for tapers, nonsymmetrical candles, and novelty candles. This kind of wick tends to

▼▼

Wicking at a Glance

Flat braid wicks: Wicks that bend while burning

Square braid wicks: Wicks that stay upright while burning

Core wicks: Wicks with built-in support for burning in soft wax

▲▲

fold over to aid in burning; without proper trimming, it can drown itself out. Flat braid wicks are identified by the total number of threads of string making up the wick. For example, a 15-ply wick contains three strands of five threads each, for a total of 15 threads.

Square Braid Wicks

A square braid wick is woven tighter than a flat braid wick. It stands upright and burns evenly. Although mainly used for symmetrical candles, it is a good all-purpose cotton wick. It comes in numbered sizes from 1 to 6. The lower the number, the smaller the wick.

Core Wicks

A core wick is a square braid wick with a core that supports the wick in soft wax so that it stands straight. The core is made of zinc, paper, or cotton. It is possible to obtain wicking with a lead core, but you should not use this type for candlemaking due to lead toxicity issues. In 1974, most U.S. candle manufacturers voluntarily agreed to stop using lead in wicks, but some candles made in the U.S. or made in other countries and sold in the U.S. still may have lead core wicks.

The majority of wicks manufactured today in the U.S. are made of cotton; those wicks with metal cores are typically zinc core wicks and pose no known health risk when burned properly. Zinc core wicks are the easiest to use, and burn as well as paper and cotton, but consumers who don't know the difference may confuse the zinc core with the lead core. If you choose to use core wicks, make sure you find out the content of the core and inform your customers of the difference.

Candle Molds

There are so many molds out there to choose from. You can buy professional candlemaking molds, investigate improvised molds, or even make your own molds (just another craft to explore!). Your collection of molds will comprise the main long-term assets of your workshop, so choose them carefully for quality and take care of them.

Metal Molds

Metal molds are the most widely used professional-quality molds today, and with proper care can last a lifetime. I still use the metal molds I bought 9 years ago! Most metal molds are slightly tapered to ensure easy removal of the candle from the mold. They come in a variety of symmetrical shapes and can produce an unlimited number of candles. Metal molds can also withstand high heat and the mistakes of beginning candlemakers.

What to look for in a metal mold:

- The metal should be heavy and durable.

- Tall molds should have a wide base plate to help prevent the mold from tipping over.

- Metal molds are available with or without seams. Seamless molds are usually more expensive, but, depending on the manufacturer and mold shape, the seam may be unnoticeable and may not need trimming.

You can buy a metal mold from some companies complete with the following necessary items:

- A wick rod to position the wick within the mold. (This can be any rod like a pencil, skewer, or knitting needle.)

- A wick screw to hold the wick in place and plug the wick entrance to the mold. This screw is actually a small Phillips or flathead screw; some merchants provide rubber plugs instead.

- Mold sealer to cover the wick screw and prevent leakage. You'll need to replace mold sealer periodically. I've found that white poster putty (an adhesive used to hang things on a wall without nails or tacks) works well for this purpose.

- Some retailers include a few feet of wick of the recommended size with each mold. Use the suggested size until you are comfortable with moving up or down a size to modify your recipes.

Caring for Metal Molds

- Never scratch or dig at the inside of the mold.
- Never hit the outside or bang it on the floor or a table to remove a candle. Dented molds make dented candles.
- Make a hot candle (230 degrees Fahrenheit) in the mold to clean out interior wax buildup.

Plastic Molds

Plastic molds come in a variety of novelty shapes and are made by forming plastic around an object. Due to the irregularity of novelty shapes, plastic molds come in two pieces and are held together by a groove that locks the two halves together or by clamps fitted along the sides of the mold, depending on the manufacturer. You position the mold in a special stand to keep it upright for pouring. Plastic molds can produce many candles if you treat them gently and make sure not to pour wax that is too hot. Eventually, they will need to be replaced by fresh molds, but plastic molds are relatively inexpensive.

What to look for in a plastic mold: Thick, sturdy-walled plastic with no visible weak points (white areas along the candle seams and around any undercuts).

Don't forget to buy the stand and clamps that the manufacturer recommends for its plastic mold. Improvising the stand and clamps is quite tricky, and may cause you much leakage and frustration.

Acrylic Molds

Like metal molds, acrylic molds come in a variety of symmetrical shapes, but have advantages over them. Acrylic molds are always seamless and can be handled when filled with hot wax without danger to your hands. They are also clear, which is a great tool for embedding objects in candles in just the right place. I like them because you don't have to wait until you pull out the candle from the mold to see what the candle will look like! Most acrylic shapes are round, square, and hexagonal; interesting shapes like stars are hard to find. What to look for in an acrylic mold: Ensure that there are no visible cracks or scratches on the interior of the mold, especially around the mold base, which will be the top of your candle.

Polycarbonate Molds

Polycarbonate molds are easy to use, but don't confuse polycarbonate molds with acrylic molds! Due to their clear walls and symmetrical shapes, they may look acrylic, but are actually made of a rigid plastic that does not withstand the high pouring temperatures that acrylic molds can. Polycarbonate molds have vertical support columns instead of wide mold bases, so these molds can be tipped over easily. They do come in interesting shapes such as cones, spheres, and pyramids, and are less expensive than acrylic molds. What to look for in a polycarbonate mold: Ensure that there are no visible cracks or scratches on the interior of the mold, especially around the mold base, which will be the top of your candle.

Flexible Molds

Flexible molds are made of materials such as rubber or PVC (polyvinyl chloride). These molds come in a variety of novelty shapes and are best for shapes that have finely detailed surfaces in relief. Candles may be difficult to remove from new flexible molds, but the molds stretch with use. What to look for: Thick mold walls are best, and scrutinize any deep undercuts for possible holes; small holes are difficult to see in flexible molds until wax starts leaking from one!

Plastic Floater Molds

Plastic floater molds come in one or two pieces, depending on the candle shape. These novelty molds are shaped specifically to minimize water contact with the wick and keep it aflame while floating. If the candle is a small floater, you can find two to six floater molds on a single sheet.

Glass Molds

Professional tempered-glass molds are cylindrical in shape and have pointed tops. They are fragile; you need to treat them with great care to make them last. They are hard to find in the United States, but are more available in the European community.

Improvised Molds

Improvised molds are any heat-tolerant item you can imagine that will allow you to remove the candle from the candle mold or break the mold away from the candle, if it is of a disposable kind. The opening of the mold must be its largest part. Depending on the type of mold, you may need a mold-releasing agent (see pages 39 and 51) to help prevent sticking. Here's a short list of household items you can use as improvised candle molds:

- Paper cups and cones

- Metal or plastic kitchen molds: Jell-O molds, cornbread pans, muffin tins, pie and cake dishes, ice trays, and bread molds

- Milk cartons or similar containers

- Plastic egg halves

- Small bowls and glasses

Did you know???

The tradition of Christmas lights dates back to the day when Christians were persecuted for saying Mass. A simple candle in the window would let other Christians know that Mass would be celebrated there that night.

Candle Containers

Candle containers must be heat-tolerant containers (clay, glass, metal, etc.). Generally, if it can stand boiling water, it should be alright. Woods and plastics are generally not a good idea. If the con-

Molds at a Glance

Metal: Symmetrically shaped molds

Plastic (acrylic, polycarbonate): Novelty shapes

Flexible: Seamless novelty shapes with fine detail

Plastic floater: Novelty molds shaped specifically to minimize water contact with the wick and keep it aflame while floating

Glass: Cylindrical-shaped molds with pointed tops

Improvised: Molds of all kinds of shapes—anything that can stand up to the heat

tainer is made out of a porous material such as a terracotta flower-pot, it must be sealed to prevent seepage. Candle containers must also have a mouth opening at least 2 to 3 inches wide to allow the candle to burn well. Again, use your imagination!

Other Candlemaking Materials

Releasing Agents: Releasing agents are various substances that help prevent the candle from sticking in the mold. They can be added to the wax as a powder or sprayed into the mold before pouring.

Dipping Rings or Frames: These dipping contraptions allow you to make many hand-dipped taper pairs connected together at the wick. Dipping candles one at a time can be time consuming, so making many at once saves a lot of time.

Wick Clips: Wick clips are small square or round metal tabs with a hole in the center used to support and hold the wick in place in containers, votives, and tea lights.

Candle Decorating Materials

With the variety of crafts that can be utilized in decorating candles, a supply list could go on forever.

Commonly used decorating items:

Acrylic paints and paintbrushes

Decorative glues

Découpage supplies

Dried or pressed flowers

Gold leaf or foil

Raffia

Rub-on or water-based transfers

Seashells or decorative stones

Candle Glaze: Candle glazes are various finishes that may be applied to candles by brushing, overdipping, or spraying. These glazes give a candle a shiny, lustrous surface and a protective coating.

Insert Plugs: These plugs, available in votive and tea light sizes, are inserted instead of a wick in the mold prior to pouring. This produces a candle with a cavity at the top so the candle can serve as a votive or tea light container, allowing you to use the "candle" without burning it down or messing up any surface decorations.

Metal Core Inserts: These inserts are metal cylinders sized to fit various mold widths. The cylinder is placed inside the

Stencils

Stickers

Wax appliqués, appliqué molds, and shape cutters

Waxy Rub'n'Buff, colored buffing wax

Useful equipment for candle decorating:

Propane torch for marbling color or applying texture

Squeeze pen: a simple device similar to a dropper for painting and drawing with melted wax

Wax melter palette: a heatable tray with small containers to hold different colors or blends of wax for wax painting

Linoleum cutting tool for incising

mold, and the cavity between the mold wall and the cylinder can then be filled with objects and wax to form a hurricane shell.

Mold Handles: This is a sturdy wire apparatus that fits around a metal mold so you can safely transport it when the mold is filled with hot wax. A handle is especially useful when you need to place a mold in a water bath.

Buying Supplies on the Internet

Shopping for candlemaking supplies can be as easy as getting on the Internet, but every e-commerce site involves a different way of getting around the site and of purchasing. It's easy to get confused and frustrated. Here are some handy guidelines to keep in mind to help online shopping be a safe and enjoyable experience.

If a supply item's description is unclear, e-mail or call the company and ask a sales representative to explain the item further. A sales rep should be knowledgeable enough to tell you specifics, such as a mold's capacity and recommended wick size, or an ingredient's melting point and recommendations for usage. A good candlemaking supply site will also provide technical support for using their products.

If you can't find a particular item, that doesn't necessarily mean that a company doesn't carry it. Sometimes companies only advertise their most popular items on their Web sites. Also, an item search engine on a merchant site may not give accurate search results if it does not understand your search criteria. Finally, a company may have the item, but call it something completely different from the name you're using. If you can't find what you're looking for, contact the company to inquire about it. Request a full printed catalog as well (some companies may not have a catalog).

Shop different Web sites and check to see how far the physical location of their shipping site is from you. A company closer to you can save you money on shipping, which can add up if you have to purchase heavy wax.

If you haven't purchased from a Web site before, first buy a few inexpensive items from a reputable retailer. You'll want to see how good their service is before buying from them in quantity.

Look for security guarantees in regard to order processing. Don't shop at stores that don't feature online shopping security. A Web form that you fill out and e-mail is NOT always completely secure, so never include your credit card information on such a form. A reputable store will prompt you with security information before ordering, and your Web browser will indicate if the store has the security

Temperature Tools

The most important factor when working with wax is temperature! If you're interested in using heat to decorate candle surfaces, use these heating tools:

Propane torch

Woodburning tool

Soldering iron or gun

Heated metal objects, such as utensils, and others with interesting textures

features in place. A good merchant site will e-mail you a confirmation with the details of your purchase almost immediately after the order is processed, and periodically update you as to your order status.

Use a credit card when shopping online. It is the best way to track an order down and get your money back if you need to do so.

Write down contact information for the merchant. Web site address, a physical address, and a customer service number are useful when you need to inquire about your order.

Once you've found a merchant you're comfortable with, you'll want to reorder from that company when you need more supplies. Remember that the same type of wax and additives from different companies may slightly vary, and using different brands will affect your recipe.

Conclusion

This chapter introduced you to the basic ingredients of a candle and the materials needed for candlemaking. You've learned a lot so far, and this knowledge will help you greatly when buying candle-making items and creating your candle recipes. The next chapter will familiarize you with the environment, equipment, and supplies needed to set up a candlemaking workshop at home.

chapter 3

Setting Up Your Personal Workspace

▼▼

WHEN I TAUGHT MYSELF how to make candles, I used my kitchen. I lived by myself at the time, so it was easy for me to transform my food kitchen into a candlemaking kitchen without worrying about being in anyone's way except my own. When I started to teach my friend Katie how to make candles, we chose to situate our workshop in the old-fashioned wooden storage shed in her backyard, away from the commotion of the house. Katie cleaned up the clutter and arranged the stored knickknacks around us in a comfy, clubhouse atmosphere. We had a great time making candles and learning new techniques in that little room. Later, we moved into a small studio warehouse in a local artist community, where we make and sell our candles today. Looking back on our start, I am amazed at how much we learned in our first workshop.

This chapter explains how to transform an area of your home into a comfortable working environment and what equipment and supplies you will need for your candlemaking workshop. You'll learn how to choose the right space in your home, how to set up different types of melting systems, and how to efficiently organize and store your equipment and supplies.

Choosing Your Workspace

Where you choose to set up your personal workspace is an important decision. Pick your site carefully. Choose a space where you can relax and let your creativity and imagination flow. Choose a time to make candles when it is most convenient for you and when you are least likely to be interrupted. Your work area should give you plenty of room where you can work free of the distractions of home. It should be a refuge for you when you want to get away from the rest of the world. Creating your ideal uninhibited workspace is essential. For you to enjoy candlemaking enough for it to grow into a hobby capable of sustaining itself through sales of your work, your workshop needs to be a space where you can feel as free as possible to grow as an artisan.

> **Did you know???**
>
> Ultraviolet (UV) rays cause candle colors to fade. Using a UV light absorber additive helps alleviate this problem.

Setting Up Your Workspace

A kitchen, garage, basement, shed, or any space can be transformed into a workshop as long as some specific requirements are considered. You'll need to designate three different work areas: a preparation and finishing area, a melting area, and a pouring area.

The Preparation and Finishing Area

This area should have all the wicking, molds, and supplies you need for your candlemaking project, as well as storage for other candlemaking equipment. This is where you will set up and wick your molds, containers, or dipping racks, as well as finish and/or decorate freshly made candles.

In addition to your wicks and molds, you will need the following preparatory and finishing supplies:

- Mold accessories (wick screw and wick sealer)
- Tape to help wick plastic molds
- Sharp scissors for wicking and finishing
- Knife for cleaning seam lines (an Exacto or any smooth-edged, unserrated knife)
- Pantyhose, excellent for buffing to remove fingerprints and surface imperfections
- Recycling bucket for storing clean wax drippings, scraps, and candle nubs to be used again.

The Melting Area

This area is where you will prepare your wax formulas. It will contain your heat source, melting utensils, and all your wax ingredients—wax, additives, dye, and any scent. Your melting area should function just like a typical home kitchen. It must be capable of withstanding heat, have good ventilation, and have an adequate source of electricity. Your heat source for melting wax may use a lot of power; so make sure your space has enough juice to keep your heat setup going without blowing a fuse. Make sure air can circulate in your shop either through an open window or by the use of a fan, because some scents may give you a headache when heated.

Try not to use your kitchen stove if possible, especially if you don't like craft clutter around your stove and food.

> **Handy Hint**
>
> Post a notepad somewhere in your workshop where you can list items you need to replenish in your workshop.

The Heat Source

Your heat source should be able to boil water quickly and have a numbered temperature control. A portable heat source is ideal for home candlemaking. Place your heat source in a safe place where the work surface is level, capable of withstanding heat, and where the electrical cord is not in the way. Keep a box of baking powder handy to extinguish a possible wax fire. Cover the work surface adequately with heavy-duty aluminum foil or wax paper. These work well because they keep wax droppings clean, so you can easily peel them off and recycle them for other projects.

There are a variety of sizes and types of portable heat sources you can use.

Single Burner or Buffet Range

These heat sources are good for making a small batch of candles at a time. Look for smooth-surface burners as opposed to heat coils because they're easier to clean. If you have to use heat coils, you can get an aluminum cover to place over the coils; this will not only keep wax away from the coils, but also distributes heat more evenly. If you use a dual-burner buffet range, be aware that some kinds have two different burners, one for heating and keeping food warm and one for cooking. The cooking burner gets much hotter faster than the other. For safety's sake, avoid open-flame heat sources such as camping stoves.

Concealed Element Heater

With a concealed element heater such as a deep-fat fryer or slow cooker, you can melt wax directly in the fryer, but you will have to ladle the wax into a pouring container.

Electric Griddle or Grill

Using an electric griddle or grill is a great way to melt large quantities of wax and multiple types of wax formulas in different pots all at the same time. These griddles usually have a cast-aluminum base with a nonstick surface that's easy to clean, and a numbered temperature control. An electric skillet works the same way for smaller quantities of wax.

Professional Wax Melters

Small-scale professional wax melters similar to restaurant-style coffee urns with spigots can melt many pounds of wax at once. These are much more costly than the other heat sources, but are useful when you get to the stage of preparing large quantities of wax at a time.

Choosing a Melting System for Your Projects

You will want to set up a system for melting wax or gel according to the size and requirements of your projects. Before you start any project, read the directions carefully to decide which arrangement will work best.

The Double-Boiler Method

The double-boiler method is an arrangement of two vessels, one of which fits above and partly inside the other. Wax is melted inside the upper vessel by the water boiling in the lower one. With this arrangement, you will be able to melt wax up to the temperature of boiling water (212 degrees Fahrenheit or 100 degrees Celsius). Although this method is slower than the direct-heat method described later, it is best for beginners and children because wax cannot reach its flash point when heated in this way. The flash point is the temperature at which the wax becomes volatile and catches on fire (around 300 degrees Fahrenheit).

At kitchen or restaurant supply shops, you can find pot pairs specifically designed for double boiling. You can also improvise a double boiler in a number of ways. Use any pot large enough to contain an amount of water to reach about one-half to two-thirds of the way up the sides of the inner melting pot, but no higher. You don't want the water jumping into the melting pot!

The melting pot must sit inside the outer pot on a trivet or riser to prevent direct contact with the heat source. The melting pot can be any pot large enough to contain the amount of wax you will need for your project, such as a saucepan, a camping pot, or even an aluminum food can, but it's better to use a container with a handle for safety.

My favorite melting pot is a nonelectric coffee percolator with the percolating equipment removed. It fits the description of an ideal melting pot: tall, seamless, with a pouring handle and a pouring lip with a built-in strainer. This pot is very similar to the wax melting pots sold by candlemaking supply and craft stores.

The Direct-Heat Method

If you have to melt wax to temperatures higher than the boiling point of water (212 degrees Fahrenheit), then you need to use the direct-heat method. For this, the melting pot is placed directly on the heat source, or the wax is melted directly in a concealed element heater. This method also works even if you don't need heat higher than 212 degrees Fahrenheit, but you must make sure that you do not overheat your wax. Overheated wax smells bad, may affect the color and scent quality, and can catch on fire.

Warning: With the direct-heat method, the materials you will melt have the capability to catch on fire. To use this method, you must be an experienced candlemaker, and be very familiar with making the particular project.

Tracking Wax Temperature

Whichever melting system and heat source you choose, it is essential that you use a thermometer to measure the temperature of wax at all times. If you use more than one melting pot at a time, have a thermometer for each melting pot. A thermometer for candlemaking must be capable of measurement up to 350 degrees Fahren-

Handy Hint

Don't let the water in your pot boil dry! Make sure that you maintain the level of water in the pot while your wax is melting.

heit, similar to a candy thermometer. The thermometer can be traditional or digital. I have found digital cooking thermometers with
alarms that beep when your wax reaches a specified temperature
extremely handy. With these thermometers, you won't
have to worry about overheating your wax and you can
precisely control your pouring temperature. For a more
accurate temperature reading, always place your thermometer in your melting pot when you begin melting
the wax.

> **Handy Hint**
>
> Keep a clock in your
> workshop for time
> measurement
> of your projects.

Melting Area Equipment and Supplies

In addition to wax and additives, the melting area also needs to have
the following utensils and supplies:

- Hammer and bin to break up and store large wax slabs

- Measurement scale to weigh wax and additives

- Mold releasing agent (This can be a silicone spray made
  specifically for candlemaking, or a light, unflavored vegetable
  oil spray.)

- Measuring spoons for measuring additives; the most commonly used are ½ teaspoon (tsp), 1 teaspoon (tsp), and
  1 tablespoon (tbsp)

- Wooden skewers (heavy duty is best), chopsticks, or knitting
  needles for stirring and mixing the wax

- Pot holders for handling hot pots safely

- Ladle for moving wax from one pot to another

- Paper towels to quickly clean up liquid wax in pitchers or on
  your heat source

- Baking soda or a small fire extinguisher. Use baking soda as a wax fire extinguisher by throwing it on a fire to extinguish the flame. *Never use water to extinguish a wax fire.* It only spreads the flame.

- Large metal pot cover, similar flat object, or a large damp towel that can be used to smother a fire

- Small, flat griddle pan or pot that can be easily heated and cleaned, to level the bottoms of candles

The Pouring Area

The pouring area is where you will transform your prepared wax into candles. Situate the melting area and the pouring area as close as possible to each other so you won't have to carry hot wax very far. Your pouring area must have a level surface, so your candles can cool safely and evenly; poured candles must not be disturbed or moved around. If you're making more than one candle, have enough room to space your molds out so that the heat of one candle won't interfere with the cooling of another.

▼▼▼▼▼▼▼▼▼▼▼▼▼▼▼▼▼▼▼▼▼▼▼▼▼

Did you know???

Lemon oil removes beeswax from countertops and tables. The beeswax mixes with the oil and wipes right off.

▲▲▲▲▲▲▲▲▲▲▲▲▲▲▲▲▲▲▲▲▲▲▲▲▲

The pouring area needs the following supplies:

- Heavy-duty aluminum foil or wax paper to cover the pouring area. This protects the surface from wax spills and allows you to easily remove scraps to recycle them. Get heavy-duty aluminum foil because it is much easier to use with wax and tears less readily than the regular kind.

- Wax paper cups. If a melting pot is needed for another candle project, pour extra wax into wax paper cups (4-ounce cups or

▼▼

Building a Wax Trap

A good way to save wax that has spilled from pouring pots is to build a wax trap:

1. Cover the top of a level wooden box, crate, or old dresser drawer with a heavy wire screen (about ¼-inch squares).

2. Staple all around the box with a staple gun, securing the screen.

3. Line the bottom with wax paper or aluminum foil. (If your box has no bottom, place it on top of a foil-lined tray.) This way, you can set your pouring pitcher on the screen and save any wax that drips from the pitcher onto the lining.

▲▲

larger). Cups can easily be peeled off when the wax is needed to be melted again for additional pourings. This is also a great way to store small amounts of leftover colored or scented wax to use at another time.

■ Skewers for stirring and poking the wax inside the mold.

A Workspace for Rolling Candles

If you will be making rolled candles or using wax sheets for candle decoration, it is necessary to have a clean, flat surface covered with heavy-duty aluminum foil or wax paper to work on.

In addition to your wax sheets and wick, you will need the following supplies:

■ Blow-dryer to soften the sheets

■ Sharp unserrated knife to cut wax sheets

■ Cutting mat board, a self-healing mat board or a piece of cardboard to protect your working surface to withstand knife cuts

■ Metal straightedge as long as the length of your rolled candle

Equipment Storage

Whether you set up a temporary or permanent workshop in your home, it is important to keep all your supplies neat and organized. The last thing you want to do in your workshop is stress yourself out by not being able to find something when you're in the middle of a project.

Storage Tips

■ Keep all equipment clean, and keep unused materials in containers protected from dust and dirt.

■ If your workshop is temporary, use a large plastic bin with handles to store all your equipment in one place.

■ A toolbox, compartmental drawer cabinet, or tackle box is handy for storing materials and supplies such as wicking, mold sealer, color chips, etc. Label everything, especially wicks and color chips, so you'll know exactly what you have when you need it.

■ When you first buy your wax additives, use recycled food jars to store each one and save the directions label. You can tape the label to the jar so you can easily refer to it when you're ready to measure out the additive for your project. Leaving additives in the plastic bags they were purchased in can be tricky; because once the label is gone it may be difficult to tell them apart from each other.

Storing Candles

■ When storing candles, keep them in a cool, dark place away from sunlight to prevent discoloration. Store them flat to prevent warping. Keep scented candles in a separate plastic bag or wrapper of some sort until you use them. Leaving a candle unwrapped as a home fragrance is up to you, but keep in mind that it won't smell as strong when you burn it as it would have if you had wrapped it up.

- If your stored candles have gotten dusty or dirty, you can clean them before lighting with a soft cloth and a little rubbing alcohol. Depending on the surface decoration, you can shine your candles with a drop of olive oil or by buffing them with some pantyhose.

Safety

Always remember that you are working with flammable materials around a heat source when you are making candles. For this reason, you must take every precaution possible in your workshop to make your craft time safe and enjoyable.

Preparatory Safety

- Wear old clothes and/or an apron to protect yourself from spillage and decorating materials.

- Have at hand all the materials and equipment you will need for whatever project you are working on.

- When breaking up slabs of wax with a hammer, put the wax in a bin and either cover the wax with a thin cloth to prevent wax from flying out or wear safety glasses.

- Keep pets and children out of your workshop. Imagine your horror if a child touched or grabbed a hot pot of wax or a cat jumped on your pouring table!

Handy Hint

Your wax should never smoke on the burner. This means the wax is too hot and must be removed from the heat source. A burner with spilled wax is a fire hazard and must be cleaned up before it starts smoking.

Safety with Heated Wax

- Never leave wax unattended while it is on a heat source.

- Always, always use a thermometer in each melting pot.

- Treat wax as you would hot cooking oil. Don't allow it to overheat and smoke.

- As soon as wax spills around an electric burner or grill, use paper towels to clean up the wax before it starts to overheat.

- Reheat wax in a melting pot slowly at first. The wax at the bottom of the pot will heat and expand, and may spurt out if heated too quickly.

- If your wax does catch on fire, don't panic and remember to do the following:

  1. Immediately turn off the heat and unplug it from the electrical outlet.

  2. Throw baking soda over the fire or try to smother it with a pot cover or damp towel. Never use water to extinguish the fire. It will only spread the flame.

  3. Don't move the wax.

Handy Hint

Pour hot candle wax (230 degrees Fahrenheit) into a metal or acrylic mold to clean interior wax buildup.

Warning: If you spill hot wax on your skin, immediately run it under cold water and gently peel the wax away. As long as the wax is below the boiling point of water, it should not scald or burn. If the wax is hotter, apply first-aid burn procedures immediately.

Cleaning Up

Cleaning up after candlemaking isn't as simple as cleaning up after most other projects. There is lots of equipment and many chemicals and melted items that need to be disposed of. Here are some tips to help you.

Cleaning Melting Equipment

You can clean colored wax from a melting pot easily by carefully wiping the inside with paper towels while the wax is still liquid. Wear pot holders—don't burn your hands! It is easier to clean tools and equipment if you wipe off the wax while it is still liquid.

Never pour wax down the sink. Once the wax cools, it will clog your drain. Pour the wax into paper cups to save and recycle the wax.

Cleaning Carpet or Rug Wax Spills

Protect work surfaces and floors by covering them with aluminum foil or wax paper. In case of wax spills on a carpet or rug:

1. Let the wax cool completely.

2. Remove by hand as much wax as you can.

3. Rub the spot with an ice cube and try to break off more wax.

4. Place a paper towel or clean rag on top of the wax and carefully iron over the spill. This will transfer the wax to the towel or rag.

5. Repeat step 4 until the wax is removed.

Did you know???

The popular children's nursery rhyme saying, "Jack jumped over the candlestick," was derived from a tradition in medieval England. People would actually jump over lighted candles as a means of predicting the future. If the candle stayed lit, it meant brighter times were ahead; if the flame went out, it meant darker days were to come.

If the wax contains candle dyes, it may be difficult to remove from the carpet and might require a heavy-duty or professional carpet stain remover. Apply this before the above iron method or you will set the dye in the carpet.

Cleaning Wax Drippings on Candleholders and Other Objects

Dip the object in or run it under hot water to soften the wax for easy removal, or place the object in the freezer for about an hour to make the wax brittle so you can break it off. You can also buy remover specifically for candle wax from department stores.

Candlemaking How-To's

▼▼▼

CANDLEMAKING IS FUN AND EASY, and it can be even more fun and easy if you know the tips and tricks of each part of the candlemaking process. This chapter will show you the best ways to do all the common candlemaking tasks.

Wick Picking

Selecting the correct wick is essential for making a quality candle that burns well. Knowing the candle diameter, style, and melting point (MP) of the wax aids in determining which wick to use. Generally, a properly burning wick is one that consumes the melted wax as rapidly as it accumulates. The rule of thumb is 2 inches in candle width for each size wick (a small wick for a 1- to 2-inch-wide candle, medium wick for a 2- to 4-inch, etc.). Your wick and wax recipe determines how your candle will burn, so choosing the correct wick for your candle project is critical. To keep your candle wall intact while your candle burns, for example, you may want to use a smaller wick than normal for the candle width so the flame will not melt the wax to the edge of the candle.

How Does Wick Size Affect a Candle?

Not taking into account your wax recipe, which of course also determines how your candle comes out, wick size generally affects your candle in the following ways:

- A wick that is too large will smoke excessively, elongate, and flicker. The wick absorbs wax faster than it can burn off the wax.

- A proper-size wick will produce a melting pool that consumes the entire width of the candle without dripping. The wick burns off the wax as rapidly as it absorbs the wax.

- A wick that is too small will drip excessively. The wick cannot absorb the melted wax fast enough.

- A wick that is way too small will sink the flame in a crater inside the candle and may burn out.

Wick Tips

Flat braid wicks (see figure 1) are best for nondrip tapers, large block candles, nonsymmetrical candles, and novelty candles. This wick bends so the tip is exposed outside the flame.

Square braid wicks (see figure 2) are best for small-diameter candles, symmetrical candles, beeswax candles, and molded candles. This wick is tighter and more compact in structure than a flat braid wick. Beeswax and soy wax candles require a wick to be about double the thickness of the wick that's used for paraffin candles of the same diameter.

Core wicks (see figure 3) are best for containers, gel candles, extra-large candles, sand candles, and votives.

Priming the Wick

It's important to prime a wick before using it to saturate the wick with wax. This improves the burning quality of the wick and pre-

Use the following chart as a general guideline for selecting a flat braid wick:

15 ply   for extra-small diameter candles

18 ply   for candles up to 2 inches in diameter

24 ply   for candles 2 inches to 2½ inches in diameter

30 ply   for candles 2½ inches to 3 inches in diameter

Figure 1. Flat braid wick.

Figure 2. Square braid wick.

vents air bubbles from sticking to the wick during pouring. To prime a wick, just dip it in melted wax and allow it to dry thoroughly before using it.

Different Wicking Methods

The different types of candle molds are each wicked in a slightly different way. It's important to remember to do all the little steps when wicking a mold in order to make candlemaking a pleasant, fun time rather than a frustrating one.

Wicking and Preparing a Commercial Metal Mold

A commercial metal mold is the easiest type of mold to use for candlemaking. Keep in mind, when working with a metal mold, that the top (open part) of the mold will be the bottom of the candle and the bottom (closed part) of the mold will be the top of the candle (see figure 4).

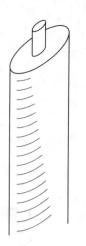

Figure 3. Core wick.

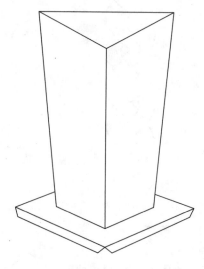

Figure 4. Standard metal mold.

Materials

Primed wick (proper type and size, depending on mold), metal mold, wick rod, wick screw, scissors, mold sealer

Instructions

1. Without cutting the wick from your supply (you will do this after you've inserted it and secured it inside the mold), insert the wick through the hole in the underside of the mold (see step MM-1) and thread it through until it reaches the top of the mold (see step MM-2).

2. Securely tie the wick to the wick rod, which will lie across the opening of the mold (see step MM-3).

3. Pull the wick tightly in the mold from the point of insertion and secure the wick on the outside of the mold with the wick screw (see step MM-4).

4. Center the wick all the way up to the top of the mold.

5. Cut the wick about an inch from the screw on the outside of the mold (see step MM-5), leaving about an inch to light (remember, the bottom of the mold is the top of the candle).

6. Wind the wick around the screw (see step MM-6) and *completely* cover the wick and screw with mold sealer (see step MM-7). (You'll remove the mold sealer after you make your candle.) If you don't cover the wick completely, wax may seep through the wick hole, travel through the wick, and jeopardize the mold seal. The metal mold is now ready for pouring.

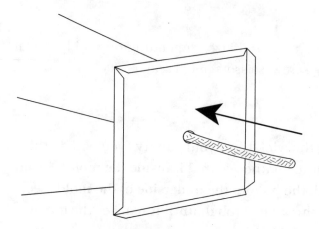

Step MM-1. Without cutting the wick from your supply, insert the wick through the hole in the underside of the mold.

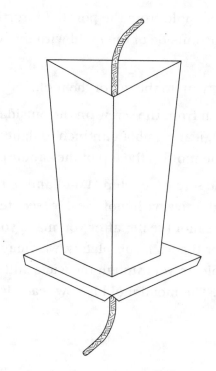

Step MM-2. Thread the wick through until it reaches the top of the mold.

Step MM-3. Securely tie the wick to the wick rod, which will lie across the opening of the mold.

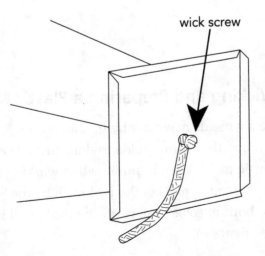

wick screw

Step MM-4. Pull the wick tightly in the mold from the point of insertion and secure the wick on the outside of the mold with the wick screw.

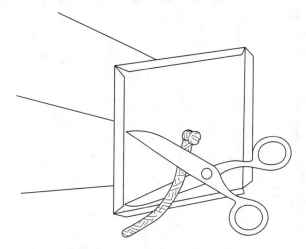

Step MM-5. Cut the wick about an inch from the screw on the outside of the mold.

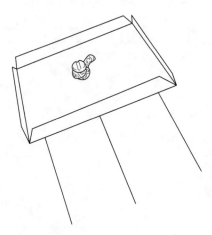

Step MM-6. Wind the wick around the screw.

Wicking and Preparing a Plastic Mold

Plastic molds may vary by manufacturer, so read the directions that come with plastic molds to determine the best way to wick your plastic mold. Keep in mind, when working with a plastic mold, that the top (open part) of the mold will be the bottom of the candle and the bottom (closed part) of the mold will be the top of the candle (see figure 5).

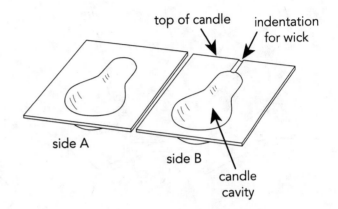

top of candle   indentation for wick

side A

side B

candle cavity

Step MM-7. *Completely* cover the wick and screw with mold sealer.

Figure 5. Standard plastic mold.

Materials

Mold, scissors, primed wick (proper type and size, depending on mold), tape, mold clamps, mold stand

Instructions

1. Plastic molds come in two halves. At the top of one of the halves, you'll see an indentation for the wick, as shown in

side A

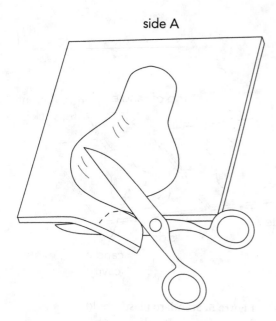

Step PM-1. Take the half of the mold that does not have the wick indentation (side A) and carefully cut around the base to provide a pouring entrance.

side B

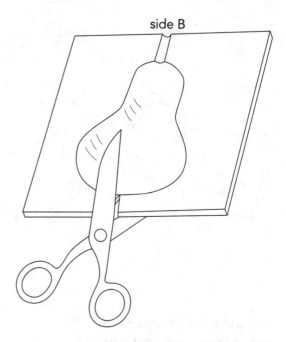

Step PM-2. Take the half of the mold that has the indentation for the wick (side B) and, at the base of the mold, cut a small slit on the plastic sheet.

figure 5. The candle is poured upside down, with the pouring entrance at the base of the candle.

2. Take the half that does not have the wick indentation (side A) and carefully cut around the base to provide a pouring entrance (see step PM-1). This may already have been done if the mold was used before.

3. Take the half that has the indentation for the wick (side B) and, at the base of the mold, cut a small slit on the plastic sheet (see step PM-2); don't cut up to the candle cavity, just a small slit will do.

side B

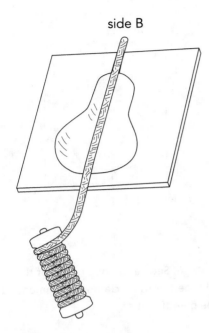

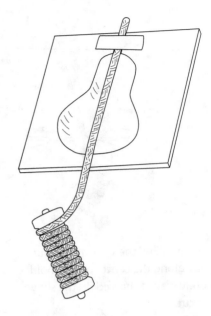

Step PM-3. Without cutting the wick from your supply, take side B of the mold and place the end of the wick on top of the indentation.

Step PM-4. Secure the top of the wick to the outside of the mold by taping it.

4. Without cutting the wick from your supply (you will do this after you've inserted it and secured it inside the mold), take side B of the mold and place the end of the wick on top of the indentation (see step PM-3).

5. Secure the top of the wick to the outside of the mold by taping it (see step PM-4). Make sure not to leave any tape hanging in the candle cavity.

6. Pull the wick gently but tightly along the center of the mold, and securely wedge the wick in the slit you have cut (see

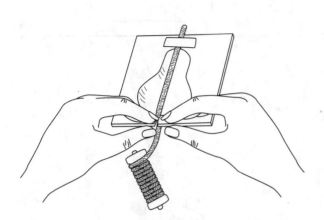

Step PM-5. Pull the wick gently but tightly along the center of the mold, and securely wedge the wick in the slit you have cut.

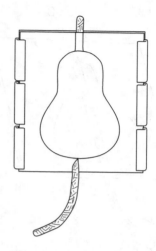

Step PM-6. Secure the two halves of the mold together using clamps recommended by the manufacturer.

step PM-5). You can tape the wick to the bottom of the base instead of cutting a slit, but I have found that sometimes the tape loses its adhesion when wax is poured over it, causing the wick to disengage from the mold and get lost in the candle.

7. Secure the two halves of the mold together using clamps recommended by the manufacturer (see step PM-6). If you don't have recommended clamps, use office binder clips as clamps all along the sides of the mold.

8. Place the two halves in the mold stand recommended by the manufacturer. If you don't have the recommended mold stand, clamp the bottom of the mold (the top of the candle) and carefully wedge the mold in a bowl of sand (see step

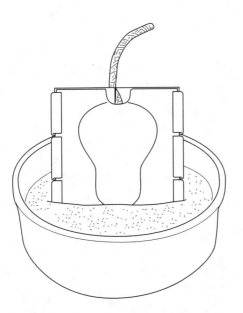

Step PM-7. If you don't have the recommended mold stand, clamp the bottom of the mold (the top of the candle) and carefully wedge the mold in a bowl of sand.

PM-7). Make sure the bottom of the mold is completely secure so sand cannot seep into the mold. The plastic mold is now ready for pouring.

Wicking and Preparing a Flexible Mold

Preparing a flexible mold is different from preparing other types of molds because you must use a container to support the mold. Flexible molds are usually made of rubber or some other flexible material. Keep in mind when working with a flexible mold that the top (open part) of the mold will be the bottom of the candle and the bottom (closed part) of the mold will be the top of the candle (see figure 6).

Figure 6. Standard flexible mold.

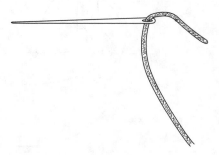

Step FM-1. Without cutting the wick from your supply, thread the wick into the darning needle.

Materials

Primed wick, darning needle, mold, wick rod, scissors, mold sealer, box deep enough to accommodate the length and width of the mold, and a piece of heavy-duty cardboard larger than the width of the mold and wide enough to sit on top of the box (or instead of the box and cardboard, use a plastic lid and can deep enough to accommodate the length and width of the mold)

Instructions

1. Without cutting the wick from your supply (you will do this after you've inserted it and secured it inside the mold), thread the wick into the darning needle (see step FM-1).

2. If the mold is new, use the darning needle to create the wick hole by inserting the wick from the underside of the mold (see step FM-2). If the mold has been used before, carefully examine the mold to find the wick hole.

3. Remove the needle and leave about ¾ inch of wick above the top of the mold for lighting (see step FM-3).

4. Pull the wick tightly in the mold from the open end, being careful not to pull too tightly so you don't pull the wick out of the hole or disfigure the mold (see step FM-4).

5. Securely tie the wick to the wick rod, which will lie across the opening (bottom) of the mold (see step FM-5).

6. Cover the other end of the wick completely with mold sealer (see step FM-6). (You will remove the mold sealer after you make the candle.) Make sure the sealer bonds tightly to the mold with no air pockets.

7. Cut out a hole in the center of cardboard or the can lid just big enough for the candle cavity to fit through (see step FM-7). The mold lip should be able to rest on the lid/cardboard (see step FM-8).

8. Place the mold with the lid/cardboard support in the can or box (see step FM-9). The mold is now ready for pouring.

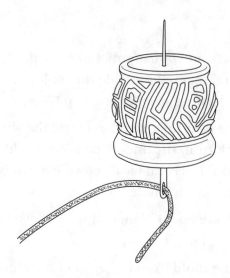

Step FM-2. If the mold is new, use the darning needle to create the wick hole by inserting the wick from the underside of the mold.

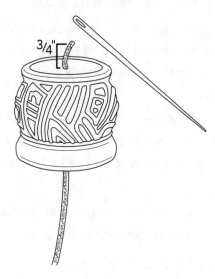

3/4"

Step FM-3. Remove the needle and leave about ¾ inch of wick above the top of the mold for lighting.

Step FM-4. Pull the wick tightly in the mold from the open end, being careful not to pull too tightly so you don't pull the wick out of the hole or disfigure the mold.

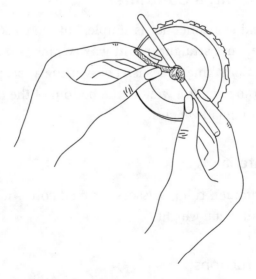

Step FM-5. Securely tie the wick to the wick rod, which will lie across the opening (bottom) of the mold.

Step FM-6. Cover the wick completely with mold sealer.

Step FM-7. Cut out a hole in the center of cardboard or the can lid just big enough for the candle cavity to fit through.

Wicking a Container

Wicking a container is simple, but the trick is to keep the wick centered and straight in soft wax (which is usually used in container candlemaking). This isn't easy using a receptacle that makes it difficult to anchor a wick to the bottom of the candle using only a wick tab or small weight.

Materials

Container, ruler, scissors, primed core wick, wick rod, wick tab or small metal weight

Instructions

1. Measure the height of the container with the ruler.

Step FM-8. The mold lip should be able to rest on the lid/cardboard.

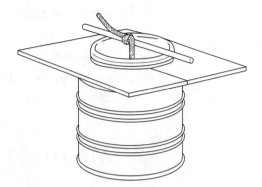

Step FM-9. Place the mold with the lid/cardboard support in the can or box.

2. Cut an appropriately sized piece of wick from your supply, adding an extra inch or two allowance.

3. Tie one end of the wick to the wick rod and attach a wick tab or tie a small metal weight to the other end.

4. Lower the wick assembly into the container, allowing the wick rod to rest on the top, and adjust the size of the wick if it does not stand straight in the container.

5. Secure the wick assembly to the container prior to pouring the entire candle by pouring a little wax over the wick tab or weight.

6. The container is now ready for pouring.

Wicking an Improvised Mold

Study the improvised mold you have chosen and decide what kind of setup—metal, flexible, or container—most closely approximates the improvised mold. Follow the directions for that setup. If it is the metal- or flexible-mold method, you may need to use an awl, nail, or other device suitable for the mold to create a wick hole.

Melting Wax

Following I'll discuss the two ways to melt wax. No matter which method you use, refer to my discussion about safety in chapter 3 and keep all the safety supplies within your reach.

Melting Wax Using the Double-Boiler Method

If you're a beginner, you must use the double-boiler method while you learn candlemaking. It is dangerous for you to attempt the direct-heat method of melting wax until you are completely comfortable with the properties of wax and additives. If you are an experienced candlemaker trying a technique or ingredient with which you have not had prior experience, it is better to be safe than sorry and use a double boiler for experimenting.

Materials

Wax (type depends on what you're making), thermometer, double boiler, permanent marker (optional), water, salt (optional), heat source

Instructions

1. Measure the amount of wax that you will need for your project and place the wax and the thermometer in the melting pot (the top half of the double boiler).

2. If you choose to, carefully mark the inside of your melting pot with a permanent marker to indicate the level of wax for each pound melted. This way you can approximate the amount of wax in your melting pot just by looking at the pot!

3. Add water to the boiling pot (see step DB-1) and situate the melting pot inside it (see step DB-2). Adjust the water level if it is too high (if the water overflows from the pot) once you have placed the melting pot inside it.

4. You can double boil over high heat and add salt to the water to speed up the boiling process, but watch it carefully. If it starts to boil rapidly and spurt water into your melting pot, lower the heat to a controllable temperature.

5. Never leave melting wax unattended!

Melting Wax Using the Direct-Heat Method

Certain projects and techniques, such as making sand candles, require wax to be heated higher than the boiling point of water, necessitating melting the wax over direct heat.

Again, to use this method, you must be an experienced candlemaker who has done this particular project before, since the risk of fire increases with the higher heat applied to candlemaking's flammable materials.

Step DB-1. Add water to the boiling pot.

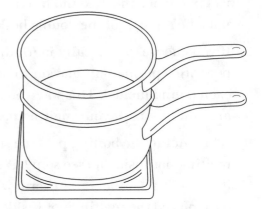

Step DB-2. Situate the melting pot inside the boiling pot.

Materials

Wax (type depends on what you're making), thermometer, melting pot, heat source

Instructions

1. Measure the amount of wax you need for your project and place the wax and the thermometer in the melting pot. If you are using any additive with a high melting point, melt it first and then add it to your wax (see Melting High MP Wax Additives section on page 81).

2. Melt the mixture over low heat while carefully monitoring the temperature. If the temperature rises too quickly and the

wax still has a long way to go before liquefying, turn down the heat.

3. Stir the wax mixture frequently to make sure all the additives are completely blended with the wax and not just sitting at the bottom of the melting pot. I like to make sure my melted wax mixture is completely clear before I add color, so I know it is thoroughly blended.

Melting High MP Wax Additives

Any wax additive with a melting point (MP) higher than 212 degrees Fahrenheit (the boiling point of water) must be melted separately over direct heat. Such additives include clear crystals and hot melt glue sticks.

Materials

Wax additive, stainless steel measuring cup with a handle, heat source

Instructions

1. Measure the amount of additive needed for your project.

2. Melt the additive over low heat in a stainless steel measuring cup with a handle (see step WA-1). I advise against using a can or something without a handle because it can be difficult to hold over the heat without burning your hand.

3. Melting the additive should not take very long, so watch it carefully. As soon as it melts completely, add it to your melted wax in the double boiler.

Step WA-1. Melt the additive over low heat in a stainless steel measuring cup with a handle.

Creating and Choosing Candle Color

With the variety of candlemaking dyes available, you have the possibility to create any color you want. A few color definitions can help you understand color variations and how to mix and match color.

Primary colors: Red, yellow, and blue. These colors cannot be mixed from any other colors.

Secondary colors: Two primary colors mixed together result in orange (yellow + red), green (yellow + blue), and violet (red + blue).

Tertiary (intermediate) colors: One primary color and one secondary color mixed together (yellow-green, blue-green, blue-violet, red-violet, red-orange, and yellow-orange).

Complementary colors: Opposite colors (orange and blue, red and green, yellow and violet). Mixing complementary colors together always gives you a brown color. To darken a color, mix in a little of its complementary color (for example: 1 part blue + ¼ part orange = darker blue).

Key color: Dominant color in a color scheme or mixture.

Intensity: The brightness or dullness of a color.

Value: The lightness or darkness of a color.

Tone: The quality or value of a color; color + gray.

Shade: The degree of darkness of a color; color + black.

Tint: A gradation of a color with reference to its mixture with white; color + white.

Aggressive (warm) colors: Reds, oranges, and yellows.

Receding (cool) colors: Greens, blues, and violets.

Neutral grey: Black + white.

> ## Handy Hint
> You can use a little stearic acid as a whitener if you need to tint a color.

Experimenting with Color

Remember, if you want to replicate a color batch, you must repeat the candle recipe for the new batch exactly, as well as replicate the environment and cooling conditions that occurred with the previous batch. Any variation from the original recipe will produce different results. If you're keeping a detailed workshop journal, this should be no problem (see page 90).

Color the Occasion

When creating a candle recipe, I like to think of who may be using the candle and why that person will light it. There are many different uses for candles, and many different ideas for color for each use.

Candles as aromatherapy: Consider a natural color to match an aromatherapy scent, such as a grassy green for a mint or a sage oil, or consider no color at all and rely on the natural beauty of soy or beeswax.

Candles as gifts: Consider the person's favorite color, zodiac color, birth month color, or home colors.

Candles for a party: Consider colors to match the festive atmosphere or theme of the party, such as pink and blue for a baby shower.

Candles for a wedding: Consider white, or colors to match or complement the wedding colors.

Candles for religious purposes: Consider the natural color of beeswax, or traditional colors such as the pink, purple, and white of Advent or the blue and white of Hanukkah.

Candles for a holiday: Consider red, green, silver, white, gold, and blue for Christmas; pinks, lavender, cream, and other pastels for Easter; and reds, pinks, blushes, and cream for Valentine's Day.

Candles for the seasons: Consider burgundy, orange, rust, navy, black, and cream for fall and winter; pastels and garden colors for spring; and bright, sunny colors and primary colors for summer.

Candles as representations: Consider realistic color when making novelty representations, such as green for frog candles and Christmas trees.

Candles to decorate: Consider items that you will use to decorate the candle. Choose a color that may contrast the decoration to highlight it, or a complementary color for a more subtle effect. Or, you can choose not to color the candle at all if the candle is going to be covered by the surface decoration.

Candles for fun: Consider that there is no rule that candles have to match or complement anything! Candles can be whatever color you choose.

Adding Candle Color

The best time to add color is when the wax is about to reach pouring temperature. Once you have carefully measured the color and added it to the wax, stir the wax and scrape the bottom with your stirrer to make sure the color is thoroughly blended rather than sitting at the bottom of the melting pot. The color of liquid is never the same as the color of the wax solidified. Liquid wax is always darker and lightens when cooled.

Factors That Affect Candle Color

Surprisingly, many things can affect your candle color besides color additives. Here's a list of some things to think about when you're trying to reach that perfect shade.

▼▼▼▼▼▼▼▼▼▼▼▼▼▼▼▼▼

Handy Hint

A good way to determine the color of your wax is to pour about ¼ inch of your colored wax into a white paper cup. Allow it to cool and you'll have a good idea of your candle color, and a color swatch to save for future reference.

▲▲▲▲▲▲▲▲▲▲▲▲▲▲▲▲▲

- Temperature: An excessively high melting temperature can dull colors.

- Addition technique: Candle color should be added and thoroughly blended right before pouring. To reduce the softening effect of stearic acid on color, you may be able to get a brighter color by melting the stearic and color first before adding them to the wax.

- Cooling: The cooling rate of the candle can affect color intensity. Remember that certain candle shapes cool more rapidly than others; for example, a cone will cool quickly at the narrower end of the cone than its wider base.

- Wax and additives: Different types, grades, and brands of wax produce different color shades. Wax additives also render certain color effects to the wax recipe. Stearic acid, for example, softens color and can accelerate fading, while clear additives can brighten color and slow fading.

- Scent: The amount and type of scent can affect candle color, especially if the oil is even slightly tinted. Colors of scents vary from clear to dark brown.

Creating Scent Recipes

Experimenting with fragrance is one of the great joys of candlemaking. Many candlemakers believe scent to be one of the most appealing qualities of a candle because of its powerful effect. Scientists have studied the role of fragrance and found that smells are indelibly imprinted in the human brain. Research shows that scents can be soothing, stimulating, or even healing.

▼▼▼▼▼▼▼▼▼▼▼▼▼▼▼▼▼▼▼▼

Did you know???

Some candlemaking dyes deepen in color up to 3 days after the candle hardens and is removed from the mold.

▲▲▲▲▲▲▲▲▲▲▲▲▲▲▲▲▲▲▲▲

Scenting a living space has become quite popular and the options today are limitless, with a wide array of scent options available, from herbal potpourri and essential oils to artificial air fresheners. The scent options in the candle world are vast as well, with flavors ranging from individual natural scents such as lavender and strawberry to scent blends invoking complex aromas such as the scent of a fresh-baked blueberry pie.

There are two general categories of candlemaking scents: essential oils and fragrance oils. An essential oil is obtained by distilling an extraction from a plant; the resulting oil retains the characteristic scent of the plant. A fragrance oil is an artificial fragrance in a carrier oil, usually a petroleum-based solvent. Both types of oils are volatile, meaning they are easily converted to a vapor, hence allowing them to give off a scent.

When scenting candles, one usually thinks of the term "aromatherapy," which has been loosely used in candle labeling to describe any scented candle. But since all scented candles are not aromatherapy candles in the traditional definition, I differentiate the term into two classifications for candlemaking purposes: traditional aromatherapy and popular aromatherapy.

Traditional Versus Popular Aromatherapy

Aromatherapy is the branch of herbal medicine that utilizes the therapeutic properties of essential oils. Aromatherapy candles are meant to deliver the power of essential oils as the scent is emitted from the burning candle and gently inhaled. All scented candles labeled as aromatherapy do not follow this traditional approach, however. Since true aromatherapy candles contain essential oils, they can be quite expensive to produce given the high cost of quality oils.

Fragrance oils are artificial, so they do not possess the therapeutic effects of true essential oils. Many manufacturers and retailers tout these inexpensive-to-make candles as aromatherapy anyway, confusing consumers who are looking for true aromatherapy products for healing purposes.

Aromatherapy Recipe Ideas

Remember, if you're a beginner, first try a single inexpensive oil or a simple blend to experiment on what proportion you should use in your candle recipe to obtain a satisfactory strength. When you're comfortable with the strength of the aroma, move on and try a more complex or pricier scent blend. Try a half-ounce of oil per pound to start; for the aromatherapy blends, use the recommended proportion first and then adjust it to suit your needs. The following are traditional aromatherapy blends—each used to invoke the healing property described in its name.

Common Aromatherapy Oils

Sensual oils: sandalwood, patchouli, rose, ylang ylang, jasmine

Relaxation oils: lavender, chamomile, geranium, ylang ylang, marjoram

Energy oils: rosemary, peppermint, ginger, basil

Meditative oils: sandalwood, cedarwood, patchouli, myrrh

Simple Combinations

For headaches: 3 drops lavender + 4 drops peppermint + 3 drops chamomile

For stress/tension relief: 4 drops lavender + 3 drops ylang ylang + 3 drops clary sage

For meditation: 6 drops frankincense + 2 drops lavender + 2 drops bergamot

For grief: 2 drops frankincense + 4 drops chamomile + 4 drops rose

For moodiness: 2 drops patchouli + 5 drops rose + 3 drops lemon

Fragrance Oil Blends

Fragrance oils give you the variety of creating your own special scents. Instead of just using vanilla, for example, you can blend vanilla with many other scents to sweeten the aroma. Here are a few ideas to try:

Sugar cookie + cinnamon = sweet and spicy, like cinnamon candies

Orange + vanilla = an orange creamsicle

Mint + chocolate + vanilla = mint chocolate chip ice cream

Almond + coconut + chocolate = a yummy chocolate candy bar

Rose + carnation + jasmine = a sweetly scented garden

Herbal Color and Scent

A great way to add natural and complementary color and scent to a candle batch is to add dried or powdered herbs to the wax (preferably soy or beeswax) and then strain the wax through a fine metal strainer or muslin to get rid of the herb bits. This method not only scents the wax, but can also leave behind a natural hint of color.

Adding Candle Scent

Different types and grades of wax have different "throwing" capabilities (the ability of the wax to give off the scent). Vybar is a wax additive utilized to increase the ability of a wax to contain and throw more scent. Watch out, because too much scent (too much of any additive, really) can damage your mold or affect the quality of your wax recipe. Candle soot can also become a problem when too much scent oil is added to the wax as well. Mix scent in with your candle wax right before you pour.

It's the Little Things That Count the Most

Variations in all the topics we've just discussed (the type of wax and any measurement involved in the making of a candle, such as pouring temperature and amount of additives, scent, and color) will produce different results every time. Even leftover wax may not look the same when it is used again. It is essential to keep track of all these dimensions in order to duplicate a candle project. That's why it's so important to keep a workshop journal. Then you'll have that great recipe to use again when you create the perfect candle.

Keeping a Workshop Journal

With a written record of your candlemaking experiences, you'll have on paper what you did when you got something right or did something wrong. You'll save a lot of time and effort in trial-and-error learning by analyzing the entries in your workshop journal. Essential entries include:

Date/time/weather: It's helpful to look back to see when exactly you created a certain project. It's also possible that environmental factors such as cold or humidity contributed to your success or failure.

Project: The type of candle you were attempting to create. In the end, you may have created something totally different than what you were hoping for, but at least you'll know what got you there.

Mold and wick used: Specify size, shape, and style of both mold and wick.

Wax: Type and amount used. Even different grades of the same kind of wax produce different results.

Additives: Type and amount used. If you use different brands of additives, specify the brand as well, since additives can vary by manufacturer.

Color: The exact color formula, type, and amount used.

Scent: The type and amount used.

Melting notes: You may look back at your process and ask, "When did I add the additive? Color? Scent? Did I overheat the wax?"

Pouring temperature: The temperature at which the wax was poured.

Pouring notes: Did I pour slowly? Fast? Did I make a mess?

Cooling notes: How long did it take to cool? How long did I wait before I repoured or poured another layer? It's helpful to know for future reference how long it took to make the candle from start to finish.

Final outcome: What did the candle end up looking like? Was it what I expected it to be? Take a photo or Polaroid of each project and add it to a candle portfolio of your projects.

Candle notes: If you burned the candle, which you should really do to see how well it turned out, describe its burning qualities—smoky, drippy, low flame, etc.

Candlemaking Techniques

The following are general candlemaking procedures used in most candlemaking projects. Use these instructions as guidelines for the techniques required by each candle project. In some cases you may need to modify a procedure as it is described here to gain the particular quality or appearance you desire.

Pouring a Molded Candle or Container

We already discussed wicking, now the next stage is pouring. This is the general technique for pouring a candle.

Materials

Melted wax (type depends on what you're making), wicked mold, pouring pitcher (if project requires you to transfer the wax from the double boiler), paper cup, pot holders, stirrer

Instructions

1. Once your wax has reached the pouring temperature, take one last look at your mold and pouring area to make

Candle Math

There will come a time when you will have to alter a wax recipe in order to accommodate the size of your own recipe batch. To do this, you need to understand measurement conversion and proportion calculations.

Measurement Chart

3 teaspoons (tsp) = 1 tablespoon (tbsp)

2 teaspoons = 1 fluid ounce (not the same as a weighted ounce)

8 fluid ounces = 1 cup

2 cups = 1 pint

2 pints = 1 quart

4 quarts = 1 gallon

16 ounces = 1 pound dry weight

½ ounce = approximately 3% of a pound

1 ounce = approximately 6% of a pound

Proportionally Speaking

To calculate proportion values, convert the part amount called for into decimal form and multiply it by the total amount of the recipe batch. For example:

If a wax formula calls for 60% paraffin, 30% beeswax, and 10% microwax, and you want to make a 6-pound batch:

sure you haven't forgotten any steps (such as forgetting to apply the mold sealer). Make sure the wick is centered.

2. Make sure your pouring pitcher (if you're not pouring directly from the melting pot) is positioned over the covered pouring area and not over the floor or table.

60% paraffin = 0.6 x 6 pounds = 3.6 pounds of paraffin = 3 pounds, 9.6 ounces of paraffin (see chart below)

30% beeswax = 0.3 x 6 pounds = 1.8 pounds of paraffin = 1 pound, 12.8 ounces of beeswax (see chart below)

10% microwax = 0.1 x 6 pounds = 0.6 pounds of paraffin = 9.6 ounces of microwax (see chart below)

Pound Percentage to Ounce Conversion Chart

Pound (%)		Ounces
0.1	=	1.6
0.2	=	3.2
0.3	=	4.8
0.4	=	6.4
0.5	=	8
0.6	=	9.6
0.7	=	11.2
0.8	=	12.8
0.9	=	14.4
1	=	16

3. Make sure your wax is thoroughly blended, but allow it to settle for a few minutes, so any undissolved particles won't get in your candle.

4. Depending on the size of the candle(s), pour 4 to 8 ounces of wax into a paper cup and set aside (this wax will be used

later for your subsequent pours to refill any cavities caused by shrinkage).

5. Pour slowly! It's easy to get excited and pour too fast, but it's important to pour slowly to minimize air bubbles in the candle. For an even candle appearance, aim at the centered wick and try not to splash along the walls of the mold. To aid in pouring, you can tilt the mold slightly while carefully holding it with pot holders unless this will affect the candle's appearance. Metal is conductive by nature and can burn you if you try to move or hold a mold filled with hot wax without protecting your hands.

6. With your stirrer, tap the sides of the mold gently (don't dent the mold) to help release any air bubbles that might be caught in the candle.

Cooling a Molded Candle

Though you'll immediately want to see your beautiful piece of work, you must take the proper precautions of cooling the candle before you remove it from the mold. This is the general technique of cooling a molded candle.

Materials

Skewer, pouring pitcher, reserved wax (in paper cup)

Instructions

1. As soon as the candle starts to congeal and thicken on the surface, poke the candle with a skewer, making sure not to disturb the wick or the sides of the candle (see step CC-1).

Cooling Tips

If the workshop environment is cold and you want the candle to cool slowly, make an aluminum-foil shell and wrap it around the mold while it cools.

If the environment is warm and you want the candle to cool quickly, wait until the poured candle is cool to the touch, then place the mold in a cool place such as a refrigerator or a water bath. For a water bath, partially fill a container taller than the mold with cold water and carefully lower the mold into it. The water should be level with the height of the candle, but not able to get into the mold. Cover the mold with a weight or apply weights at the mold base to prevent it from floating or tipping.

This relieves the surface tension and prevents the sides of the mold from possibly caving in. It also enables additional pourings to reach any air pockets inside the candle.

2. Allow the candle to cool for a couple of hours. It is normal to see the wax cave in and form a depression around the wick. This shrinkage phenomenon occurs as the wax molecules cool from their heated, excited state and settle down to a more compact solid.

3. Using the cup of wax you set aside in the pouring method, refill this well until the cavity is filled almost up to the original pouring level. Don't pour all the way to the original level, or liquid wax might seep between the solid candle and the mold, making it difficult to remove the candle. Poke the well every time you pour to make sure you fill any air pockets that may form in the candle.

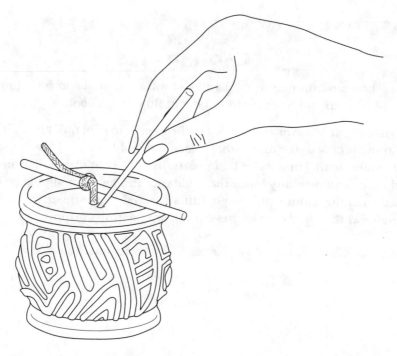

Step CC-1. As soon as the candle starts to congeal and thicken on the surface, poke the candle with a skewer, making sure not to disturb the wick or the sides of the candle.

Finishing a Molded Candle

Now you've made it through the cooling . . . only one more step before you get to see what you've made. This is the general technique of finishing a molded candle.

Materials

Scissors, flat griddle pan or skillet, heat source

Instructions

1. Once the shrinkage well is filled and the candle is completely cooled, the candle is now ready to be removed from the mold.

2. Metal mold: Supporting the open end of the mold with your hand, remove the mold sealer and the wick screw. The candle should slide out easily. Squeeze the mold and gently pull on the wick rod if the candle doesn't just slide out.

   Plastic mold: Remove the wick stand and clamps from the two halves. Dislodge the wick from the wick slit, remove one half of the mold from the candle, and support it while removing the other half.

   Flexible mold: Remove the mold sealer and the wick screw and gently pull the sides of the mold away from the candle. Carefully peel the mold off the candle.

> ▼▼▼▼▼▼▼▼▼▼▼▼▼▼▼▼▼▼
> ## Handy Hint
> Never bang on a mold to release a candle. It will only make it more difficult to remove the candle and may damage the mold.
> ▲▲▲▲▲▲▲▲▲▲▲▲▲▲▲▲▲▲

3. Once you have removed the candle from the mold, remove the wick rod and cut the wick, including any knots, away from the base of the candle (see step FC-1).

4. To give your candle a level base, place it on a flat griddle pan or skillet set at low heat.

5. With the top of the candle at eye level, rotate it gently and quickly (see step FC-2).

6. Remove the candle from the heat, hold the candle while the base cools (a few seconds), and set the candle upright. Repeat this process until the candle is level. Make sure you use a low heat setting or the base will melt too fast.

7. Allow a candle to set at least for a couple of days before lighting it to give the candle a chance to settle chemically and improve its burning quality. Some dyes have to set for a few days in order to show their true color.

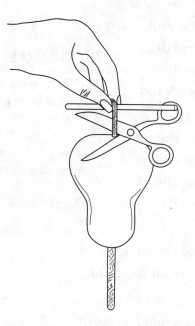

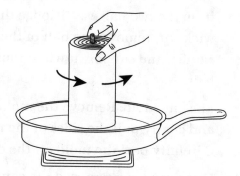

Step FC-1. Once you have removed the candle from the mold, remove the wick rod and cut the wick, including any knots, away from the base of the candle.

Step FC-2. With the top of the candle at eye level, rotate it gently and quickly.

Rolling a Candle

There are other ways to make candles without using a mold. Following are standard instructions for rolling a candle.

Materials

Wax sheets (beeswax or make your own), hair-dryer, wick (remember beeswax requires a larger wick than paraffin requires). Optional: straightedge, mat board, sharp, unserrated knife

Instructions

1. Lay a wax sheet on a clean, flat surface.

2. Soften the wax using a hair-dryer set on low heat.

3. Lay a length of wick along one edge of the sheet so that it sticks out on one side about ¼ inch (see step RC-1). This will be the top of your candle.

4. Fold the edge of the sheet over the wick and gently but firmly roll the sheet up around the wick, working evenly and taking care to keep the fold straight (see step RC-2).

5. When you reach the end of the sheet, press the edge gently down to seal the sheet to the candle.

> ### Did you know???
> Using beeswax for church candles was so important through the Middle Ages and afterward that practically every monastery and abbey had its own apiary for producing beeswax.

   Variations: Slant the top edge of the wax sheet to make taper or spiral rolled candles. Or roll a sheet of wax around a ready-made candle as a surface decoration.

Making Your Own Wax Sheets

You can really get creative and "start from scratch." Following is the general technique for making your own wax sheets.

Materials

   2.5 pounds paraffin wax (130 to 135 degrees Fahrenheit), heat source, 11 × 17" shallow baking pan, wax paper larger than pans, 0.5 pounds beeswax additive (or a dip and carve type wax), color and scent (optional)

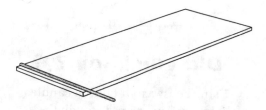

Step RC-1. Lay a length of wick along one edge of the sheet so that it sticks out on one side about ¼ inch.

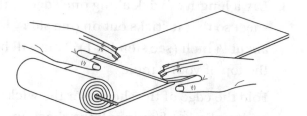

Step RC-2. Fold the edge of the sheet over the wick and gently but firmly roll the sheet up around the wick, working evenly and taking care to keep the fold straight.

Instructions

1. Line baking pan with wax paper.

2. Melt the wax and additive to 150 degrees Fahrenheit and pour into the baking pan lined with wax paper to about ¾ inch.

3. Once the wax is pliable and not runny, pick up the wax with the wax paper and lay it on a flat surface. The candle is now ready to be rolled.

    Variation: Press flowers or other objects such as seeds or coffee beans onto the outside of the sheet to roll around a ready-made candle. Sheets with embedments must only be used as a surface decoration.

Dipping a Candle

Here's another method of candlemaking that is simple and fun.

Materials

Primed wick, wick rod, small weight, wax (145 degrees Fahrenheit; type depends on what you're making; you'll need a lot of wax, depending on the height and diameter of the dipping can), hardening additive, double boiler (the melting pot/dipping can must be a few inches taller than the height of the candle), heat source

Instructions

1. Tie one end of the wick to the wick rod and the other to the small weight. If you're making more than one taper, space the wicks on the rod at least 4 inches apart.

2. Heat the wax and additives together to 160 degrees Fahrenheit in the double boiler.

Overdipping a Candle

You can overdip any candle to seal the surface and surface decorations. Dip the candle into wax a few times as you would finish a taper. Use the same color as the candle for the overdip or experiment with different additives and wax for interesting effects.

3. Hold the rod perpendicular to the dipping can and lower the wick into the wax with a swift, smooth movement.

4. Allow the wax to cool between dippings. Dip each wick repeatedly until you reach the desired thickness.

5. To finish the taper, heat the wax to 180 degrees Fahrenheit for the final few dips, and dip longer than usual for a smooth finish.

Variations: Dip layers in different colors for multicolored drips, or alternate colors and dip in successively shorter dips for striped tapers.

Testing Your Candle Recipes

There are no standards, regulations, or laws governing the manufacture of candles. Therefore, as a candlemaker, you are responsible to the consumer of your candles for the quality of every candle you make. Without common standards of quality, how do you know what makes a good candle? It is more than just appearance; a candle should burn in an excellent manner. A well-burning candle is one that consumes the melted wax as rapidly as it accumulates and minimizes toxic emissions from the fuel and/or ingredients used in the making of the candle.

Candle Soot

Candle soot is the environmental hazard arising from the use of petroleum-based candles (candles made from paraffin and gel). All candles that emit a yellow flame produce soot, but usually at a rate that does not cause damage. An improper recipe of wax, wick, and additives can cause excessive candle soot. Candle soot is microscopic hydrocarbon particles that can penetrate air-conditioning filters as well as the deepest recesses of our lungs. When excessively

An Easy Way to Test for Candle Soot

This is an easy (although not entirely scientific) way to test for excessively sooty candles.

Materials: test candle, small stack of about 10 white disposable plastic plates

Light the candle in a confined area, such as a utility or bathroom. Right after lighting the candle, separate the plates into 2 or 3 stacks (this will create a static charge) and place them near or around the burning candle. Let the candle burn for about an hour (depending on the carbon emission rates of the candle, the time needed for results could be as short as 10 minutes), monitoring the candle so it doesn't start a fire. If the candle is excessively sooty, you will notice a thin, dark film collecting on the top plate of each stack. This type of soot has a strong attraction to plastics, especially when the plastic is charged.

sooty candles are burned in the home, deposits of aggregated soot build up on all interior surfaces. This can cause much smoke damage not covered by homeowners insurance, not to mention smoke inhalation is a personal health hazard.

It is not only the rate at which these candles produce soot that is dangerous, but also the type of soot produced. A petroleum-based candle, depending on the type and grade of the wax, can also emit substances similar to the emissions of its sister by-products—gasoline and kerosene. Since soy wax and beeswax are not petroleum based, they do not produce such emissions and are cleaner burning.

Needless to say, paraffin and gel candles that smoke excessively are indoor air pollutants and health hazards, and you must do everything you can to minimize these risks.

As a manufacturer of petroleum-based candles, you can make it a point to use quality ingredients and test a candle from each batch for safety. If you do find a batch that does not meet your quality standards, melt the candles down and repeatedly adjust the recipe until they burn well.

Here are a few things you can do in a candle recipe to minimize soot:

Reduce the amount of paraffin in your recipe by blending it with soy or beeswax, or eliminate paraffin altogether from the mix.

If you do use paraffin, use a hard wax containing mostly saturated hydrocarbons. (Saturated hydrocarbons do not emit as readily as unsaturated hydrocarbons.)

Use a braided wick that curls over when burned.

Cut down the amount of artificial oil you use. Many artificial oils are petroleum based as well.

Use a cotton core wick in container candles.

When test-burning a candle for safety, look for these signs that your candle may produce excessive soot:

Excessively oily wax due to wax type or too much scent oil

Pockets of unmixed additives or pools of oil

An oversized wick that produces a large, smoky flame

Soot deposits on the mouth of a container candle

A flame that spits, sputters, flickers, or dances when not burning in a draft

Visible soot from an erratic flame

Burning Your Candles Safely

The following are important issues with regards to fire safety.

Candle containers should be capable of withstanding the high heat of candles. Champagne glasses, for example, are not manufactured to hold up to heat and are also questionable when it comes to the stability of the glass. If the candle is allowed to burn to the bottom of the container, metal wick tabs can heat up to high temperatures and cause the container to break.

Candle-Quality Troubleshooting

Flaws/Burning Flaws	Possible Reasons	Possible Solutions
Burns too fast	Wax is too soft Air cavities around the wick	Add hardening additives Poke the surface when pouring even if there is little shrinkage to make sure you pour into any air cavities
Dripping	Candle burning in a draft Wax recipe is too soft Wick too large Wick not centered	Burn away from drafts Use harder wax recipe Use smaller wick Make sure wick is centered in mold
Flame flickers or sputters	Water in the wax Wick not primed	Keep water out of mold if using a water bath. Prime wick.
New candle will not light	Wick not primed	Hold lighter flame to wick until it starts to draw wax Prime the wick
Small flame	Wax is too hard	Use less hardening additive
Small melt pool	Wick is too small	Use larger wick
Wick burns out	Air cavities around the wick	Poke the surface when pouring even if there is little shrinkage to make sure you pour into any air cavities
Smokes/produces soot	Candle burning in a draft Too much oil in candle Wick too large Poor quality wax Poor quality wick	Burn away from drafts Use less oil Use smaller wick Use better quality wax Use properly treated wick

(continued)

Molding Problems	Possible Reasons	Possible Solutions
Air bubbles	Poor quality wax	Use better quality wax
	Poured too fast	Tip mold when pouring to minimize bubbles
	Not sufficiently tapped to release air bubbles	Tap mold to release air bubbles
	Dirty mold	Make sure mold is thoroughly clean
Bleeding or running color layers	Previous layer not adequately cooled	Allow a layer to cool until it forms a strong but pliable surface
	Layer poured too hot	Pour at a lower temperature
	Previous layer contracted away from the mold	Pour next layer while wax is still warm
Bulges	Mold wall not strong enough (cardboard mold)	Reinforce cardboard mold
	Not poked to relieve surface tension (flexible mold)	Poke the mold to relieve surface tension
Caved-in sides	Not poked to relieve surface tension	Poke the mold to relieve surface tension
	Not poked soon enough	Poke the surface when pouring even if there is little shrinkage to make sure you pour into any air cavities
	Air cavities around the wick	
Crumbly bottom	Additional pourings poured too late	Pour additional pourings before the candle has set
	Additional pourings not poured hot enough	Pour additional pourings a little hotter than the original pour so the pouring adheres to the candle
Difficult to remove candle	Damaged mold	Put mold in refrigerator and try every ½ hour to remove candle
	Additional pouring seeped in between the candle and the mold	

	Wax too soft	Use a harder wax recipe
	Not enough mold release	Spray mold release prior to pouring
	Poured too hot for type of mold or type of wax recipe	Pour at a lower temperature
Frost or pit marks	Poured too cool	Raise pouring temperature
	Dirty mold	Make sure the mold is free of wax residue
	Not enough mold release	Use mold release
Little or no scent	Not enough scent	Add more scent
	Scent not compatible with wax mixture	Try a different scent
	Scent vaporized before pouring	Add scent right before you pour
Mottling	Small melt pool	Use a softer wax that will produce a larger melt pool
Oily candle	Too much oil in the wax	Add vybar to the wax recipe Decrease scent oil
	Too much mold releasing agent	Use less mold release
Ring around the candle	Mold was too cold	Warm the mold prior to pouring
	Low pouring temperature	Raise pouring temperature
Thermal cracks	Cooled too quickly	Wrap aluminum-foil shell around mold to slow cooling Cool in a warmer place
"Wet spots" in glass containers	Wax not adhering to the glass	Use a softer wax
	Wax is too hard	or softening additives Heat the container prior to pouring

Always make sure that any surface decorations you use are nonflammable and will not come in contact with the flame. If the candle is not meant to be burned, don't put a wick in it, or label it as such.

Even if you are not selling your candles, it is still important to educate each user about candle safety. You should assume nothing when it comes to the consumer's knowledge of the proper use and safety of your candles. Here's what you can tell your candle users to do to minimize soot and prevent fire accidents:

Put a candle in a nonflammable holder and in a safe place.
Trim the wick to ¼ inch before every lighting. Wicks in soy wax candles can be trimmed to ⅛ inch.

Never leave a burning candle unattended.
Never move a candle while it is burning.
Store candles in the refrigerator (wrapped in foil or plastic wrap to protect them from moisture) to lengthen burning times.
To increase the burning quality of a new candle, allow the candle to burn up to the edge of the candle (but not over the edge) before extinguishing it the first time.
Generally, allow a candle to burn 1 hour at a time for every inch in diameter.
Burn candles away from drafts to prevent dripping and uneven burning.
Turn candles before every lighting to burn the candle evenly.
Reduce the amount of smoke when extinguishing a candle by dipping the wick in the melt pool to snuff it out.
Keep candles clean and free of dust and dirt. Buff the candle with a nylon stocking to refresh candle gloss.

Of course you can't fit all this safety information on a little candle label. But as a relatively small-time candlemaker, you have the

> **Handy Hint**
>
> Decorate the candle surface or overdip the candle (see page 101) to hide surface flaws.

intimate opportunity to educate candle lovers to be better consumers and candle users. When giving or selling your candles, attach a simple label describing the candle, the most important points to remember when burning that particular candle, and a friendly safety reminder.

Creating Your Candlemaking Projects

▼▼

IT'S TIME TO PUT what you've learned so far into practice! This chapter will show you how to make a few projects that will allow you to create all kinds of candles as your experience grows. See the color insert in the center of the book for a look at these finished projects.

Fun and Simple Projects

These projects are great eye-openers to the wonderful world of candlemaking. Each is simple to learn and easy to adapt to your own technique and skill. I've chosen these recipes because each one focuses on a different and popular facet of contemporary candlemaking. These types of candles are the candles you see everywhere, and it only takes basic modifications of each process illustrated here to make many styles of candles.

Read through the whole recipe first before you begin to gain an understanding of what's involved. You must also first read chapter 4 and know the basic how-to's before you begin these projects. If you have any question about the materials needed, look back to the

Candlemaking Using Soy-Based Waxes

The following are tips specifically for using Ecowax novelty blend wax (MP 174 degrees Fahrenheit). Other soy wax blends have similar properties, but may differ in temperature considerations.

- Ecowax slides out of the bucket it comes in or it can be broken up inside the bucket with a chisel-like tool, digging and prying from the center out.

- Soy-based waxes do not shrink as much as paraffin; for example Ecowax shrinks approximately 3%, requiring only one pour.

- Additives such as vybar and stearic acid in general are not necessary with Ecowax. It removes easily from molds, not requiring a mold-releasing agent.

- Your molds may need "conditioning" before using Ecowax. If your candle does not release well after cooling, clean the mold of excess wax, remelt the Ecowax, and re-pour. This first pouring will have "conditioned" the mold.

- Melting Ecowax to 210 degrees Fahrenheit to mix in your color works well. The wax should then be cooled to your desired pour temperature for the addition of scent. Ecowaxes can be melted in the microwave.

previous chapters for more information. Pay close attention to safety and detail to have the most pleasurable time in your workshop. Make sure you never leave the wax on the heat source unattended while you move through each step of your project. If you need to leave the melting area, turn off the heat source and remove the double boiler from the heat. Don't forget to take journal notes at each step of the process.

Pottery Container Candles

Smelling the aroma of rosemary, lavender, and tea tree is a great way to freshen up and energize. This project creates a true aromatherapy candle in handmade pottery that anyone would appreciate.

- Pouring at lower temperatures creates a harder candle exterior, and may cause fracturing when the candle is burning.

- Ecowax does not produce bubbles when poured, and tapping the mold may not be necessary.

- The natural mottling effects that occur with Ecowax can be varied by using very dark coloring, very light coloring, or increasing the amount of any coloring to reduce or eliminate the mottling. The effects are most intense with moderate use of mid-range colors and quick cooling.

- As Ecowax is more viscous than paraffin when melted and has a higher melting point, the use of a much larger wick is necessary. For example, a #6 square braid wick can be used in a 3-inch pillar candle; whereas with a paraffin candle of the same size, you would use a smaller sized square braid wick.

- For hurricane and embedded candles, pour Ecowax at about 180 degrees Fahrenheit along the sides of the mold. Stick your embedded material to the cooling wax. Using a smaller wick, pour the rest of the candle at 170 degrees Fahrenheit after the sides have cooled but are not fully hardened.

Makes 1 candle

Time

1 to 1½ hours, plus a few hours of cooling time and 24 hours for curing/drying

Materials

16-ounce ceramic container at least 3 inches in diameter (waterproof and able to withstand high temperatures)
Primed cotton core wick or square braid wick of appropriate size (one to two sizes larger for soy wax and beeswax than standard size used for paraffin)

Wick rod

1 pound Ecowax CB soy wax (or 12 ounces soy wax + 4 ounces
    beeswax blend)*

Double boiler

Heat source

Thermometer

Rosemary Refresher scent oil blend (6 drops rosemary +
    2 drops lavender + 2 drops tea tree)

Dropper

Skewer or knitting needle stirrer

4- to 5-ounce paper cups for color tests and excess wax

Pot holders

Instructions

1. Wick and prepare the ceramic container by following the
   steps outlined in chapter 4.

2. With the thermometer in place, melt the wax in the double
   boiler, making sure that no water gets into the melting pot.
   Heat the wax to 180 degrees Fahrenheit.

3. Once the wax has melted, add color (if desired).

4. Add the drops of rosemary, lavender, and tea tree, one scent
   at a time, and slowly stir the mixture.

5. Double-check the container to make sure it is fully prepared
   and ready for pouring.

6. Using pot holders, pour the wax at 160 degrees Fahrenheit.
   Pour slowly, close to the container to minimize splattering.

7. Cool the container undisturbed at room temperature. Soy
   wax has very little shrinkage and should not require additional pourings to level the pouring surface. However, if

If you can't find soy wax, see Variations on page 115 for other options.

you're using paraffin wax, as the wax cools, keep filling the mold with leftover wax until the surface is level.

8. Allow the candle to set for a day or so before lighting it.

Variations

■ For a true aromatherapy candle, make sure your fragrance is a true essential oil and use a soy wax or beeswax. Soy wax is excellent for aromatherapy products because of its vegetable base and compatibility with essential oils. You can substitute paraffin or gel and/or use artificial fragrance oils, but the candle will not contain the therapeutic properties of a true aromatherapy product. Soy wax blends from different manufacturers may vary in color and scent throw even when poured at the same temperature. Check with the wax's distributor for recommendations on using their wax.

■ Try a different aromatherapy blend. If the aroma was not strong enough, gradually increase the recipe proportions, not to exceed 6% (1 ounce per pound) of the wax mixture.

■ Instead of an aromatherapy candle, try a whimsical approach. Experiment with a container candle in an interesting tin or recycled container with a cheerful color and fragrance. There are many blends of container waxes available, so pay attention to the manufacturer's recommendations for pouring temperatures.

Gel Candle Seascapes

The gel candle variations in this project will present illusions of pretty underwater scenes.

Makes 2 candles

Time

1 to 2 hours, plus 1 hour of cooling time

Materials

Thermometer
16 ounces Versagel MP or HP gel
Double boiler
Heat source
Large metal spoon
2 core wicks
2 wick tabs
Small seashells
Wax paper
Two 8-ounce clear glass containers
1 cup natural color aquarium sand
1 ounce fragrance
A few shavings of sky blue block dye or a drop of blue liquid dye
Pot holders

Tips for Selecting and Handling Materials

- Make sure your glass is sturdy and able to withstand high temperatures (tempered glass is best). The glass should also have a mouth at least 2 to 3 inches in diameter to allow for proper burning.

- Wicks for gel candles should be a size larger than wicks for paraffin candles.

- Make sure your fragrance is clear. A colored scent can make the gel cloudy.

- Rinse and thoroughly dry the sand to make sure that it is completely free of dust and dirt.

- You only need a small amount of dye, since the beauty of gel is its clarity.

- Use a metal spoon instead of a wooden spoon because wood retains moisture and can cause bubbles in the gel.

- Gel melts slower than wax in a double boiler. Once you get the hang of making gel candles, you can try melting the wax over very low direct heat, but you must be extra careful.

- Make sure your melting pot has no wax residue from any wax candlemaking. Any wax in your pot will make the gel cloudy.

Instructions

1. With the thermometer in place, melt the gel in the double boiler, making sure that no water gets into the melting pot. Melt the gel to the maximum temperature a double boiler allows—212 degrees Fahrenheit.

2. With the metal spoon, dip wicks, wick tabs, and shells, one at a time into the gel to lightly coat each object. This coating helps prevent the object from creating bubbles in the gel. You may be able to hand-dip each wick and wick tab (attach them to each other first) into the gel instead of using the spoon. Allow each coated item to cool on a sheet of wax paper.

3. Pre-warm both glass containers by carefully running warm to hot water over the outside of the glass. This will minimize stress on the glass and bubbles in the gel.

4. Center the wick in each container.

5. Hold the wick in place while you cover the bottom of the container with a thin layer of sand, concealing the wick tab.

6. Place a few of the coated shells on the gravel toward the sides of the container, away from the wick. This placement will maximize the shells' visibility in the gel and minimize interference with the wick as it burns.

7. Check the temperature of the gel. When it has reached 205 degrees Fahrenheit, you can add color and scent. Don't be tempted to add more than a few shavings or a drop of color or more than an ounce of scent. (Any more makes the gel cloudy.) Slowly stir the mixture and make sure the color and scent are thoroughly blended with the gel.

8. Double-check to make sure the glass containers are ready for pouring and the shells and gravel are situated where you want them.

9. Using pot holders, pour the gel at 210 degrees Fahrenheit. Pour slowly and as close to the container as possible to minimize bubbles. If the gel has cooled to a lower temperature from being off the heat, reheat it to the proper pouring temperature, or you'll get lots of bubbles.

10. Allow the candles to cool undisturbed for a few hours. They should then be ready to light.

Variations

■ Instead of shells and gravel, you can use any embedments that are nonflammable. Stones, glass objects, glitter, crystals, and metal items are good choices.

■ Instead of placing the shells on top of the gravel, suspend the shells in the gel by pouring a shallow layer of gel, allowing it

Fragrance and Gel Candle Safety

Here's where scenting gel gets tricky! The scent you use in your recipe must be both compatible and soluble in the gel. Check with your scent retailer to find out the flash point (temperature at which it catches fire) of your scent. Any scent with a flash point of 170 degrees Fahrenheit or higher is okay for candle gel. Lower flash points can cause the scent to combust before the gel while the candle is burning, and that's dangerous!

You'll also want to make sure the oil is completely soluble in the gel. To test if your oil is soluble, mix 1 part fragrance with 3 parts mineral oil (these can be very small amounts, as long as the proportions are correct). If the fragrance separates from the mineral oil, then the oil is not soluble enough for the gel and should not be used. You can also make a test candle and allow it to sit for a few days. If the fragrance starts to travel to the top of the candle, then the oil is not suitable for the gel.

to get a little sticky, and then dropping each shell into the candle. Be sure to minimize bubbles as in step 9 and use Versagel HP. You may have to experiment with other brands to determine how well other consistencies of gel hold suspended objects.

■ Pour different color layers of gel for a multicolored look. Allow the layers to cool to different levels of hardness before pouring the next color to experiment with interesting color variations.

■ Make gel chunks by pouring gel into a shallow baking pan and cutting it into squares or other shapes. After the shapes cool, fill the container with the chunks and pour a different color gel over the chunks.

3 Mosaic Candles

There are many names for this type of candle (chunk, landscape, watercolor), which is simply created by pouring wax over wax chunks of a contrasting color. You'll have to beg people to burn these colorful candles.

Makes 2 candles

Time

1 to 1½ hours to make and the cool chunks, 1 to 2 hours to make the candles, a few hours of cooling time and 24 hours for curing/drying

Materials

Shallow baking pan

Thermometer

2 pounds medium MP (135 to 145 degrees Fahrenheit) paraffin
    wax divided in half

Double boiler

Heat source

1 teaspoon translucent or clear additive divided in half

¼ cup stainless steel measuring cup

Skewer or knitting needle stirrer

2 contrasting color dyes (one for the chunks and one for the
    overpour)

Pot holders

Unserrated knife

2 primed wicks of appropriate size

Two 1-pound symmetrical metal molds and accessories (wick
    rod, screw, and sealer)

1 teaspoon vybar for molded candles (if fragrance is added)

1 ounce fragrance (optional)

Two 4- to 5-ounce $1/2$ wax paper cups
Griddle pan or skillet

Making Wax Chunks

1. Place the baking pan on a covered surface.

2. With the thermometer in place, melt 1 pound of the wax in the double boiler, making sure that no water gets into the melting pot.

3. When the wax has reached its melting point, melt $1/2$ teaspoon of clear additive in the measuring cup over direct heat. As soon as the additive has melted, add it to the wax. The additive may sink to the bottom of the melting pot. Stir the mixture and scrape the bottom of the melting pot with your stirrer to ensure that the additive is completely blended with the wax.

4. Once the wax mixture is completely clear, add color (using manufacturer instructions). Stir the mixture and scrape the bottom of the melting pot with your stirrer to ensure that the color is completely blended with the wax.

5. Using pot holders, pour the wax slowly and carefully into the baking pan to a $1/2$-inch thickness. Pour close to the pan to minimize splatter.

6. Allow the wax sheet to cool and thicken. The surface of the wax should be solid but warm to the touch when slicing. Test the sheet for thickness by poking it with the knife in a corner of the pan. The sheet should be semisolid throughout the layer, leaving no liquid wax residue on the knife.

7. When the wax has suitably thickened, slice the wax into small squares. (This is like making brownies!) Pay attention to time and make sure the sheet has not completely hardened or you will not be able to slice through it.

8. Allow the sheet to completely harden after slicing. This should take from ½ an hour to an hour.

9. Once the sheet has completely hardened, break the sheet into chunks. The sheet should be easy to break apart.

Making the Candles

1. Wick and prepare the molds, following the directions as outlined in chapter 4. You do not need a mold release.

2. Fill the wicked molds with the wax chunks. Gently shake each mold to settle the chunks and continue to add chunks until the molds are completely filled. Make sure the wick stays centered as you fill the mold.

3. To prepare the overpour, repeat steps 2–4 in the instructions on page 121 for making wax chunks, using the other pound of wax.

4. Add vybar first, then scent, if desired. Stir the mixture and scrape the bottom of the melting pot with your stirrer to ensure that the additive is completely blended with the wax.

5. Once the mixture is completely blended, fill the two paper cups with wax. This wax will either be stored as leftover wax, or remelted for additional pourings after the candle has cooled.

6. Using pot holders, pour the wax at 200 degrees Fahrenheit into each mold. Pour slowly, aiming at the wick. If the wax has cooled to a lower temperature from being off the heat after pouring the first candle, reheat the wax to the proper pouring temperature before pouring the second candle, or the candles may look different.

7. Tap along the side of each mold from top to bottom with your stirrer immediately after pouring to help the wax fill any air pockets inside the mold.

8. Allow the molds to cool undisturbed. Once the surface of the wax inside the mold has formed a thick skin, poke into the mold away from the edges to allow additional pourings to reach any air pockets and to relieve the surface tension. Don't poke to the bottom of the mold, which is the top of your candle or you'll see a blemish on the top of the candle.

9. At this point, you can turn off the heat source.

10. As the wax settles and cools, keep filling the mold with left-over wax until surface is level. If you run out of wax in your pitcher, allow the wax in the paper cups to cool. Remove the cup by tearing it away from the wax, and remelt it in your melting pot.

    Do not pour higher than the original pouring level. Pour each successive pouring at 210 degrees Fahrenheit. This process is repeated during the next 3- to 4-hour period until the pouring surface is level. The temperature is a little higher than the first pouring to ensure that the new wax binds well with the hardened wax.

11. Each time the surface of the wax inside the mold has formed a thick skin, poke into the mold again. This is where most of your time will be spent. You won't see a shrinkage well form as much with chunks in the mold, but there will be air pockets. Don't wait too long to pour additional pourings. If you do, and the sides of the candle have cooled sufficiently to shrink away from the mold, you may accidentally pour liquid wax into the cavity between the candle and the mold, blemishing the candle surface and making it difficult to remove the candle from the mold.

12. Once each candle has completely cooled and the pouring surface is level, you can remove the candle from the mold. Supporting the open end of the mold with your hand, remove the mold sealer and the wick screw. The candle should slide easily out of the mold.

13. Place each candle on the griddle pan or skillet set at low heat, one at a time.

14. With the top of the candle at eye level, rotate it gently and quickly.

15. Remove the candle from the heat, hold the candle while the base cools (a few seconds), and set the candle upright. Repeat this process until the candle is level. Make sure you use a low heat setting or the base will melt too fast.

16. Allow the candles to set for at least a couple of days before lighting to give them a chance to settle chemically and improve their burning quality. Some dyes may also have to set for a few days before true colors surface.

Variations

- Instead of clear additives, experiment with other additives to attain different effects. I used clear additives in this recipe to make the whole candle translucent, but you can add opaque additives instead. Try substituting opaque additives such as stearine or luster additive when making chunks and keep the clear additive for the overpour. This will make the chunks stand out even more.

- Experiment with different types of wax blends. Soy wax can also be used as an alternative to paraffin. No additives are needed for soy wax.

- Experiment with different pouring temperatures. You can make overdyed chunks without hardening additive and pour at a higher temperature, melting the chunks and creating a beautiful watercolor effect.

- Try all kinds of color combinations. Use different color wax chunks and randomly fill, make a design, or layer different colors however you like.

- Pack the molds tightly for a real chunky look, or pack them lightly for a more subtle effect.

- Try another type of mold—it doesn't have to be metal. Just be sure not to pour at too high of a temperature for the type of mold you use.

- Make a mosaic candle as a container candle, using container-type wax.

 Project 4

Textured Stripe Candles

These candles are pretty layered candles with a textured look attained by whipping each wax layer to a creamy consistency. Well-made candles of this type are popular gifts because of their handmade attractiveness.

Time

1 to 2 hours, plus a few hours of cooling time and 24 hours for curing/drying

Materials

Primed wick of appropriate size
Two 1-pound round metal molds and accessories (wick rod, screw, and sealer)

2 pounds medium MP (135 to 145 degrees Fahrenheit) paraffin wax divided in half

Thermometer

6 tablespoons stearic acid divided in half

2 contrasting color dyes (one for the chunks and one for the overpour)

2 double boiler setups

Heat source

1 teaspoon vybar for molded candles (if fragrance is added)

1 ounce fragrance (optional)

Skewer or knitting needle stirrer

¼ cup stainless steel measuring cup

Manual rotary beater (optional)

Pot holders

Griddle pan or skillet

Two 4- to 5-ounce wax paper cups

Unserrated knife

Instructions

1. Wick the molds, following the directions as outlined in chapter 4. You do not need a mold release.

2. Follow steps 3–5 to melt 2 batches of wax individually, one for each color.

3. With the thermometer in place, melt 3 tablespoons of stearic acid with the color dye in the double boiler, making sure that no water gets into the melting pot. Stir the mixture until thoroughly melted. Add 1 pound of wax.

4. Add ½ teaspoon vybar first, then ½ ounce scent, if desired. Stir the mixture and scrape the bottom of the melting pot with your stirrer to ensure that the additive is completely blended with the wax.

5. When the additives are thoroughly blended, turn off the heat and remove the melting pot from the double boiler.

6. When the wax forms a thin skin on the liquid surface, vigorously whip the wax with your stirrer or a manual rotary beater, until the wax becomes a thick creamy consistency. Scrape the sides of the pot to reintroduce the thickening wax back into the mixture. The wax should be slightly liquid and runny. It should not be so cool that it has hard lumps. If this occurs, reheat the wax, and cool the mixture again to the proper consistency.

7. Double-check the molds to make sure they are fully prepared and ready for pouring.

8. Using pot holders, pour the thick wax mixture to fill ⅓ of each mold, pouring slowly down the center to avoid splattering inside the mold.

9. Allow the layer to cool slightly. The skin should thicken quickly because the wax is already cool.

10. Heat the wax again and repeat steps 5–7 for the next layers. After you have poured both the second and third layers, poke the wax around the wick to relieve surface tension and allow additional pourings to reach any interior air pockets.

11. As the wax settles and cools, keep filling the mold with leftover wax until surface is level.

12. When each candle has completely cooled and the pouring surface is level, you can now remove the candle from the mold. Supporting the open end of the mold with your hand, remove the mold sealer and the wick screw. The candle should slide easily out of the mold.

13. Place each candle on the griddle pan or skillet set at low heat, one at a time.

14. With the top of the candle at eye level, rotate it gently and quickly.

15. Remove the candle from the heat, hold the candle while the base cools (a few seconds), and set the candle upright. Repeat this process until the candle is level. Make sure you use a low heat setting or the base will melt too fast.

16. Trim the seam line with a knife, if necessary, holding the knife at a 45-degree angle to minimize nicks.

17. Allow the candles to set for at least a couple of days before lighting to give them a chance to settle chemically and improve their burning quality. Some dyes may also have to set for a few days in order to show their true colors.

Variations

- Pour more layers and/or colors.

- Experiment with different wax consistencies for varied textures.

- Tilt each layer by leaning the mold against a sturdy object, or if the mold has a suitable base, tilt the mold in a coffee can.

- Make one-color textured candles: Instead of layers, just pour one color for a simple textured look.

- Make frosted candles: Prepare the wax as in the above project. Allow the wax to cool until lumpy, but still runny. Dip a premade candle into the lumpy wax with one smooth movement, holding the candle by its wick with pliers. Dip repeatedly until the candle forms a lumpy, frosted looking surface. Or, instead of dipping the candle, you can apply the whipped wax with a spatula as if you were frosting a cake.

Novelty Candles

Novelty candles are sold everywhere; they are any candles you see that are representations of objects. Here are a few ideas, but the novelty possibilities are endless. This is a fun and simple way to make candles, much similar to making most novelty candles made with plastic molds.

Amount varies depending on mold(s)

Time

2 hours, plus a few hours of cooling time and 24 hours for curing/ drying

Materials

2 wicks appropriate for soy wax and size of mold

One 2-pound two-piece plastic mold or two 1-pound plastic molds

Plastic mold accessories (tape, clamps, stand, shoebox)

Thermometer

2 pounds Ecowax soy wax (MP 174 degrees Fahrenheit) or paraffin wax combination (see Variations on page 131)

Double boiler setup

Heat source

Color dye (optional)

1 ounce fragrance (optional)

Skewer or knitting needle stirrer

Pot holders

Unserrated knife

Nylon stocking

Griddle pan or skillet

Instructions

1. Wick and prepare each mold according to the manufacturer's directions, or follow the steps for wicking a plastic mold outlined in chapter 4.

2. With the thermometer in place, melt the wax in the double boiler, making sure that no water gets into the melting pot. Melt the wax to 210 degrees Fahrenheit.

3. When the wax has reached 210 degrees Fahrenheit, add color and scent, if desired, according to manufacturer's instructions. Stir the mixture and scrape the bottom of the melting pot with your stirrer to ensure that the additive is completely blended with the wax.

4. Double-check the molds to make sure they are fully prepared and ready for pouring.

5. Using pot holders, pour the wax at 180 degrees Fahrenheit into the molds. Ecowax does not produce bubbles when used alone, so tapping the mold is not necessary.

6. Cool the molds at room temperature. Soy wax has very little shrinkage and should not require additional pourings to level the pouring surface.

7. When the molds have completely cooled, remove the wick stand and clamps from the two halves. Dislodge the wick from the wick slit, remove one half of the mold from the candle, and support the candle while removing the other half.

8. Smooth any visible seam lines with the knife, holding the knife at a 45-degree angle to minimize nicks.

9. Buff the seams and any fingerprints with a nylon stocking.

10. Place each candle on the griddle pan or skillet set at low heat, one at a time.

11. With the top of the candle at eye level, rotate it gently and quickly.

12. Remove the candle from the heat, hold the candle while the base cools (a few seconds), and set the candle upright. Repeat this process until the candle is level. Make sure you use a low heat setting or the base will melt too fast.

13. Allow the candles to set for at least a couple of days before lighting to give them a chance to settle chemically and improve their burning quality. Some dyes may also have to set for a few days in order to show their true colors.

> **Handy Hint**
>
> If the candle does not release well after cooling, clean the excess wax from the mold with a soft cloth. Your molds may need "conditioning" before using Ecowax. Remelt the wax and repour. This first pouring should "condition" the mold.

Variations

- For a shiny appearance, dip the candle in a candle glaze or spray with a candle luster glaze.

- You can use paraffin instead of soy wax. Add ½ teaspoon of luster additive per pound of wax and ½ teaspoon of vybar per pound (if fragrance is added).

Project 6 Glowing Coffee Candle Lantern

This "hurricane" lantern shell is a popular decorative enclosure for votives and tea lights. This project doesn't make a candle, but a wax shell embedded with coffee beans and scented with a coffee fragrance that glows when a votive or tea light is lit inside it. This project is a little more complex than the previous ones, but it just takes some practice to get your technique right. Be sure to test your shell for safety. If it is too narrow, the flame of the tea light or votive might melt the wax and the embedments could catch fire.

Makes 1 lantern

Time

1 to 2 hours to make and cool shell, plus a few hours of cooling time and 24 hours for curing/drying

Materials

Cold water bath (water in a container taller and wider than the
   mold)
1 wide symmetrical metal mold with metal core insert (see Tips
   for Selecting Materials below, if you have trouble finding a
   mold with insert)
Mold sealer
1 cup coffee beans
Thermometer
4 pounds high MP (145 degrees Fahrenheit) paraffin wax
Double boiler
Heat source
3 teaspoons translucent or clear additive
¼ cup stainless steel measuring cup
1 ounce fragrance (optional)
Skewer or knitting needle stirrer
Pot holders
Griddle pan or skillet

Tips for Selecting and Handling Materials

■ The mold should be at least 5 inches wide to allow a tea light
   or votive to burn inside the shell without melting it.

■ The core insert should be a smooth surface cylinder wide
   enough to allow only about a 1-inch cavity between the insert
   and the mold.

■ Using a hardening additive is necessary to make the lantern walls strong. Translucent or clear additive is used to make the wax glow and highlight the coffee beans when a tea light or votive is lit inside.

Instructions

1. Prepare the water bath by filling the bath container about halfway with cold water and placing it in an area where it can sit undisturbed.

2. Seal the wick hole of the mold with mold sealer and center the insert inside the mold.

3. Fill the shell cavity with a small layer of coffee beans (see step CL-1). The insert will keep the embedded coffee beans in place while the wax cools.

4. With the thermometer in place, melt 4 pounds of wax in the double boiler, making sure that no water gets into the melting pot, heating the wax to 210 degrees Fahrenheit.

5. When the wax has thoroughly melted, melt 3 teaspoons of clear additive in the measuring cup over direct heat. As soon as the additive has melted, add it to the wax.

6. Add scent, if desired.

7. The additive may sink to the bottom of the melting pot. Stir the mixture and scrape the bottom of the melting pot with your stirrer to ensure that the additive is completely blended with the wax.

8. Double-check the mold and insert to make sure they are fully prepared and ready for pouring.

9. Using pot holders, pour the wax into the cavity between the mold and the insert at 190 degrees Fahrenheit. It's all right for the wax to seep into the inner cavity.

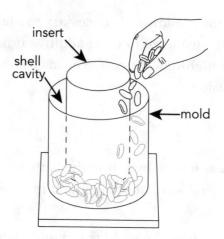

Step CL-1. Fill the shell cavity with a small layer of coffee beans.

10. Tap along the side of each mold from top to bottom of the mold with your stirrer immediately after pouring to help the wax fill any air pockets inside the mold.

11. With pot holders, carefully place the cooling mold into the water bath.

12. As soon as the wax inside the mold begins to form a skin on its surface, grasp the insert and lift it out of the mold at a rate of about an inch a minute. If you poured at a temperature hotter than 190 degrees Fahrenheit, removing the insert might take longer. Don't wait until the wax is too solid to remove the insert or it will break the shell.

13. The wax shell will cool and thicken starting from the mold walls, going inward toward the center of the mold. Once you have removed the insert, allow the shell to cool until the walls thicken to about ½ to ¾ of an inch thick, then immediately pour the molten wax out of the center of the mold

and back into the melting pot. Pour slowly and close to the pot to minimize splattering.

14. Allow the shell to cool completely (a few hours).

15. When the shell has cooled, it should slide easily out of the mold.

16. To smooth out the top and bottom of the shell, place it on the griddle pan or skillet.

17. With the top of the shell at eye level, rotate it gently and quickly.

18. Remove the shell from the heat, hold the shell while the base cools (a few seconds), and set the shell upright. Repeat this process until the shell is level. Make sure you use a low heat setting or the base will melt too fast. Repeat this process for the top, placing the shell upside down on the pan or skillet.

Variations

- If you use embedments that might float, lodge the items between the shell walls.

- Making the wall of the shell a little thicker strengthens the lantern, while a thinner wall allows the shell to glow more.

- Try different embedments and fragrances. Adding a touch of color can also add appeal.

Candle Decorating Ideas

Always remember that if you're applying anything to a candle's surface that may be flammable, make sure the consumer of the candle knows to remove the decoration before lighting the candle to avoid accidental fires.

- Acrylic paints are good for painting novelty candles that are not meant to be burned.

- Découpage is a great way to decorate smooth candle surfaces such as round pillars.

- Decorative glues (colored and metallic) are easy to use and suitable for applying fine decorative designs to candles.

- Dried flowers wrapped around a candle with raffia are a classic candle decoration. Be sure to warn consumers to avoid accidental fires by removing the flowers before lighting the candle.

- Gold leaf or foil applied with a heated metal spoon is an easy decoration. The heated spoon melts the wax underneath the foil, causing the foil to adhere to the candle.

- A linoleum cutting tool is useful for carving fine designs on a candle surface. Overdip a candle in a contrasting color and carve through the overdip layer to expose the color beneath.

- Pressed flowers can be applied with clear glue or by the same method used for gold leaf or foil. Plan out your design carefully and overdip the candle in a clear glaze to give the surface a glossy finish.

- Propane torch marbling (a propane torch with a crafter's point) is handy for the experienced candlemaker. Powdered dyes can be lightly torched onto the candle surface for a marble look with bold color. A blemished candle can also be saved by lightly torching the surface, giving the candle a new, textured appearance.

- Rub'n'Buff waxes are a great way to highlight candle details on novelty candles. Apply the wax buff in small amounts with your finger, smudging your finger first on a piece of paper to remove excess wax.

- Rub-on transfers are one of the easiest ways to decorate a smooth-surfaced candle. Simply cut out the design, tape it to the candle, and carefully rub the design off of the transfer film and onto the candle.

- Seashells or decorative stones are pretty items to decorate candle bases.

- Stencils are easily applied to a smooth-surfaced candle by positioning the design, taping the stencil to the candle, and painting or wax-buffing the design.

- Stickers are also one of the easiest candle decorations.

- Wax appliqués (small wax shapes) are easily applied to candles with glue or a sticky blend of wax (beeswax also works well).

Your Crafts Vision

▼▼

NOW THAT YOU KNOW HOW to make candles, where do you want this craft to take you? Learning a hobby and practicing it enough to become a skilled artisan can lead you along diverse pathways of creative self-expression and possibly to a means of making money from your craft. I didn't even think about selling my candles until a friend of mine paid me a visit and, while admiring the display of my work that I had set up in my living room, asked if he could buy one of my candles. Before then, my only goal in my candle-making hobby was to learn as much as I could about the craft. After that first impromptu sale, however, I got more interested in the prospect of making candles that people wanted to buy. The experience motivated me to learn new techniques. With each successive candle batch, my skill developed beyond what I had originally thought I could accomplish when I had made candles just for fun.

▼▼▼

KIM'S STORY

W hen I first started making candles, I found a lot of frustration," says Kim Beth-Poe from Wick-It Craft Originals, a part-time home-based business. "Every candle I made came out with surface flaws. It was devastating. Pretty soon I had a large collection of rejects. As friends and family came by and saw my work, they marveled and fell in love with candles I considered terrible failures. I was afraid to even give them away, let alone sell them.

"Soon I found the imperfections were what made each candle unique and appealing. They became a signature ensuring buyers that each candle

Transforming Your Craft Vision into Reality

The decision to go further with your candlemaking hobby is an important one. Before you take this step, it's a good idea to make sure that your decision will not impede on your enjoyment of your craft and the rest of your life. As a happy balance of the different roles in your life is a necessity for a healthy lifestyle, you must ask yourself how well your candlemaking will fit into your life. Undoubtedly, you will give time to candlemaking that otherwise would have been spent on home, career, and other life activities. Discuss your personal goals for success with the important people in your life and incorporate their feedback in your decision making. Ultimately, however, you must do whatever allows your creative expression to flow in all the facets of your life.

was a handcrafted original. Over the years I've experimented with color and additives and learned to manipulate those imperfections to create some marvelous textures and appearances.

Today, a museum gift shop and other stores sell my candles alongside other original works of art!"

Here are some questions to consider when turning your candlemaking into a business:

Do you know what you're doing?

Will you take the time to sharpen your candlemaking skills? Can you make the same candles repeatedly? Do you know how to adjust candle wax formulas to create a specific candle technique or color? Do you know the proper wicking for each kind of candle you will make? It takes discipline to make a batch of the same candle style over and over again. Whether you'll be making candles by yourself or working with others, you will have to know what's going on in your workshop. Even if you produce small-scale batches for sale, you must keep quality consistent to keep customers coming back. Candlemaking for profit requires not only an artistic vision, but also a good deal of technical knowledge that can only be acquired through practice.

Can you make candlemaking part of your normal routine?

Candlemaking is a time-consuming process; therefore, time management is essential for candlemaking as a business. From experience you'll learn how long it takes you to make a batch of candles. Review your schedule to see where you can set a time for candlemaking that is best for you. The ability to devote a specific time to candlemaking is important. If you can keep that time free of interruptions, the time you spend in your workshop will be higher quality.

The beauty of a part-time craft business is that you can set your own time for selling. For some candlemakers, the only time they devote daily or weekly attention to selling candles is during the holiday season, which they supplement by sporadic sales at craft markets throughout the year. If one good sales event is sufficient to fulfill your year-long goal, that's great. Nowhere is it written that you have to work continuously. It's *your* part-time business!

What are your candlemaking goals?

It's easy to say "I want to sell a lot of candles," but that statement is difficult to measure in results. Put your dreams of success into words on paper and translate them into small attainable goals within your capabilities. These goals should be measurable with a due date; for example, "I want to sell 15 candles at the church Christmas fair," or "I want to make 60% over my cost of materials." It's so important to start small and work your way up to more challenging goals. Achieving even the little goals you set for yourself will give you the confidence to attain higher levels of success.

A dream worksheet is a great way to organize your thoughts into attainable goals. Use the table at the end of this chapter as a template to state your goals and begin transforming your dream into a reality.

Did you know???

Candlemaking in factories started in the 1800s. Before this time most people made their own household candles.

Ten Great Reasons to Own a Part-Time Craft Business:

1. Crafting is known to be less stressful than other types of work

2. You can make money working at home

3. Having someone buy your work is the ultimate compliment

4. You are your own boss and make your own schedule

5. You're free from the downsides of the traditional workplace (distractions, designated work space, etc.)

6. Your creativity actually produces something of value to you

7. Handcrafted products are always in demand

8. There are tax breaks associated with home-based businesses

9. You can do what you like doing, rather than doing designated tasks

10. You'll discover more about yourself and your capabilities

Your Motivation to Create

What motivates you to make candles? Is it your desire to fuel a feeling of accomplishment? Is it the compliments on your work from friends and family? Does candlemaking prompt fantasies about your candles on sale at a retail store or artisans' gallery? Do you dream of having your sole career someday be your candlemaking? Finding these answers can help you realize the best future for your craft.

Whatever path you choose to advance your candlemaking hobby, that road is the on-ramp to a future that could blossom into a lifelong journey of creativity, one that will take you as far as you allow it to go. Fulfilling your creative urge can be the most relaxing and fun part of your life. Getting away to your candlemaking workshop is your own personal time away from all your other responsibilities. A part-time business in candlemaking is an ideal home-based business. To work where you live—and nourish your creativity—is a double blessing, so if making money from your handmade candles appeals to you, it's time for you to discover your capabilities as a business owner and artisan. The next step in becoming a more successful artisan is to explore beyond the comfortable safety zone of sharing your candles with your family and friends and discover other patrons of your art outside your social circle.

A Dream Worksheet and Timeline	
My Dream:	
Goal Translation:	Due Date:
Task/Sub-Goal:	Due Date:
Progress Notes:	
Task/Sub-Goal:	Due Date:
Progress Notes:	
Task/Sub-Goal:	Due Date:
Progress Notes:	
Task/Sub-Goal:	Due Date:
Progress Notes:	

Part Two

For Profit

Profiting from Your Talent

▼▼

AS A CANDLEMAKER, YOU HAVE numerous options for earning money with your abilities. Whether you choose to work part time or full time, sustaining yourself as professional crafter and artist is a big responsibility. Running your own business can disrupt your life in ways that you never expected. Once you've turned your candlemaking talents into a moneymaking venture, it's no longer "just a hobby." It will often eat into your personal finances and overwhelm your time well beyond the conventional workday. Now that you're in it for the money as well as your love of the craft, your candlemaking skills must also answer to your customers, which means your "spare time" may not be enough.

But the payoffs are worth all your efforts. You'll have more independence and control of your schedule. You decide how to spend your profits. How much money you want to make is also up to you. I should stress here that the purpose of the second half of this book is not just to encourage you to become a full-time professional candle crafter. These chapters are also meant to give you inspirational ideas for making money from your candles in any capacity, whether your desire is to earn hobby income or build a business that allows you to live comfortably off your craft.

Your Candles vs. All the Others

Your candles reflect your passion for candlemaking. A handmade candle also mirrors the personality of its owner and becomes an extension of his or her identity. Today, candles are a form of household art—both useful and beautiful. For your candles to shine over the competition and make you money, they must be more than practical and ordinary. For your candles to stay afloat in a sea of commercial candles similar to yours, they must be well designed, not just handmade. As you continue to make candles, you will find the urge to continuously innovate and strengthen your artistry. Creative minds constantly think imaginative thoughts—ideas that become reality through research and experimentation.

When candlemaking for profit, what your creative mind works at most is achieving the balance between making candles you enjoy making and producing for your target market. Finding that market is essential for small-time candlemakers. Since your time is limited, you don't want, nor have the ability, to appeal to the whole candle market. Instead, your business should focus on a select group of people who have a specific need for your candles and are willing to buy them.

To find this target market, you need to answer specific questions about your possible market niche. The following questions provide you with the profile of your "perfect" candle customer.

> What need do your candles fill for your customers?
> Are your customers looking to buy locally produced,
> handmade crafts for personal use?
> Do your customers need unique candle gifts for the
> holiday season?
> Will your customers choose handmade quality over
> a discounted price?

Did you know???

The Colgate company started out making starch, soap, and candles.

You also need to consider where you want to sell your candles. Selling at craft shows, fairs, and artisan galleries, for example, directs your sales to the specific audiences attracted to these types of marketplaces. To sell at a certain show or shop, it's best to study the crowds who frequent it, their spending habits, and what they might value in your work. Before selling at a particular craft show, I participate in the show first as a customer and observer. By investigating who actually goes to the show and what they buy, I get great insight into what I need to do to prepare for the show.

As a student selling my first candles at Florida State University's weekly campus flea market, I quickly learned that fellow students were willing to buy small, unique novelty candles that were affordable to a shallow-pocket budget. They were most willing to buy these candles and sometimes more expensive ones at gift-giving times of the year, such as Valentine's Day and Christmas, or when financial aid checks were disbursed at the beginning of the semester. So instead of setting up every Wednesday at the student union, I went only when it was most profitable for me to sell.

Creating a Professional Crafter Image

When you find your market niche, you need to promote yourself as a businessperson and artisan worthy of your candle prices. For the artisan, good design and quality materials are essential in producing marketable candles. For the businessperson, professional promotional materials are indispensable in selling yourself to your buying audience. Everything associated with your business that the buying public sees—from your business cards to your craft show display—reflects you and gives people an initial impression of you.

A simple way to begin promoting yourself as a candlemaker/businessperson is to use business cards. A business card shows

Selling Inexperience

Are you worried about selling your candles because you've never sold anything? You shouldn't be. Most crafters don't know much about selling or marketing when they start out either. Books and research are very helpful resources, but experience is your best educator. If you're proud of your candles, have worked hard to develop a good product, and offer great services, your selling will be a lot easier. Undoubtedly, you will have to take risks—both big and small—in order to succeed in selling your candles. However, the sense of accomplishment and money in your pocket derived from your efforts are well worth the risks.

people that you have made a commitment to being in business, which is especially important when selling to family and friends who may have previously viewed you as only a hobbyist.

Be a Community Artisan

Being involved in your local community and building a network of contacts is essential in establishing yourself as an artisan. Joining a local artisans' guild, art center, or just getting out and participating in arts and crafts events allows you to connect to the resources of the local creative crowd. Friendships with other artisans and art patrons are invaluable in gaining local support of your work. This will build your confidence to attempt markets outside your community.

I am fortunate that my candlemaking studio, Waxed Out Candles, which I share with my friend Katie who I introduced to you earlier, is located in a neighborhood of warehouses in Tallahassee, Florida. Since this community has historically been a center for the studio and living spaces of many artists in the area, just being around other people who share the same energetic attitude toward their art gives me the inspiration to create. Sometimes it feels as though creativity and imagination linger in the air there. Whenever other studios and galleries are open for shows, we try to be accessible and show our working studio space as well. Participating in arts and crafts shows as a group of artists also provides local support and recognition of our small art community.

Crafting in the Digital Age

Even though candlemaking may not involve the latest digital know-how, it can benefit from new technology. Due to the quick development of electronic technologies, the average family can now afford a personal computer and access to the Internet. Some PC owners are a little afraid of their machines and a little overwhelmed by the sheer amount of resources available with them. Can you get by without a computer and still make money? The answer is yes. But crafters who want to take full advantage of their possibilities for profit must learn to make a computer work as a personal assistant. Following are some of the ways your personal computer can help you in your activities.

Organize Your Life

Personal information management software (Microsoft Outlook, Day-Timer Organizer) is great for juggling the duties of a career, family, and a part-time business. This kind of program can make your life easier by organizing all your day-to-day information. It can:

- Plan your personal and business calendars
- Improve your communication via e-mail (e-mail is a quick and efficient way to communicate with existing and potential clients)
- Store and maintain all your lists—clients, suppliers, networking contacts, friends, family, and to-do tasks
- Set reminders for all your to-do tasks

KATIE'S STORY

Katie Maseri discovered she loved candlemaking from the moment I introduced her to the craft 5 years ago. Today, Katie and I share a studio business, Waxed Out Candles, and Katie also works full time as art education director for a nonprofit art foundation. "When we moved into the studio, we weren't ready to quit our jobs to become full-time candlemakers. But we knew we could make enough money selling in our free time to at least cover our expenses," Katie says.

Every year since, sales have grown steadily, mostly due to a diversified sales strategy of sales to private clients, wholesale and consignment accounts, the occasional craft show, and a variety of candlemaking classes and workshops. "Teaching candlemaking classes has given me more confidence in my skills. Every year I build on what I've learned myself and share it in the next season of classes," Katie explains.

Maintain Your Inventory or Sales

Simple database programs such as Microsoft Access or electronic spreadsheets such as Excel are powerful tools. They enable you to analyze your candlemaking assets and break down information about your business into meaningful statistics that can help you improve its success. Accounting packages such as QuickBooks can be used to maintain accurate bookkeeping and other fiscal information for your business, as well as help you recognize financial ways of improving profits. Other ways your PC can help you:

"Building our business slowly is what we need to do to keep having fun together and to best incorporate our knowledge from all our mistakes and successes into our plans for growth," Katie adds. "Word-of-mouth sales have worked so well for us, our returning customer base grows yearly. Since we know our buyers well, we can make candles specifically with them in mind, knowing they'll want them. Catering directly to consumers gets us out of producing large lots and gives  us the creative ability to design every type of candle they would use in their home, from votives to novelties.

"As long as I'm having fun in the shop, that's all that matters."

- Design and print your own advertising and marketing materials, such as signage and information flyers
- Keep a digital portfolio or catalog of your candle work and designs
- Write thank-you letters and maintain other professional correspondence with clients and suppliers

Use the Internet

The Internet is a valuable tool for efficiently developing both your talents and your business. It is also a cost-effective way of doing many of the things your business needs in order to grow. On the Internet, you can:

- Educate yourself about running a business
- Communicate with other candlemakers for help and to share ideas
- Promote your business via a Web site
- Order supplies for your craft and business
- Research the candle market for a competitive analysis and explore trends in the industry

Utilizing a Web Site for Your Profit Venture

If used properly, a Web site can be very profitable. If you don't have the time to maintain a site, you can establish yourself on the Internet by contributing to candlemaking message boards, list serves (mailing lists), and news groups.

If you set up a Web site, you should choose its content based on the profit avenue of choice that appeals to your target market. For example, if you make artistic candles that you think would do well in artisan galleries or museum gift shops, you may want your site to be an online gallery of your work that will appeal to museum and gallery buyers. The following three types of Web-site content are most suited to the craftsperson:

Internet presence site: The content of an Internet presence site is your online business card or brochure. A few simple Web pages can contain a sample candle portfolio, marketing information about you and your candles, and important contact information so existing and potential clients can reach you easily. You'll find more information about this type of Web site in chapter 10.

Candlemaking information site: Sharing your love of candlemaking and knowledge of the art and business proves your skill and ability to your clients, and establishes you as an expert in your field and a reliable source for candlemaking information. It can also help you sell yourself as a capable instructor if you teach candlemaking classes. An information site doesn't have to be comprehensive. Sharing detailed information about what you know well may be more beneficial to a visitor than trying to cover every aspect of candlemaking.

E-commerce site: An e-commerce site is an online storefront for selling your candles. Whether your store site contains a few candles or multiple product lines, it should look as professional as possible, and offer secure ordering (a protected online area where customers may safely conduct credit card sales). To make an e-commerce investment a worthwhile venture for you as either a part-time or full-time business, you must be able to attract visitors who will buy from your Web site. You want to make your customers as comfortable as possible while shopping and give them the confidence to share their personal information. Research your target market carefully and even consult with an e-commerce design business to help you with this type of Web site. Making a good initial online impression goes a long way in attracting return visits. More information about this type of Web site is discussed in chapter 9.

> **Handy Hint**
>
> Remember to set aside time for your administrative duties, such as paying bills, organizing your calendar, and answering e-mail, to keep tasks from piling up and slowing you down.

Creating a Web site is more intensive in terms of time in the preparation stage than in the physical setting up of the site on the computer. The more time you spend planning your site in your head and on paper, the easier it will be for you to set up and maintain your site when it's time to do actual PC work. Sitting in front of your monitor without an initial plan will only waste your time.

Other Profit-Making Avenues

Making money with candlemaking may seem a little discouraging, especially if you're a beginner, but once you learn the art of candlemaking—and hopefully realize how well you do it, there are many ways to make money with the talent alone.

Teaching Candlemaking

Sharing your knowledge of candlemaking through teaching can be a profitable means of making money from your know-how. Teaching is one of the more satisfying avenues for profiting from the craft. You can teach by leading classes, holding workshops, and providing demonstrations.

Having a sincere desire to share your talents with others is an essential trait of a teacher. If this profit technique appeals to you, start by showing friends how to make candles in your own workshop. Once you're comfortable with simultaneously teaching and candlemaking, volunteer your instruction by holding a candlemaking demonstration at a Girl Scout troop, church, or other community organization. If you're comfortable with the group, offer to volunteer-run a small candlemaking workshop. Volunteering can improve your teaching skills, establish yourself as a specialist, and eventually qualify you to earn money as a teacher. My first attempt at teaching was a volunteer effort with Florida State University's Center for Participant Education (CPE), an organization run by students that offered a variety of free workshops and classes to anyone. My first class only had three students, but I learned a lot from teaching that class which I carry to all the workshops I lead.

Writing About Candlemaking

Once you are expertly skilled in candlemaking, you can also earn money by writing how-to candlemaking articles. Candles are contemporary decorating items popularized by many home-decor and craft magazines. If you enjoy writing, publishing articles of this type is a possible avenue for you to pursue. Writing articles can lead to larger publications, such as informative leaflets or how-to books, as your confidence grows.

Selling Candlemaking Supplies

Another avenue to consider is selling candlemaking supplies instead of or in addition to candles. This is ideal for candlemakers who are expert in the technical aspects of their craft and are interested in expanding their business. Such candlemakers can make money from candlemaking, but shift the focus of sales away from actual candle production to the sale of supplies. This enables them to spend more time in the workshop on research and for their own enjoyment. Information about candle making equipment and materials, as well as the candle business, is a great service to provide. It also sets up a strong reason for customers to return to you for repeat business. Adding candlemaking class instruction to selling supplies and candles on the side is a solid, well-rounded approach to candlemaking for profit.

Handy Hint

Find another candlemaker who can help mentor you in developing your craftsmanship.

Pricing Your Candles

▼▼▼

PRICING IS NOT AN EASY thing to do. In fact, deciding how much to charge for your candles can be one of the most difficult tasks you face as an artisan. Just pricing your own work is difficult in itself. That aside, you need to take into consideration several cost and value factors. To figure out the best price to charge for your candles, you'll need to get your calculator out and do some number crunching, as well as spend some time researching your candle market. In essence, your pricing goals are to cover your expenses, determine the market value of your candles, and make a healthy profit from each candle sold. The price you determine for each of your candles must be a price fair to both you and the consumer.

Covering Your Costs

The first step in pricing your candles is to determine how much it costs you to produce and sell each candle. Costs arising from making and selling candles fall into three expense categories: the cost of goods, labor, and overhead. The cost of goods is the expense incurred in the making and packaging of each candle. Labor is the price of your time and effort expended in the making and selling of each candle. Overhead costs are all the fixed expenses that keep you in business.

Cost of Goods

You must take into account the cost of each ingredient used in producing your finished candle product. The following is a list of direct costs to consider when determining candle prices:

- Wax
- Additives
- Wicking
- Wick tabs
- Coloring
- Scent
- Labels
- Wrapping
- Decorations
- Container

Make a list of all your candlemaking ingredients and break down the total cost you paid for each ingredient into smaller measurement units. Direct production costs involving reusable but eventually consumable materials, such as the cost of the mold, mold sealer, mold release, etc., can be estimated by dividing the price of the material by the number of candles produced during its usable life. Metal molds that are well cared for can produce hundreds of candles, for example. Plastic molds do not last that long and may affect costs more than metal molds because of their shorter life. Mold sealer eventually needs to be replaced. If the candle is made from an improvised mold that is disposable after a single use, take into account the total price of the improvised mold. Even though the amount of these ingredients may seem miniscule, it's important to include their cost because it can add up! Scents, one of the more expensive ingredients, for example, can particularly make a big difference in candle price. An 8-ounce bottle of scent that costs $10.00 is $1.25 per ounce. If you're pricing a 2-pound candle that contains two ounces of scent, that's already $2.50 in scent cost alone.

The following table provides an example of figuring out the cost of the materials for one candle.

Determining the cost of goods for a 2-pound scented pillar candle.		
Candle Material	**Supply Cost**	**Candle Cost**
2 pounds of wax	59-pound case @ $0.89 per pound = $52.51 + $26.00 shipping = $78.51 per case ($78.51 ÷ 59 pounds) = $1.33 per pound	$2.66 ($1.33 × 2 pounds)
6 inches of wicking	75 yards for $10.00 = $0.13 per yard ($10.00 ÷ 75 yards) = $0.04 per foot	$0.02 ($0.04 per foot × 0.5 feet)
½ ounce of strawberry scent	8-ounce bottle = $13.00 = $1.63 per ounce ($13.00 ÷ 8 ounce)	$0.82 ($1.63 ÷ 2)
1 teaspoon vybar	16-ounce bag = $4.95 $4.95 ÷ 16 ounce = $0.31 per ounce 1 teaspoon = 0.17 ounces (⅙ of an ounce) 1 teaspoon = 0.17 ounces × $0.31 = $0.05	$0.05
6 tablespoons stearine	16-ounce bag = $2.95 $2.95 ÷ 16 ounces = $0.18 per ounce 1 tablespoon = 0.5 ounces 1 tablespoon = 0.5 × $0.18 = $0.09	$0.54 ($0.09 × 6 tablespoons)
½ block dye	$0.75 per block ½ block = $0.38	$0.38
label and packaging	$0.03 per label $0.10 per candle wrap	$0.13
	Total candle cost of goods:	$ 4.60

Overhead Costs

Overhead is the catchall category for all the other expenses not related to the cost of goods. Not recognizing these indirect costs is where many business owners lose money. Overlooking several small costs quickly adds up and results in poor profits. To figure your actual overhead costs, calculate the total of all your overhead costs (including phone, Internet, mall rent, and others that are easily overlooked) per month and divide by the total number of candles made during the month. Add that number to the cost of goods for each candle. Don't include start-up costs if you are just beginning to sell candles, since this will inflate your monthly overhead cost. Instead, spread your start-up costs over a 12-month period and include that monthly figure in your overhead to accommodate for these expenses over a longer period of time.

One way to estimate your overhead costs is to add a markup of 30 to 35% of the cost of goods to your goods and labor. (Once you have a few months of steady business, you can figure your actual cost of doing business and adjust the percentage accordingly.) With the previous example of the cost of goods for a 2-pound candle, the calculation using this method is as follows:

30% of $4.60 (cost of goods) = $1.38 (overhead cost for one candle)

$4.60 + $1.38 = $5.98 (cost of goods + overhead costs for one candle)

Labor

To estimate your labor costs, track the number of candles you make in a week and how many hours you spend weekly on candlemaking-

Handy Hint

When looking up the costs of your candle ingredients, don't just look at your supplier's price list for your costs. Make sure you take into account any shipping and handling costs you incurred with your supply order. These costs can add up, especially with shipped wax!

Frequently Overlooked Costs

- **Shrinkage:** The cost of lost, stolen, or damaged goods; also, if you decide to remelt a candle and start over again, you've lost money in the effort and materials used to produce the original candle.

- **Miscellaneous packaging costs:** Tissue paper, bubble wrap, bags, labels, etc.

- **Travel costs:** Gas for driving to craft shows, deliveries, and buying supplies; meal costs incurred when traveling "on business"; baby-sitting charges while you're away on business.

- **Storage costs:** The cost of storage units for materials, equipment, and your candle inventory.

- **Office supplies:** Thank-you notes, pens, receipt books, computer supplies, etc.

related activities. These activities should not only include the time spent making the candles, but also time spent working on other tasks such as preparing marketing materials, purchasing supplies, or selling candles. As a beginner, pay yourself the minimum wage to start. Once your skill increases and you become a more established artisan, you can pay yourself a higher rate. A good rule of thumb is to consider how much it would cost you to hire someone to do your work for you. Some candles are also more complex and take a considerable amount of time to make. As your candlemaking skills develop, however, you will become more efficient and spend less amount of time in the shop.

Here is an example of figuring labor costs. If you can make 20 candles in a week and you spend about 4 hours per week doing candle work, use this formula (minimum wage may vary among states): (4 hours × $6 per hour) ÷ 20 candles = $1.20 per candle in labor costs. To continue with the previous example, if you made 20 of those 2-pound pillar candles, the total cost of goods, overhead, and labor per candle would be:

$4.60 + $1.38 + $1.20 = $7.18 (cost of goods + overhead + labor)

This total is the basic break-even price, the price that just covers your expenses; you neither make nor lose money. Any price for the candle above this price is profit, and any price below it is lost money. The biggest mistake crafters make in figuring out what they will charge for a candle is in the area of determining the cost of their time and efforts. Many crafters undersell themselves in this regard. They think that, since they enjoy the time and effort spent on their craft, their labor is not worth as much as it would be if the work was less pleasant. Crafters who really profit from their labor understand the true value of their efforts. Beginner crafters usually value their labor based on confidence in their talents. As their confidence grows with experience, they do better at estimating the cost of their labor.

Creatively Controlling Costs

In applying these pricing principles, you'll soon find that costs can add up quickly and eat into possible profits. It's up to you to find creative ways to control these expenses. Look over the numbers and research where you can lower them. Here are some questions to consider to streamline costs:

- Can you group similar tasks into a more efficient means of production that will save time and effort? (One time-saving trick is to wick all your molds at once while your wax is melting.)

- Can you buy supplies in larger quantities or in bulk to lower the cost of materials?

Five Ways to Control Costs

1. Pay wholesale for everything you buy for resale.

2. Shop for the best prices on equipment and supplies.

3. Take advantage of invoice discounts for early payment.

4. Recognize ALL costs, not just the obvious ones.

5. Carefully control your candle inventory to reduce shrinkage.

- Can a different heating system melt your wax faster?

- Can you substitute less expensive ingredients and still maintain quality?

- Can you make larger batches at once to save time?

Retail Pricing

Retail pricing adds an extra standard markup that should cover profit and all the costs incurred in selling your candles. This includes the hours it takes to prepare and set up a craft show, gas you purchase to get to and from the show, and any advertising and marketing expenses. The following is the general formula for retail pricing:

Cost of goods + overhead + labor + selling costs + profit = retail price

Multiple pricing: Multiple pricing is pricing a group of candles together for a single price. For example, you may make a batch of candles of the same color and style, but from molds of various shapes and sizes. You can price these candles to sell as a group based on the total cost and market value of the batch, or arrange them in attractively matched gift sets. **Prices for specially made candles:** Candles that individual clients commission can command higher prices than those in a normal batch because of exclusivity in design, special production arrangements such as special-order molds, and unique handling (personal delivery or private appointments).

Market Value

Market value is what people will pay for your candles, and what they will pay is a subjective matter. Each person perceives value differently among varying dimensions of measurement. I have found, for example, that some people believe that a taller candle is more valuable than a shorter one. The shorter candle may be wider, weigh more, and may burn longer than the taller, more slender candle that weighs less, but height is a value dimension that can command a higher price. Some shoppers consider price above all, while others consider service as well.

> **Handy Hint**
>
> Shop the competition and find out what prices you would have to pay for candles similar to yours.

Pricing candles by market value is better than pricing them solely based on cost because the market approach also considers how much customers are willing to pay. Handmade candles are normally priced above mass-produced, competitively priced candles. Since candles are essentially luxury merchandise, handmade candles are even more special, demanding a higher price. People tend to pay higher prices for gifts, and candles are no exception. A candlemaker I recently spoke to told me that she prices her jar candles by comparing hers to others sold in the shops where her candles are sold. "I consider the other candles' container quality and scent, and determine how they compare to my candles. If I feel my candles have a more interesting container or scent, I price them a little higher than the others."

In pricing your candles, you should also take into account these items of perceived value:

- **Selling location:** Selling at an artisan's gallery in an affluent part of town or tourist spot will command higher prices than selling at a less prestigious location such as a flea market or discount store. Selling particular designs at an exclusive location in a particular market area can also command higher prices.

- **Geographic location:** Your candles may sell differently based on how much competition you have, or the cultural influences in a particular area.

- **Candle design:** An unusually shaped novelty candle or unique candle technique can command a higher price than an ordinary candle.

- **A good product name:** Naming your design or product line can also add perceived value. A product name can set your candles apart from others. "Watercolor Landscapes," for example, can describe a multicolored chunk candle in an artistic and more creative manner than just calling it a "chunk" candle.

Markdowns

There are times when you have to lower prices. This is a necessary part of doing business that results from the following factors:

- Overestimating the market value of your candle product
- Shopworn candles
- Too much competition

- Selling to the wrong market
- Bad selling practices
- Lack of marketing or advertising
- Lack of service
- Overproducing seasonal candle styles

If your candles are seasonal and outdated, mark them down as soon as they become outdated to move them quickly and avoid a loss. A rule of thumb is to lower the price by half of your original profit on the candle. For example, if the total cost of a seasonal candle is $8 and the original retail markup is $8, lower the markup by half to $4. This marks the candle price down to $12. To avoid markdowns, research your market more carefully in the beginning. If your candles are not selling, try to discover the reasons. When and how much to mark down your candles depends on the information you find. If you're selling to a completely wrong market, you may not have to mark down at all; simply offer your candles in a different marketplace.

Conclusion

Regardless of your pricing method, you should feel comfortable with the prices you place on your products. If you don't feel comfortable about them, your selling disposition may reflect your discomfort and shoppers will pick up on it. If you feel you cannot price your candles objectively, run your prices by someone else who could pose as a consumer. Remember that there is no rule for pricing, only guidelines. With experience, your understanding of pricing will grow and allow your profits to grow as well.

Selling Your Candles

▼▼▼

OVER THE YEARS, CANDLE SALES have become a multi-billion-dollar industry. People are using more candles these days, due to the popularity of the candle as a home fashion accessory and fragrance medium. While the majority of candles sold are produced by mass manufacturers, small candle businesses are gaining an increased share of the market due to their low start-up costs and the ease of acquiring supplies.

This chapter explores the variety of markets available and selling considerations for the candle merchant. Selling profitably in each type of market requires an understanding of the basic aspects of candle sales and how to choose the right market, create a selling environment, and maintain a supportive customer base.

About Candle Sales

The market for candles is so broad and diverse that there are literally thousands of product lines available to the candle consumer. Some mass manufacturers have hundreds of styles in their product lines. Candles make great gifts, most are affordably priced, and they're consumable. Consumers have become increasingly sophisticated in judging which candles burn well. Stores that specialize in candles are on the rise; franchised candle stores as well as independent shops continue to populate the retail landscape. Given these facts, how can you compete and maintain a viable candle business? You can—just as many other candlemakers like you have—by finding the target markets for your candles and effectively selling to those markets.

The Candle Marketplace

Fall and winter have traditionally been the best seasons for selling candles. After the expansion of electricity to every modern home, candle use tended to be limited to holiday decorating. In recent times, however, candles have become so popular that there is no slow season for these items as more and more people burn them year-round and buy more to replenish their supply.

Candles excel in popularity in two main retail categories. The home fragrance market, a billion-dollar market, with scented candles as the fastest growing and largest segment of the industry and the home accessory market, which has seen candles emerge as a popular household item embraced by most demographic classifications. From teenagers to senior citizens, low-income families to the wealthy, country to contemporary homes, there is a candle product for everyone.

▼▼▼▼▼▼▼▼▼▼▼▼▼▼▼▼▼▼▼▼▼▼▼

Did you know???

The craft industry contributes approximately 2 billion dollars yearly in sales to the U.S. economy.

▲▲▲▲▲▲▲▲▲▲▲▲▲▲▲▲▲▲▲▲▲▲▲

Choosing Markets for Your Candles

Which types of markets to choose depends on your production level, the target markets for your particular candles, and your selling style.

Candle Versatility

The versatility of candles makes them attractive to consumers.

- Candles are a beautiful source of light.
- They have a rich history in rituals and tradition.
- They are used in ceremony and celebration.
- Candles are the most popular carriers of home fragrance.

It's no wonder candles are favorite home accessories today.

Your Production Level

As a beginner, consider your experience and production level when selecting a candle market. Pick a venue that you can quickly re-stock as your inventory decreases. A weekend arts and crafts market may be good for a small inventory of candles, for example, and also a good place to start selling as a beginner. Once you get the hang of things you can move on to a larger venue. There is a variety of market options for each candlemaker's level of experience. You may want to experiment in a setting that allows you to gain confidence that you can build on as your exposure to selling grows.

Your Target Market

Your target market consists of the people who will most likely buy your candles. For example, if you make wedding candles, your target market would be future brides and wedding planners. In this case, you would commonly find these people frequenting bridal outlets, party stores, or bridal Web sites. The places your potential best customers or target market members visit are places you should go to make direct contact with them.

To get your feet wet, consider first selling in your local community where you can get direct contact with your customers. The best way to research an event is to visit in advance and see who's buying and what's selling. You may find that the event may not attract the target market you are attempting to reach. Ask other local artisans' advice on the event to see if it's really the right place for selling your candles.

The experience you get from these initial events gives you valuable insight into the direction you should take with your craft. You'll know firsthand how well your hard work has paid off, and in which areas you need to further refine your salesmanship and artistry. Local selling can be accomplished with a relatively small inventory, a beginner's selling experience level, and low initial investment. Your first few selling events will give you a good idea of your overall candle market and how to develop your sales strategy. You'll quickly see a valuable tool in recognizing demographic trends in who's looking, who's buying, how much each person spends, and which sales venues attract these people.

Did you know???

Women buy the vast majority of all candles sold.

Your Selling Style

You may love candlemaking, but how much do you love candle selling? Candle markets range from no direct consumer contact, as with Internet sales and mail order, to face-to-face contact with the consumer, as at arts and crafts shows, studio sales, and holiday boutiques. Selling candles can take a tremendous amount of time, and your schedule may already be jammed full with a full-time job and hours in your workshop, so choose an outlet that allows you to be comfortable in your activities as a selling artisan.

Don't expect your candle business to take off right away! Have a back-up plan and be prepared to take time off if things aren't going well. Disappointing sales might mean that selling just isn't in the stars for you at this time in your life, or maybe you need more candlemaking exploration and experience.

Your Candle Marketing Options

The following sections describe a variety of ways in which you might sell your candle creations. Note that some of these markets have a higher consumer contact level than others.

Candle Parties

Selling at a candle party is more relaxing than selling your candles at a public venue. Have fun and promote candle sales by demonstrating candle culture to friends and acquaintances. Host your own party or ask someone else to host it for you. A candle party is a great way to introduce people you know to your new products and money making efforts. Set up pretty, lighted displays throughout your home and have a story or interesting anecdote to tell about each one. Research ritual candle burning and share your knowledge with your friends. Have extra, unlit candles available for anyone who wants to buy one. Arrange a small table of information about you and the candles displayed at the party.

Consider giving your party a theme such as a luau, an evening pool party, a twilight dinner party, or a cocktail lounge get-together.

I love this kind of soft selling and have these parties when I feel the need to promote my work with friends, but don't want to feel the pressure of concentrating on sales. I think you will also find that

Handy Hint

On your party invitations, use the name of your studio or business as well as your own name as the host of the party.

parties generate interest in your candles and serve as a reminder to your friends and acquaintances to think of you when they need to buy candles. It's also a great way to gain essential consumer feedback directly from potential buyers. After the party, try to remember and write down all the comments and reactions people had to your candles and party efforts. You can incorporate this feedback to develop further your candle styles and marketing plan.

Open Houses

Open houses have a more specific purpose than candle parties—to open your workshop and your candlemaking process to the public. I've found studio open-house sales great for selling my candles. Sharing a studio with another candlemaker in a studio neighborhood provides a lot of exposure and traffic when we need it. More people come every year, as our studio, Waxed Out Candles, becomes more established in the community.

People are often curious to see inside an artist's studio, so clean your space and actually "open" your studio to the public. Allow people to see your setup and answer any questions they have. Do everything you can to impress your visitors and promote your artisan image, so they'll talk about you positively after they leave the studio.

Do you have some candles that require a complex production technique but are damaged with surface imperfections? If so, instead of remelting them, specially price them and sell them to move them out. Don't put out improperly formulated candles or ones with incorrectly sized wicks that will smoke excessively—these candles are better recycled than sold. While you should not try to sell a candle that is environmentally unsafe, you *can* make a good impression even with an ugly candle.

Sell by promoting yourself as a candlemaker instead of concentrating on selling your inventory. Give a how-to demonstration on making a particular type of candle. To really wow your visitors and sell yourself as a real expert, plan ahead and polish your most impressive candlemaking technique, if it's not too complex to demonstrate.

Appointment Sales

If you've found regular return customers who love to burn your candles and buy more from you, you've acquired true patrons of your art. As such, you must treat these special buyers as customer royalty. Give them priority and shower them with your thankfulness. These are the customers who will gladly advertise your candles by word of mouth and refer others to you. Try to be as accommodating as possible with private showings. When making sales appointments with your clients, you're better off meeting them in your studio or home workshop. Even if the customer is interested in you making them a particular type of candle or candle batch, show them your latest efforts and techniques. You may spark additional sales just by showing them what you've been up to.

Commissioned Sales

If clients request candles to be specially made, ask many questions to make sure you know exactly what they want, so they'll be completely satisfied with the finished product. If a client asks for a specific color or style that you do not normally make or have not made before, tell your customer that. Then when offering a price quote, make sure you've included in your costs sufficient additional production time, especially if the request will take some experimentation or specially ordered materials.

If you don't have an exact idea of what your customer requires, consider designing a sample to show your client before you make a large-quantity special order. Getting feedback from the buyer before you produce the whole lot can prevent frustration and lost sales if the results are not what the buyer expected. Remember that you and your customer may be using the same words to describe different candles, so clarify what the customer wants as much as possible. There is a big difference, for example, between a hurricane style candle and a wax hurricane lamp! I once helped a customer who specially ordered blue and green chunk candles for some gift baskets she was assembling. I didn't know she was making color-matching gift baskets, so when I gave her the finished candles with blue and green chunks combined, she was disappointed that they were not solid green and solid blue. If I had asked more specifically what she wanted, I could have made the candles more to her liking.

Boutiques

Art and craft boutiques consist of artisans gathering together, usually seasonally, to sell at a private home or community center. All participants hope to benefit from the larger scale of this type of retail event, which should generate more customer traffic compared to a single artisan showing. The group can be formed based on geographical location, craft type, or affiliation with a particular organization. Boutiques can arise from a neighborhood gathering of crafters, a crafter co-op, or even a group of crafters belonging to a particular church or working outside of their offices for a particular company.

Boutiques can be set up as a shared display of crafts throughout a home or in separate displays for each crafter. Usually boutiques feature unique but complimentary crafts that do not compete directly with each other for sales. A small fee given to the hostess or center is usually required to cover the expenses of the event.

If you want to host a boutique, plan well in advance and contact potential participants as soon as possible to give them plenty of time to prepare. Send invitations to a list of customers you and your

Selling Tips for Your Home and Studio Events

- Don't forget to invite your neighbors! You will want their support if your home event fills up the neighborhood with cars!

- Even though you are selling from your home, offer your guest customers a return policy with their purchases.

- Lighting candles in your home during sales events as you would normally while at home adds beauty to your event and gives guests ideas for using candles.

- Make sure everyone leaves with a flyer advertising your future studio events and any craft shows in which you will be participating.

- Offer a small sample votive to guests or have door prizes of candles for people to take home.

- Offer refreshments and provide areas in which to socialize.

- Place a guest book near an entrance for people to sign in and leave their contact information, so you can build your client list.

- Plan well in advance. Since you are setting up in your own space, you can arrange and rearrange attractive merchandising displays.

- Remove small or breakable objects from guest areas and relocate them to a safer place where they can hide until the guests are gone.

- Enlist someone to help you answer questions and monitor the burning candles while you're busy with your guests. Make sure no lit candle is left unattended!

See chapter 11 for general information about the risks to take before selling in your home.

friends have collected from previous sales or shows. To set up for the boutique, survey your house and remove any personal items that customers may mistake for sales items, choose rooms that allow attractive merchandising displays and permit easy flowing foot traffic, and organize payment and refreshment areas that you can easily manage.

Fundraisers

A small-scale fundraiser or craft sale is a good beginner's market. I say small-scale, because some fundraisers can be as large as a juried craft show! Many nonprofit organizations such as churches, community centers, and service groups hold craft fundraisers. As a craftsperson, you are usually required to give a small fee and contribute a portion of your sales to the fundraiser. I've found a few candlemaking sites on the Internet that offer candles to organizations raising money for a particular cause. Usually the candle products are offered in large quantities at wholesale costs to allow the organization to profit from the sale. Again, do some research into the fundraiser and the organization sponsoring it to see if it's the right venue for you.

Selling to Interior Designers

Interior designers have a great interest in candles because of their enormous popularity as a home accessory. They can become middlemen for you if they like your candles enough to recommend them to their clients. Look up any architecture or interior design organizations in the phone book or contact your local chamber of commerce. Make a list of designers in your area and contact them with a brochure of your business (see chapter 10).

Corporate Sales

Businesses frequently offer gifts to clients as employee incentives or awards. Getting a "shoe in" from someone you know at the business helps with these types of sales, especially in contacting busy human resources personnel. A professional-looking brochure, introductory letter, and a sample gift basket or candle set can make all the difference in attracting attention and getting an order. If a company is interested in purchasing in volume, offer a special discount.

Art and Craft Shows

Art and craft shows existed long before malls and mail-order catalogs. Long ago, when everything was handcrafted, people bartered their handmade products for other handmade products that they couldn't make themselves. Today, in the age of mass production, handmade products still shine as a valuable commodity, worth more than machine-made goods. Thousands of craft shows occur yearly. Most likely, there are a few in your own hometown. The size of a show can range from a small local bazaar to a popular juried show. Here's how to find the right shows for your products:

■ **Local and regional periodicals:** Check local newspapers, local culture magazines, and state tourist magazines for craft events in your area.

■ **Craft show periodicals (available by subscription or from large booksellers):** *American Style* and the *Sunshine Artist* ("America's Premier Show and Festival Guide") are monthly magazines that list events by several categories and review shows nationwide. Look for shows specializing in bath and beauty, home accessories, and specialty crafts for markets suitable for candles. Garden shows are another potential market. See Resources for a list of these and other periodicals.

■ **Word of mouth:** Approach crafters at craft sales events and ask them their opinions or advice on the event and others they have participated in.

■ **Internet:** Many sites on the Web offer show information (see Resources).

A Different Kind of Candle

Laura Leigh is an American artist who has years of experience in health and fitness and health products. She is also experienced in the use of aromatherapy. While working in Los Angeles as a meditation and personal conflict counselor with the entertainment industry, Laura began designing "Wish Candles" to express her insight into the needs and wishes of those dealing with stress. Using her experience as a one-on-one personal empowerment consultant, Laura explores the depth of human needs and, in her creations, presents the aura of hope and wishes as they affect the daily lives of individuals.

Laura has traveled extensively in Africa, the Middle East, Asia, and Europe. In her travels she searches for colors and scents to help make or highlight a mood or a

Once you think you've found a promising show, here are some questions you need to answer:

- What has been the show's attendance in previous years? How many people are expected to attend this year?
- How many candle artisans have previously participated in the show and how different are their candle styles from yours?
- What is the daily schedule, from setup to takedown?
- What will the show provide for your booth (tables, lighting, etc.)?
- Will electricity be provided? Pipe and drape? A tent? Chairs?
- What are you requested to provide?
- What advertising will be done for this event?

A Few Words About Outdoor Shows

Remember that candles don't always stand up to the heat of a hot-summer street market or fair. Even though it may not be readily evident to you, candles can sag and discolor when exposed to direct

decisive moment. She takes great pains to combine these in her designs and to present them as a sensual part of her love of life and hope for the future.

Laura individually pours each and every wish candle in a loving environment of music, meditation, and scent. Combining colors, scents, and expression, she creates candles that provide a soft glow and a provocative scent to help set a frame of mind that helps her customers focus on their dreams.

While retaining her ties to the West Coast, Laura has returned to her roots in Leon County, Florida, where she has her main studio and administrative offices. In addition to her artistic candles, Laura continues to perform on stage and at direct local productions, while still giving her mystic tarot interpretations and providing motivational and self-enhancing consultations. She participates in art and craft shows and has sold her candles to art galleries, furniture stores, and high-fashion clothing stores.

sun or hot display lamps. If you participate in an outdoor craft show, be sure to use a covered display area. A tent with sides is ideal to shield your merchandise from damaging rays. When signing up for the event, choose and request a shady area if at all possible.

Craft Malls

Craft malls are specialized shopping centers catering to the crafts market. Most are indoor spaces allowing permanent display booths for each crafter. Mall management is responsible for actual selling and the crafter is responsible for merchandising and maintaining a local display. You can also research craft malls outside your area for those that offer to merchandise and maintain your booth for a small fee.

Make sure you can justify the cost for renting a booth at a craft mall. Figure out how many candles you must sell to break even, and how much you want to profit from your efforts. Usually you must sign a contract to lease the booth for several months. If you

Craft Show Cost Considerations

Shows can be quite costly, cutting into your profits. Keep accurate records and carefully consider these expenses before entering a show:

- Entry fee

- Photography fees for professional slides

- Travel costs (hotel, meals, gas, rental van, and incidentals)

- Money you would have made if you didn't take days off from work at another job

- Booth fee

- Merchandising and display costs

haven't sold successfully in other markets, you may not want to sign a contract that requires you to pay monthly rent when you haven't generated enough profit.

Make sure you check out each craft mall before you sign any contract. Many craft malls have been successful and in business for a long time. However, others are fairly new and may not attract enough customers to generate the sales needed to cover rental fees. Historically, more craft malls have failed than succeeded, so caution is the key word here. Investigate other booths and, whenever possible, contact crafters who are already selling for insight about that particular mall.

Selling on Consignment

In selling on consignment, you retain ownership of your candles, but place them in a retail shop for sale. The retail shop accepts the responsibility of selling and, when a sale is made, you get a previously agreed upon percentage of the retail price. The advantage of

Textured Stripe Candles
Container Candles (glass)

Container Candles (tin)

Clockwise from Right:
Novelty Candles
Gel Candle Seascapes
Container Candles (pottery)

consignment is that you don't pay the selling expense, except for the costs of maintaining an inventory at the shop. Also, if the candles sell well, the shop may want to deal with you wholesale on future orders and buy the candles outright.

Consignment should always be handled with a signed, written agreement between the shop and the artisan, specifying the following terms of consignment:

Pricing: Who has the authority to set, raise, and lower prices? When may prices be changed?

Sales commission: You should at least receive a profit over your wholesale price for each candle. A 40% sales commission, or 60/40 split of the final sales, is the norm. With any higher rate of commission, seriously consider your costs and make sure you will still make a good profit.

Payment cycle: How often will payments be made? Is there a certain date when payments are normally sent to consignors?

Merchandise responsibilities: What will the retailer do on a regular basis? What will be required of you?

Damage/theft: Who pays the price of damaged or stolen goods? How soon will you be notified when these instances occur?

> ▼▼▼▼▼▼▼▼▼▼▼▼▼▼▼▼▼
> # Handy Hint
> To prepare for a traveling show, set up your booth arrangement in your house, take it down, and pack it in your storage containers as you would at the show. By test-driving your display, you can see exactly what you'll need for the booth and if it will all fit in your vehicle. You may have to borrow or consider the expense of renting a bigger vehicle just for the show.
> ▲▲▲▲▲▲▲▲▲▲▲▲▲▲▲▲▲

Sometimes a shop will approach you about consigning your candles, while other times you must seek out consignment opportunities. Visit a potential shop several times before you sign an agreement. Make sure your candles are a good fit for the shop and that shoppers are buying them. Once you have signed an agreement, visit the shop periodically to follow up personally with the retailer and make sure the candles are well maintained. Include a note in your contract stating that the shop

▼▼

Ready-to-Go Checklist

Whichever sales arena you choose, you'll need certain items to set up a sales display. If you have to prepare for a sales event outside your home or studio, find out first what the event management will provide, and mark these items on your list. Develop easily dismantled setups that can be packed into your vehicle.

Look in craft show magazines such as *Sunshine Artist* for companies that specialize in craft show display equipment. When selecting display equipment, buy as much quality as you can afford. You will often be competing with professional artisans, and your display should look as expert as theirs.

Here's what you'll need to furnish a booth and make sales:

Table: Choose a table that is compact, level, and easy to break down.
Table cover/skirt: Choose a table cover that complements your candles and goes all the way to the ground. A busy or complex design might take the focus away from the merchandise.
Chairs: Don't forget to bring enough folding chairs for you and your help, unless chairs are provided at the show.
Wastebasket: You don't want to have your booth cluttered with trash.
Merchandising decorations: Candleholders, flowers, knickknacks.
Display shelving: Make sure the shelving is level and sturdy on the display table.

▲▲

will be responsible for loss if candles are placed in direct sun or under hot display lamps, and thus damaged for sale. Share with shop owners all the safety and care information they need to pass on to the candle consumer.

Mail Order

Specialty items such as handcrafted candles are great products for mail order, but marketing by direct mail requires either developing

Risers: Could be boxes, shelves, bricks, or anything else adjustable used to create different levels of display height. It helps to have candles at the customer's eye level as well as on the table.

Business cards and marketing materials: Provide all your contact information and a list of future sales events.

Receipt and special order books: Keep these handy to record sales and production requests.

Sales and storage packaging: This might include tissue, bags, and safe, sturdy containers for your candles and display furnishings. Candles are damaged easily by constant handling. Use plenty of cushioning materials such as foam sheets and bubble wrap to protect each candle. Don't use newspaper to wrap merchandise because it can dirty the candle with ink.

Pantyhose: These work well to clean fingerprints and buff handled candles. You should recommend this tip to your customers as well!

Small cups of instant coffee grounds: These are perfect to clear a shopper's nose so she or he can better smell candle fragrances.

Tarp: Use this to cover containers or your display in case of rain. Bring this along even if you're at an indoor show. (You may need to protect your goods from rain while transporting them from your car to the show.)

Cooler: You should keep snacks and drinks in your booth in case you can't leave to visit a food vendor.

advertisements for magazines or marketing materials for direct mailings. Before you attempt this costly method of selling, research the industry thoroughly and learn how to advertise effectively through display and classified ads. Read about how to develop good-looking marketing materials to mail to potential customers and present buyers. The easiest way to sell by mail is to simply encourage follow-up mail-order sales from craft fair shoppers and other customers. You can solicit candle orders through brochures, full-color flyers, and catalogs distributed at shows. Mail order is best suited to the organized crafter who pays attention to details and works well with paperwork and deadlines. You'll definitely want to use a personal computer to keep track of your bookkeeping if you plan to get serious about this kind of selling.

Internet Sales

Doing business via the Internet is common. Every day, people are getting on the Internet for the first time, buying online, and connecting with people all over the world for business, friendship, and information. Electronic commerce, or e-commerce, is more than just a 24-hour storefront for selling products. It is a system that not only includes buying and selling, but also those transactions that support revenue generation, such as sales support, advertising, customer service, and communication within the business and with the public.

There are a variety of ways to sell on the Internet. Two options are to set up your own Web site and to sell through online malls. Whether you choose one sales approach or a combination of methods, you must base your selection on your technical knowledge, available resources, and selling style. E-commerce is a tricky business. You really have to put some thinking into it and develop a plan for how to approach your target market online. To effectively reach these shoppers, you need to research where they congregate online, and this is something you can learn best simply by going online and exploring the Internet sites that now offer handicrafts for sale.

> **Handy Hint**
>
> Learn the basics of identifying and protecting yourself against counterfeit money and false identification at the U.S. Treasury Web site: www.ustreas.gov.

Your Own Web Site

Selling from a Web site can range from simply posting information about yourself and your candles to a full-blown storefront with online shopping. A professional-looking site can put you on a par with your big-name competitors, but you need to consider the costs of maintaining your online selling activities. If you are not computer savvy, you may have to depend on a person or a company to design your site and maintain your online business. (This could easily cost you $2,000 or more a year.)

The biggest sales challenge on the Internet is to bring visitors to your site and make those visitors buyers. Don't get discouraged if sales are slow at first. It may take a while for you to develop your site to the point where shoppers feel comfortable buying from you online; this is especially true if you do the work yourself instead of hiring a professional Web-site designer. The major problem I see with crafter sites is that some seem to think that all they need to do is set up the site, sit back, and watch the sales pour in. It just doesn't work that way. You'll have to do as much promotional/marketing work as you would when participating in other markets. The work is just of a different nature. Don't depend on anyone else to market your site.

Online Auctions

An online auction is a way to promote your candle business by placing one or a set of your candles for bid on an auction Web site. Auctions can introduce you to selling on the Internet and allow you to realize the real market value of your candles. Most auction sites provide a link to your Web site as well, which allows potential buyers to learn more about you and your business.

To obtain the best prices for your candles, choose auction sites that have heavy traffic. You can determine this by checking the craft category where you would place your items for sale. If there are a healthy number of bids in the category, it may be a good sales site. If there are many items that have no bids, look at those items and see if you can figure out why they are not selling. Many times I have found in these auction items with no bids that the link to the

DONEEN'S STORY

Doneen St. John created her own Web site called The Candle Cauldron, www.candlecauldron.com.

"I have always loved candles, for both decoration and for burning in my home. They are like an obsession for me. I collect candles and candleholders of every type, shape, color, and size imaginable. I love to find old candleholders at thrift stores and flea markets, fix them up, and make unique works of art out of them.

"A good friend of mine used to melt down the leftover wax from her old store-bought candles and fill her jars to make new ones. She inspired me to try making my own candles, so I started by melting down leftovers. Then I bought some granulated wax from a local craft store to try. I just played around with it, experimenting a little, until a relative gave me an old candlemaking kit from the seventies that she dug out of her basement. I did more experimenting and slowly learned more and more about the craft. It soon became a passion.

"I decided to search the Internet for more information. At the time, there were very few sources on candlemaking and what I did find was pretty limited. I had only recently started to use the Web, and began enjoying surfing for new information and discovering all of the wonderful things to learn and do online. I ran across a Web site that gave free space for personal home pages, and it had an easy online editor you could use to make

descriptive photo was incorrect resulting in a blank image, or the text description was poorly written.

Payments are usually by check, money order, or electronic funds transfer such as Pay Pal, which allows buyers to make secure instant payments and sellers to accept payments from anyone with a credit card and e-mail address without having to pay a service fee.

your own Web page. I thought it might be fun to create my own site, and maybe other people would enjoy it, too. I've always been creative and loved doing artistic designs and layouts, whether it was business cards or flyers. I had dreamed of having my own candle shop someday, so I decided to use the name I had thought of for my site as well. This is how The Candle Cauldron was born.

"I drew on paper a basic design for the main page, and went from there. I had to teach myself how to design pages, make my own graphics, and learn HTML code (essential for all documents placed on the Web). As time went by I just kept adding new things to the site until it grew to be one of the largest and best-known candlemaking sites on the Web. Now, 3 years later, The Candle Cauldron gets anywhere from 5,000 to 10,000 hits per day and is one of the most interactive online sites, with its message board, chat room, and classified ad section. When I first started it, I had no idea how huge it would become, or how many people would end up visiting it every day!

(continued)

Online Malls

An online mall is similar in concept to a brick-and-mortar mall. The latter usually has small specialty shops congregated around larger anchor retailers such as department stores. Online malls are retail Web sites connected by a site hosting or a site listing with a larger

"I created the site out of my love for candles and candlemaking, and simply to help other people who were interested in the same thing. It started as a nonprofit site, purely for hobby. Since at the time it didn't cost me anything to keep it up, and I was a full-time homemaker, that was fine. As time went on, the site outgrew the free Web space, so I began paying for Web space to house it. The more popular it grew, the more I put into it, eventually purchasing its own domain name and an upgraded chat room program. I have many new ideas and plans for the site in the future, such as offering advertising space and selling some finished candles, soaps, and incense.

"I have learned so much about Internet selling along the way by studying every book I could, reading whatever I could find on the Web, talking to supply manufacturers and technicians, and sharing ideas with other fellow candlemakers. Not only has my Web site been a wonderful source of information, but I've met some invaluable friends and colleagues as well. It is because of my Candle Cauldron site that I am now a partner in a large candlemaking supply business called Bitter Creek Candle Supply, Inc. The owner, Rich Hansen, contacted me through my site and hired me to create a Web site for him. Through our teamwork, business sense, and creative marketing, products, and services, we built the company into one of the largest suppliers online. After just 3 years, we now employ over 25 people

Internet presence, whose primary business may not necessarily be retail. Yahoo, an Internet search engine, for example, allows companies to build stores on their Web servers and offers customer services such as browsing all affiliated stores at once to search for items and easy price comparisons from different store merchants selling the same item. Yahoo handles payment services and passes

and ship out hundreds of orders each day to candlemakers all over the world! What started as only a part-time Web design job has become a full-time career, and will soon fulfill my dream of having my own candle shop as well! (See Resources for the Bitter Creek Candle Supply, Inc. Web site address.)

"The best advice I can give to new candlemakers is to read all you can and study up before jumping in with both feet. Take time to experiment with formulas, document them, and always test-burn each new creation before trying to sell it! Test different fragrances and supplies for yourself, and never rely only on other people's opinions. What looks or smells great to you, may not to someone else, and vice versa. And what doesn't sell for others, may be a big seller for you! Remember, mistakes in candlemaking can always be melted back down to try again. Test your new creations on friends and family, and make sure you're happy with your finished product before selling it. When you're ready to sell, always include caution labels and burning instructions with your candles! Be unique in both the product and the packaging, and don't be afraid to try something new. The candle business can be very trendy, so what's hot today may not be the hot product next week. Most important, keep an open mind and a positive attitude, and remember there are always new things to learn in candlemaking!"

sales information immediately to the individual Web site owner, who then ships the merchandise.

Smaller malls specialize in particular retail categories, such as online craft malls, and may offer limited merchant services. Unless you pay someone to maintain your site for you, you maintain your online shopping area as you would an independent site. If you choose to affiliate your business with an online mall, consider the quality of the site and the services it offers, as well as any setup and maintenance fees. If they offer online content design for you, you may be required to follow a predesigned template, which may or may not meet your marketing needs. Before you affiliate yourself with another Web site, inquire about its site statistics and how much advertising is done to promote the site.

Even though an online mall can help you gain recognition on the Web, it is still up to you to attract visitors and generate sales. If a mall site says they can do all the work for you if you don't have a computer or have limited Web access, you won't likely sell much on the Internet.

Do's and Don'ts for Online Selling

Do provide a detailed image, but not one so large that it takes too long to upload so the interested buyer gives up before actually viewing the item for sale. A poor-quality image may not accurately depict the item for sale; poor lighting or a busy background is a common reason.

Don't set up an item in the wrong merchandise category or too general of a category. Candles fall into categories such as aromatherapy, home fragrance, candles, home decor, and seasonal merchandise, for example. In which one do you list your candles? The answer is all that apply, if possible; if you must choose one, choose a general category that best approaches what your target market can identify with.

Do use creative marketing in presenting your merchandise online. Whether you're selling by mail order or on the Internet, your description can make all the difference in selling your candles. This is where your writing and selling skills come into play. The candle photo, text description, and price are all the merchandise information the shoppers have to decide whether to buy or not. You must accurately describe all the item's attributes likely to arouse interest in a potential buyer. For buyers in a normal store setting, shopping for candles is a sensory activity. They will pick up a candle they are interested in and smell it to sample its fragrance. Scent is the main reason consumers buy candles; since smell does not carry online, you must use creative writing in your description of a scent.

Online Sales Observations

I've included a lot of information about selling on the Internet because it is a sales arena that many want to try, but don't know where to begin. I think a lot of people are a little hesitant because many crafters who have tried online selling have spread the word to others that the profit—or lack of profit—wasn't worth the effort and expense. It's important to know that many people jump online and don't know what they're getting into. They don't see the shift in sales strategy they must develop in order to reach their online target market. Although their other sales venues may be successful, they are inexperienced when it comes to doing business online. Some people do not personally involve themselves in the online community by buying online themselves or participating in message boards enough to really know how it all works.

You should approach the Internet just as you would go to a craft show as an observer to see if it's the right show for you before you sign up and participate. Try buying some candles online. How did you find the site where you could buy candles? What made you choose to buy or not to buy? Visit several successful online retail giants and make some purchases. You'll see a consistency in their Web content in terms of product descriptions, site navigation, and customer service that is the basis of excellent online sales design. Use them as an example of what you should do for your own online

Give Your Internet Sales a Boost

Add power to your Web presence by enhancing communication with your customers. Offering your visitors several ways to communicate with you and making it easier for them to find your business on the Internet will increase your online customer service and most likely fuel additional sales. Seek advice from a trusted Internet service consultant for recommendations on utilizing these features on your site.

The following are other methods to help increase your sales:

Unique domain name: having your own catchy .com or .net address makes it a lot easier for customers to find you. Make it easier for customers to recall your address by using an address they'll easily remember and not confuse with another site with a similar name.

Toll-free phone number: The power of a free call is supreme in the mail-order world. Giving your visitors the option of doing business with you the old-fashioned way can

efforts. An introductory book to online commerce can further explain these ideas to you. Take the time to do the research before you take the virtual plunge!

Customer Service: Your Sales Skills

Wherever you sell your products, the first rule of selling is to be attentive to your customer. If selling face to face, always make it easy for the customer to approach you for help. The best way to break the ice with customers is to simply recognize them. A welcoming hello as they walk into your studio or booth is sufficient to let the customer know that you are there for them. If you look busy to them, they may not want to bother you, which is not how you want them to feel! Even if you don't have direct customer contact, it's still important to make customers know they are important to you by

aid sales from those who would prefer to talk with a person or pay over the phone. Make sure someone is available to answer calls within your posted available service hours. People who call to talk to a person usually prefer not to talk to a machine!

Secure online ordering system: Secure online shopping encrypts credit card data and maintains transmission safety, which gives shoppers confidence in entering their credit card number to buy online from you. Your system should include a well-maintained online inventory, an easy-to-use shopping basket, and a secure site page for processing orders.

Online contact form: This online form on a Web page contains fields for visitors to enter their information and comments online. These forms render a professional look to your site, as well as allow you to collect valuable marketing information about visitors that they might not leave in an e-mail message.

following up on all communication with a postcard or phone call with them as soon as possible.

Doing a show can be tiring—unpacking, setting up, making sales, packing up—but regardless of the work, you must keep a selling disposition for your customers. I enjoy selling and yet at times during shows I feel my face starting to hurt from all the smiling I do as I answer the same questions about my candles over and over again! Whatever you do, don't take out frustration or stress on your customers. You can lose sales, as they'll surely spread the word to other shoppers about your bad attitude.

Consumer Concerns and Customer Satisfaction

If you have customers who are concerned about candle smoke or soot, educate them as to the best practices for burning and remind them that properly maintained candles made with quality

Payment Methods

Cash: The best and quickest method of payment. Just remember to keep your cash secure at all times and make frequent trips to the bank to keep your profits safe.

Checks: Good payments with no additional costs, except for an occasional bounced check. Here are some tips when dealing with checks:

- Get the buyer's essential information: driver license number, phone number, and address.

- Don't accept starter checks or checks with numbers less than 200.

- Display your payment requirements at the point of sale and post a written fee notice for any returned checks.

- Deposit checks immediately.

Check cards or debit cards: These can be used just like credit cards. This method is more convenient for the customer than writing a check, but the merchant pays for the convenience at a regular credit card percentage (see below).

Credit cards: These allow for better sales from all shoppers who use plastic. Accepting credit cards also increases impulse buys, which frequently involve using plastic. If you decide it is important to offer the service to your customers, always ask for identification and get a phone number from credit card users. This service is paid by merchant fees, which are based on a percentage of the total sale and can add up to a substantial usage fee. You should have a significant amount of sales for this to be profitable.

ingredients produce minimal soot and smoke. Since you make your candles with your own hands, you can assure a buyer of their quality and guarantee satisfaction. If customers are not satisfied with a candle in any way, have them return the unused portion and offer a refund or exchange.

Even with test-burning each candle batch, it's still possible to get a bad egg once in a while, so research the reason for the return and work on your process to eliminate the problem. If the reason is because the candle was not properly maintained, tactfully let the customer know. If the person felt the need to return the candle, you should accept the return and do what you can to keep your customer satisfied. You're better off remelting a candle than losing a customer!

When I was the manager of a mall bath and beauty shop, one customer repeatedly returned candles for one reason or another, burning most of the candle before coming in to exchange it. This case is an exception that rarely happens, but when it does you must eventually put your foot down and not allow your customer to take undue advantage of your customer service efforts.

Soaking It All Up

The techniques I've presented in this chapter are meant to give you ideas of how and where to sell your candles. Of course these aren't all the possibilities available to you. And, in your experiences, you may find that certain methods I've outlined that have worked well for me may not work as well for you. Your best approach after reading this chapter is to read more and get as acquainted with the candle and gift business as you can. The Resources section of this book has information that can help you get started on your research.

Marketing Your Candles

Advertising and Publicity

▼▼▼

MAKING YOUR PRODUCT KNOWN to the public is the first step to getting sales. If consumers don't know your product exists, how can they even think about buying it?

In the marketing of handcrafted items, making yourself known is part of making your product known. Providing customers and prospects with background information on you, the artisan, is vital. Many candles bear the label "handmade," but the label often fails to say by whom. If a customer is interested in the handcrafted aspect of the candle, knowing some of your background and personal information is likely to strengthen the link between you and the customer.

In all the mediums that you use to advertise your business to the public, you must present a positive image in a professional manner. Pay the same special attention to fine details in all of your communications as you do to handcrafting a quality candle. If you can't afford professional design services, learn how to use a simple publishing software tool, such as Adobe PageMaker or Printshop by Broderbund, and research the fundamentals of advertising and publicity. This chapter explores the marketing methods of advertising and publicity that can promote both you and your candles. As you will see in this chapter, there are many low-cost things you can do to generate more sales; I discuss many important ones.

Business Cards

A business card is the easiest way to personally promote your business. It should be the first printed material you purchase for your profit efforts. Your business card needs to contain all your primary contact information: business name and logo, mailing or physical address, Web site address, e-mail address, phone number, and fax number. Project as professional an image as you can, so people will take you and your business seriously.

Flyers and Brochures

Flyers are inexpensive handouts, generally 8½ × 11 sheets, that you can use to advertise special occasions, such as your next sales event or candlemaking class. A brochure is a method of relaying more information than a flyer or business card can convey. It should be a handy reference on you and your candles, and can be printed in a variety of sizes and formats. Check local print shops for ideas, or buy simple computer software to design your own. A good brochure illustrates the uniqueness of your work, and lists and describes all your services as a candle artisan.

Printed Letterhead and Envelopes

A nice-looking printed letterhead and matching envelope is a little detail that goes a long way in presenting a professional image in all your written correspondence. Keep your logos and fonts consistent in each mailing you do so people can easily recognize your correspondence.

Promotional Marketing Materials

Customers like a little something extra with their purchase. Candle information cards are an inexpensive promotional item you can design and print on your computer. Such cards might illustrate a historic candle-burning ritual or list the do's and don'ts of candle safety while doubling as a business card with all your contact information. These handy cards can be as small as an eighth to a quarter of a standard letter size. Other information you can put on cards to give out to your customers includes candle and candlemaking history, holidays that celebrate light, candle terminology, or an explanation of candlemaking technique. Just think of all the candlemaking questions people ask you and put those answers as interesting candle trivia on cards. This will make your contact information more memorable than it would be on an ordinary business card.

Promotional Newsletters

Sending a little update on your activities to all those on your mailing list can keep your business fresh in the minds of your customers and inform them about your new candlemaking class, upcoming sales event, new scents you've acquired, or new candle style you've developed. Many crafters print one-page newsletters on their computers, and send them to customers and interested prospects. If you maintain a customer e-mail list, you can send electronic newsletters easily, quickly, and without postal costs.

Press Releases

A press release is an announcement, usually on one 8½ × 11-inch page, that you send to editors about something worthy of publication. Periodical editors regularly look for information that will interest their readers. Find out the editorial deadlines of the appropriate newspapers or magazines so you can send your press releases in a

Celebrations of Light Around the World

Around the world, people use light at the heart of their festivals.

All Saints'/Souls' Day: Europe, Latin America, Philippines

Bon Matsuri: Japan

Buddha's Birthday: Korea

Christmas: United States (and all around the world wherever Christians are)

Diwali: India

Hanukkah: Israel (and all around the world wherever Jewish people are)

Hungry Ghost Festival: China, Taiwan

Kwanzaa: United States, Canada, England, the Caribbean, and Africa

Lichtmesdag: Luxembourg

Loy Krathong: Thailand

Luciadagen: Sweden

New Year: China, Taiwan

New Year's Eve: United States and all around the world

Prachum Ben: Cambodia

Tet: Vietnam

timely manner. (Some magazines have closing dates several months in advance of publication.)

Make your press release look as professional as possible. Type it on the computer and double-space the document for easy reading. The standard format of a press release consists of the following:

- A catchy headline that will get an editor's attention (centered on the page)

- Your name and contact information (on the top, left-hand side of the page) and date

- An excellent opening sentence followed by the principal information stated concisely. The body of your release should be brief, but contain all the relevant facts.

(For details on how to write a good press release, see the Resources section.)

Feature Articles

Having a newspaper or magazine write something about you and your candles is a great way to gain free advertising. You can submit to the media ideas for articles that you think are worthy of notice, such as a new candlemaking class you are teaching in your area or an award you've won at a craft show. If you gain recognition on the national level, don't forget to send a press release to your local newspaper. Journalists love to feature hometown people in their local news.

Print Advertisements

Print advertisements present a direct sales approach to your target market. A small ad placed in a local newspaper can do wonders for your open house or candlemaking class. Ads do not necessarily have to be large and overly expensive to be successful. To make the most of your advertising dollar, be concise and persuasive in your writing and choose the best print medium for reaching your target market.

Word-of-Mouth Advertising

The happier your customers are with your candles, the more they'll want to spread the word for you. Personal endorsements by your customers spoken directly to potential buyers (usually friends, family, or coworkers) are the best advertising you can get. The only price you pay is the amount of effort you perform in pleasing your customers.

Internet

As discussed in the previous chapters, the Internet can be a valuable marketing and promotional tool. Learn to use it to share information, generate new business, improve your customer relations, and enhance your artisan image. (See chapter 9 for more information about using the Internet in your candlemaking business.)

Having a Web site of your own is, in effect, an online business card or brochure. Your site should have all the information about you and your candles that appeals to your target market. Even if you don't sell directly over the Web through your own site or another's, a presence on the Internet will promote your candlemaking business. One or a few simple Web pages can contain a sample candle portfolio, marketing information about you and your candles, and important contact information so existing and potential clients can reach you easily.

The way you present your information depends on the type of market you are trying to attract. The general rule is to organize information in a consistent way and in the best manner for visitors to learn about you and your candles and easily find what they're looking for. Here's the type of information you should include on your Internet presence site:

- **Artist history: Background information about you includes your candlemaking experience and activities. Your candles are more valuable because you made them!**

■ Contact information: If you don't want to publish your address and phone number, at least provide an e-mail address visible on all the pages of your Web site so visitors can contact you easily. A post office box address is a good addition for visitors who prefer snail-mail communication.

■ An online candle gallery: Even if you're not selling your candles through online ordering, your candles need to be the main focus of your Web site. Simple photos and brilliant descriptions of your candles are all you need to publish an online portfolio of your work. Keep page backgrounds simple to make your candles stand out. Museums and galleries give works of art plenty of space to maintain focus on the piece. The same technique works well online. Your photos should be high quality, but a small file size so visitors won't have to wait too long while the image downloads for viewing. Include a close-up of each candle to show off your design better. Your descriptions should support the visual images and enhance the fine details of your craftsmanship that is not so evident in your photo. An elegant explanation of texture, scent, burning quality, and size provides a more vivid representation of your candles.

> **Handy Hint**
>
> Give visitors a reason to return to your site. Post periodic updates of your sales schedule if you participate in craft shows, or maintain an online newsletter of your activities.

Making your site known is the key to the success of any online venture. You can try to depend on people finding you by chance through a search engine, but essentially you are a stranger to them if they don't know you personally. Having a few pages on the Web is great for crafters who cannot afford to give every interested person a brochure about their products, but can afford a business card with an Internet address for people to check out at their convenience. It is to your advantage to promote your site as a primary way for people to find out more about you.

E-mail

E-mail can be used in a variety of ways to support your candle sales. Get the e-mail address of anyone interested in your candles. Every time you participate in a show or hold an open house or candle party, put out a guest book for your visitors to sign that includes a column for e-mail addresses. Enter these names in your e-mail address book and categorize them as selling contacts. You can even further categorize them into where you came into contact with them—craft show, open house, or Web-site inquiry.

When it's time for your next sales event, you can publicize your event by e-mailing all these potential customers at once to let them hear all about it directly from you. You can also e-mail past customers periodically to let them know what you're up to in your studio; for example, that you've just developed a new style of candle or just acquired a special new scent. As much as possible, keep tabs on each person who has bought from you directly by making a note in your e-mail contact file for that person, stating exactly what they bought, where they bought from you, and why they bought it. After collecting a lot of this contact information, you'll be able to see trends in your sales and the demographics of your customers.

No-Cost Publicity

Free publicity is any information, dissemination, or promotion that brings notice to you and your candles without you having to pay for it. Here are some ideas for free publicity: In addition to sending press releases, you can get publicity in several other ways with only a little elbow grease on your part. It's not difficult work if you love doing it!

Hold Candlemaking Demonstrations

Sharing your candlemaking skills with a group or at an event increases your exposure in your community. Volunteer your instruction by holding a candlemaking demonstration for a Girl Scout troop, church, or other community organization. Such visibility can lead to future contacts and sales.

Promote Your Candlemaking Classes

Many newspapers, magazines, and Web sites offer free listings of art and craft workshops and classes. Having your class publicized can easily fill up your rosters and increase demand for your instruction as students spread interest by word of mouth.

Join Arts and Crafts Organizations

Arts and crafts associations support local creativity, especially the artistic works of their members. Visit a local gallery or art foundation to get more information about organizations in your community. At the national and global level, the International Guild of Candle Artisans (IGCA) is a friendly organization, dedicated to promoting the interest of candle artisans, encouraging the study of candlemaking and candle design, and fostering good will, fellowship, and the exchange of ideas among its members. The IGCA offers a monthly newsletter filled with candlemaking techniques and decorating ideas, patterns, photographs, news of members, and a hotline for problem solving. There are 12 issues per year, including a yearbook issue that gives names and addresses of members and suppliers, along with a list of wholesalers. The IGCA also offers candle networking, correspondence with a group of members about candlemaking ideas and problems. An annual convention is usually held the second week in July. It offers workshops, candle competition, and lots of great fun and camaraderie.

Donate Candles

Donating candle gifts for door prizes or auction items for charity fundraisers can enhance your image in your community and publicize your work while supporting a worthwhile cause. Always include marketing materials with your gift, such as a business card and brochure. Also leave extra materials at the event for people to pick up, but check with the organizers of the event first to make sure that it's all right.

Merchandising Your Candles

Candle display and packaging adds sales appeal to your products. "Merchandising" your candles means effectively balancing the marketing tasks of candle selection, pricing, displaying, and advertising in a way that attracts more buyers. Since many people buy candles for a specific reason and may buy numerous candles at once, you may be able to boost sales by making gift sets that appeal to such shoppers. Develop different gift sets and displays that address the different reasons consumers use candles. (See chapter 4, page 84, for the various reasons people use candles.) Since candles are most popular as a home fragrance carrier and as a decorative accessory, emphasize these attributes in eye-catching merchandising displays that attract buyers to the style, scent, and idea for using them in the home. Include a few burning candles to spark even more interest; check to make sure this is okay if you're selling at a show.

As emphasized earlier, shopping for candles is a sensory experience. Often I see customers shopping my candles as if they were carefully examining a piece of fruit to eat. Make your display as inviting as possible, and set it up so people can easily shop and sample your candles' scents and textures. People often comment that they can smell my candles before they even get to my display. After being around my candles so much, I can't smell individual scents, so I try to get away from my booth sometimes and take a walk, or sip a cup of coffee to clear my senses. (This is why I said earlier in chapter 9 to bring coffee grounds to your shows—smelling them refreshes the senses.)

> **Handy Hint**
>
> For unusual-shaped candles, offer a candleholder that can accommodate the candle as an add-on sale.

The Power of Packaging

The power of selling associated products packaged together under one price is evident in the booming sales of gift baskets. Looking for the perfect gift often means looking for a gift that offers a complete setup so the recipient doesn't need to buy any additional accessories to use the gift. Candles are so versatile that you can group them in many different ways to increase sales. Here are a few examples:

Floater gift set: A set of matching floater candles packaged in a decorative bowl to float them in.

Men's gift set: A set of candles colored in dark tones with earthy scents, with or without a candleholder.

Scent/color set: A set of complementary or matching colors and scents. Package a colorful "fruit bowl" of fruity-scented candles or line up candles to form a color rainbow.

Complementary handmade product sets: Candles packaged with other handmade products. Group scented candles with matching scented soaps or bath salts made by you or another crafter, or pair a candle with a handmade ceramic bowl as an extra craft item.

Aromatherapy sampler gift set: A set of natural aromatherapy candles in complementary colors and therapeutic effects.

Add-On Candle Accessories and Packaging

To generate additional sales and offer a complete candle package, consider these extra sales items when merchandising your candles:

Candleholders	Bowls for floating candles
Candle chandeliers	Candle wax remover
Matching flower arrangements	Candle-burning booklet
Candle storage containers	Matching scent oils
Fancy lighters	

Ritual gift set: A group of candles in the traditional color and shape necessary for performing a particular candle-burning ritual. Provide information with the set on how to perform the ritual.

Novelty theme set: A set of seasonal figures, religious figures such as angels and crosses, or other themes that fit the occasion.

Candle Labeling

There are currently no laws governing candle labeling. However, most manufacturers voluntarily place safety information on their products. Safety labels should remind the consumer of the hazards of an open flame and recommend the best practice on how to burn the particular candle to prevent fire and minimize soot.

You should provide a safety label for each candle you do not burn yourself. You cannot assume each person who lights your handmade candles has the common sense you do about candle safety. Every time I sell a candle face to face, I personally remind the consumer of candle safety as I close the sale. It seems as though

Spread Out and Diversify

To maintain good prices for your candles, spread out your retail distribution. Don't crowd the market by placing your candles in every corner gift shop. Once you think you've saturated your local target market, it may be necessary for you to expand the geographic boundaries of your business and introduce your candles to new markets. At this point you'll need to reassess your activities and further develop your business plan to accommodate these new ventures.

every new product that comes out has some sort of safety warning, but people just don't read warning labels or simply overlook them. When I think of all the candle fires from careless candle use that could have been prevented, I feel a responsibility to stress candle safety.

Safety information can be printed on packaging. If the packaging is to be removed prior to burning the candle, however, it's better to put the information on a sticker on the bottom of the candle whenever possible. That way it can be referred to when needed.

Letting Your Light Shine

All in all, the best way to advertise and promote your business is to stay visible however you can. Take advantage of free advertising, and make some of your own. Use your creativity to your benefit and explore wherever your candlemaking takes you. Who knows where you'll end up?

I never thought my college curiosity would lead to almost a decade of candlemaking. I teach candlemaking classes, though I used to think that I would never be able to speak coherently in front of a group of people. I never thought my hobby would lead to writing a candlemaking book. I've never considered myself an expert candlemaker or an expert on making money from it, but I love candlemaking so much it shows. It shows to the people I work with at my full-time job with a software development company, as well as to my candle clients, candlemaking students, friends, and family. I've worked hard to learn as much about candlemaking as I could through research and experience. If you feel a passion for candlemaking, fuel that flame inside you as I have and reap the benefits of a fully satisfying and profitable craft. If you simply enjoy candlemaking as a worthwhile pastime, I hope you will find this book a handy reference for candlemaking information and for inspiring ideas to elevate your craft to higher levels of challenge.

A Mini-Course in Crafts-Business Basics

by Barbara Brabec

▼▼

THIS SECTION OF THE BOOK will familiarize you with important areas of legal and financial concern and enable you to ask the right questions if and when it is necessary to consult with an attorney, accountant, or other business adviser. Although the tax and legal information included here has been carefully researched by the author and is accurate to the best of her knowledge, it is not the business of either the author or publisher to render professional services in the area of business law, taxes, or accounting. Readers should therefore use their own good judgment in determining when the services of a lawyer or other professional would be appropriate to their needs.

Information presented applies specifically to businesses in the United States. However, because many U.S. and Canadian laws are similar, Canadian readers can certainly use the following information as a start-up business plan and guide to questions they need to ask their own local, provincial, or federal authorities.

Contents

7. **Insurance Tips**

Homeowner's or Renter's Insurance
Liability Insurance
Insurance on Crafts Merchandise
Auto Insurance

8. **Important Regulations Affecting Artists
    and Craftspeople**

Consumer Safety Laws
Labels Required by Law
The Bedding and Upholstered Furniture Law
FTC Rule for Mail-Order Sellers

9. **Protecting Your Intellectual Property**

Perspective on Patents
What a Trademark Protects
What Copyrights Protect
Copyright Registration Tips
Respecting the Copyrights of Others
Using Commercial Patterns and Designs

10. **To Keep Growing, Keep Learning**

Motivational Tips

A "Things to Do" Checklist with Related Resources

- Business Start-Up Checklist
- Government Agencies
- Craft and Home-Business Organizations
- Recommended Crafts-Business Periodicals
- Other Services and Suppliers
- Recommended Business Books
- Helpful Library Directories

1. Starting Right

In preceding chapters of this book, you learned the techniques of a particular art or craft and realized its potential for profit. You learned what kinds of products are likely to sell, how to price them, and how and where you might sell them.

Now that you've seen how much fun a crafts business can be (and how profitable it might be if you were to get serious about selling what you make!) you need to learn about some of the "nitty-gritty stuff" that goes hand in hand with even the smallest business based at home. It's easy to start selling what you make and it's satisfying when you earn enough money to make your hobby self-supporting. Many crafters go this far and no further, which is fine. But even a hobby seller must be concerned about taxes and local, state, and federal laws. And if your goal is to build a part- or full-time business at home, you must pay even greater attention to the topics discussed in this section of the book.

Everyone loves to make money . . . but actually starting a business frightens some people because they don't understand what's involved. It's easy to come up with excuses for why we don't do certain things in life; close inspection of those excuses usually boils down to fear of the unknown. We get the shivers when we step out of our comfort zone and try something we've never done before. The simple solution to this problem lies in having the right information at the right time. As someone once said, "Knowledge is the antidote to fear."

The quickest and surest way to dispel fear is to inform yourself about the topics that frighten you. With knowledge comes a sense of power, and that power enables you to move. Whether your goal is merely to earn extra income from your craft hobby or launch a genuine home-based business, reading the following information will help you get started on the right legal foot, avoid financial pitfalls, and move forward with confidence.

When you're ready to learn more about art or crafts marketing or the operation of a home-based crafts business, a visit to your library or bookstore will turn up many interesting titles. In addition to the special resources listed by this book's author, you will find my list of recommended business books, organizations, periodicals, and other helpful resources later in this chapter. This information is arranged in a checklist you can use as a plan to get your business up and running.

Before you read my Mini-Course in Crafts-Business Basics, be assured that I understand where you're coming from because I was once there myself.

For a while I sold my craft work, and this experience led me to write my first book, *Creative Cash*. Now, 20 years later, this crafts-business classic ("my baby") has reached its sixth edition. Few of those who are totally involved in a crafts business today started out with a business in mind. Like me, most began as hobbyists looking for something interesting to do in their spare time, and one thing naturally led to another. I never imagined those many years ago

Social Security Taxes

When your crafts-business earnings are more than $400 (net), you must file a Self-Employment Tax form (Schedule SE) and pay into your personal Social Security account. This could be quite beneficial for individuals who have some previous work experience but have been out of the workplace for a while. Your re-entry into the business world as a self-employed worker, and the additional contributions to your Social Security account, could result in increased benefits on retirement.

Because so many senior citizens are starting home-based businesses these days, it should be noted that there is a limit on the amount seniors age 62 to 65 can earn before losing Social Security benefits. This dollar limit increases every year, however, and once you are past the age of 65, you can earn any amount of income and still receive full benefits. Contact your nearest Social Security office for details.

when I got serious about my craft hobby that I was putting myself on the road to a full-time career as a crafts writer, publisher, author, and speaker. Because I and thousands of others have progressed from hobbyists to professionals, I won't be at all surprised if some-day you, too, have a similar adventure.

2. Taxes and Record Keeping

"Ambition in America is still rewarded . . . with high taxes," the comics quip. Don't you long for the good old days when Uncle Sam lived within his income and without most of yours?

Seriously, taxes are one of the first things you must be con-cerned about as a new business owner, no matter how small your endeavor. This section offers a brief overview of your tax responsi-bilities as a sole proprietor.

Is Your Activity a "Hobby" or a "Business"?

Whether you are selling what you make only to get the cost of your supplies back or actually trying to build a profitable business, you need to understand the legal difference between a profitable hobby and a business, and how each is related to your annual tax return.

The IRS defines a hobby as "an activity engaged in primarily for pleasure, not for profit." Making a profit from a hobby does not automatically place you "in business" in the eyes of the Internal Revenue Service, but the activity will be *presumed* to have been en-gaged in for profit if it results in a profit in at least 3 out of 5 years. Or, to put it another way, a "hobby business" automatically becomes a "real business" in the eyes of the IRS at the point where you can state that you are (1) trying to make a profit, (2) making regular business transactions, and (3) have made a profit 3 out of 5 years.

As you know, all income must be reported on your annual tax return. How it's reported, however, has everything to do with the amount of taxes you must pay on this income. If hobby income is less than $400, it must be entered on the 1040 tax form, with taxes payable accordingly. If the amount is greater than this, you must file a Schedule C form with your 1040 tax form. This is to your advantage, however, because taxes are due only on your *net profit*. Because you can deduct expenses up to the amount of your hobby income, there may be little or no tax at all on your hobby income.

Self-Employment Taxes

Whereas a hobby cannot show a loss on a Schedule C form, a business can. Business owners must pay not only state and federal income taxes on their profits, but self-employment taxes as well. (See sidebar, Social Security Taxes, page 217.) Because self-employed people pay Social Security taxes at twice the level of regular, salaried workers, you should strive to lower your annual gross profit figure on the Schedule C form through every legal means possible. One way to do this is through careful record keeping of all expenses related to the operation of your business. To quote IRS publications, expenses are deductible if they are "ordinary, necessary, and somehow connected with the operation and potential profit of your business." In addition to being able to deduct all expenses related to the making and selling of their products, business owners can also depreciate the cost of tools and equipment, deduct the overhead costs of operating a home-based office or studio (called the Home Office Deduction), and hire their spouse or children.

> *Avoid this pitfall:* Many new businesses that end up with a nice net profit on their first year's Schedule C tax form find themselves in financial trouble when tax time rolls around because they did not make estimated quarterly tax payments throughout the year. Aside from the penalties for underpayment of taxes, it's

a terrible blow to suddenly realize that you've spent all your business profits and now have no money left for taxes. Be sure to discuss this matter with a tax adviser or accountant when you begin your business.

Given the complexity of our tax laws and the fact that they are changing all the time, a detailed discussion of all the tax deductions currently available to small-business owners cannot be included in a book of this nature. Learning, however, is as easy as reading a book such as *Small Time Operator* by Bernard Kamoroff (my favorite tax and accounting guide), visiting the IRS Web site, or consulting your regular tax adviser.

You can also get answers to specific tax questions 24 hours a day by calling the National Association of Enrolled Agents (NAEA). Enrolled agents (EAs) are licensed by the Treasury Department to represent taxpayers before the IRS. Their rates for doing tax returns are often less than those you would pay for an accountant or CPA.

Keeping Tax Records

Once you're in business, you must keep accurate records of all income and expenses, but the IRS does not require any special kind of bookkeeping system. Its primary concern is that you use a system that clearly and accurately shows true income and expenses. For the sole proprietor, a simple system consisting of a checkbook, a cash receipts journal, a cash disbursements ledger, and a petty cash fund is quite adequate. Post expenses and income regularly to avoid year-end pile-up and panic.

If you plan to keep manual records, check your local office supply store or catalogs for the *Dome* series of record-keeping books, or use the handy ledger sheets and worksheets included in *Small Time Operator*. (This classic tax and accounting guide by CPA Bernard Kamoroff includes details on how to keep good records and prepare financial reports.) If you have a computer, there are a number of accounting software programs available, such as Intuit's Quicken, MYOB (Mind Your Own Business) Accounting, and Intuit's

An important concept to remember is that even the smallest business is entitled to deduct expenses related to its business, and the same tax-saving strategies used by "the big guys" can be used by small-business owners. Your business may be small now or still in the dreaming stage, but it could be larger next year and surprisingly profitable a few years from now. Therefore it is in your best interest to always prepare for growth, profit, and taxes by learning all you can about the tax laws and deductions applicable to your business. (See the sidebar, Keeping Tax Records on page 220.)

Sales Tax Is Serious Business

If you live in a state that has a sales tax (all but five states do), and sell products directly to consumers, you are required by law to register with your state's Department of Revenue (Sales Tax division) for a resale tax number. The fee for this in most states ranges from $5 to $25, with some states requiring a bond or deposit of up to $150.

QuickBooks, the latter of which is one of the most popular and best bookkeeping systems for small businesses. The great advantage of computerized accounting is that financial statements can be created at the press of a key after accounting entries have been made.

Regardless of which system you use, always get a receipt for everything and file receipts in a monthly envelope. If you don't want to establish a petty cash fund, spindle all of your cash receipts, tally them at month's end, and reimburse your personal outlay of cash with a check written on your business account. On your checkbook stub, document the individual purchases covered by this check.

At year's end, bundle your monthly tax receipt envelopes and file them for future reference, if needed. Because the IRS can audit a return for up to 3 years after a tax return has been filed, all accounting and tax records should be kept at least this long, but 6 years is better. Personally, I believe you should keep all your tax returns, journals, and ledgers throughout the life of your business.

Depending on where you live, this tax number may also be called a Retailer's Occupation Tax Registration Number, resale license, or use tax permit. Also, depending on where you live, the place you must call to obtain this number will have different names. In California, for example, you would contact the State Board of Equalization; in Texas, it's called the State Comptroller's Office. Within your state's revenue department, the tax division may have a name such as sales and use tax division or department of taxation and finance. Generally speaking, if you check your telephone book under "Government," and look for whatever listing comes closest to "Revenue," you can find the right office.

If your state has no sales tax, you will still need a reseller's permit or tax exemption certificate to buy supplies and materials at wholesale prices from manufacturers, wholesalers, or distributors. Note that this tax number is only for supplies and materials used to make your products, not for things purchased at the retail level or for general office supplies.

Once registered with the state, you will begin to collect and remit sales and use tax (monthly, quarterly, or annually, as determined by your state) on all *taxable sales*. This does not mean *all* of your gross income. Different states tax different things. Some states put a sales tax on certain services, but generally you will never have to pay sales tax on income from articles sold to magazines, on teaching or consulting fees, or subscription income (if you happen to publish a newsletter). In addition, sales taxes are not applicable to:

- Items sold on consignment through a charitable organization, shop, or other retail outlet, including craft malls and rent-a-space shops (because the party who sells directly to the consumer is the one who must collect and pay sales tax).

- Products you wholesale to others who will be reselling them to consumers. (Be sure to get their tax-exemption ID number for your own files, however, in case you are ever questioned as to why you did not collect taxes on those sales.)

As you sell throughout the year, your record-keeping system must be set up so you can tell which income is taxable and which is tax-exempt for reporting on your sales tax return.

Collecting Sales Tax at Craft Shows

States are getting very aggressive about collecting sales tax, and agents are showing up everywhere these days, especially at the larger craft fairs, festivals, and small-business conferences. As I was writing this chapter, a posting on the Internet stated that in New Jersey the sales tax department is routinely contacting show promoters about a month before the show date to get the names and addresses of exhibitors. It is expected that other states will soon be following suit. For this reason, you should always take your resale or tax collection certificate with you to shows.

Although you must always collect sales tax at a show when you sell in a state that has a sales tax, how and when the tax is paid to the state can vary. When selling at shows in other states, you may find that the show promoter has obtained an umbrella sales tax certificate, in which case vendors would be asked to give management a check for sales tax at the end of the show for turning over to a tax agent. Or you may have to obtain a temporary sales tax certificate for a show, as advised by the show promoter. Some sellers who regularly do shows in two or three states say it's easier to get a tax ID number from each state and file an annual return instead of doing taxes on a show-by-show basis. (See sidebar, Including Tax in the Retail Price, page 224.)

Collecting Sales Tax at a Holiday Boutique

If you're involved in a holiday boutique where several sellers are offering goods to the public, each individual seller will be responsible for collecting and remitting his or her own sales tax. (This means someone has to keep very good records during the sale so each seller receives a record of the sale and the amount of tax on that sale.) A reader who regularly has home boutiques told me that in her community she must also post a sign at her "cash station" stating that sales tax is being collected on all sales, just as craft-fair sellers must do in some states. Again, it's important that you get complete details from your own state about its sales tax policies.

> ***Avoid this pitfall:*** Individuals who are selling "just for the fun of it" may think they don't have to collect sales taxes, but this is not true. As an official in my state's Department of Revenue told me, "Everyone who sells anything to consumers must collect sales tax. If you hold yourself out as a seller of merchandise, then you're subject to tax, even if you sell only a couple of times a year." The financial penalties for violating this state law can be severe. In Illinois, for example, lawbreakers are subject to a penalty of 20% over and above any normal tax obligation, and could receive for each offense (meaning each return not filed)

Including Tax in the Retail Price

Is it okay to incorporate the amount of sales tax into the retail price of items being sold directly to consumers? It's best to check with your individual state because each state's sales tax law is different.

Crafters like to use round-figure prices at fairs because this encourages cash sales and eliminates the need for taking coins to make change. Some crafters tell their customers that sales tax has been included in their rounded-off prices, but you should not do this until you check with your state. In some states, this is illegal; in others, you may find that you are required to inform your customers, by means of a sign, that sales tax has been included in your price. You may also have to print this information on customer receipts as well.

If you make such a statement and collect taxes on cash sales, be sure to report those cash sales as taxable income and remit the tax money to the state accordingly. Failure

from 1 to 6 months in prison and a fine of $5,000. As you can see, the collection of sales tax is serious business.

Collecting Tax on Internet Sales

Anything you sell that is taxable in your state is also taxable on the Internet. This is simply another method of selling, like craft fairs or mail-order sales. You don't have to break out Internet sales separately; simply include them in your total taxable sales.

3. The Legal Forms of Business

Every business must take one of four legal forms:

Sole Proprietorship
Partnership
LLC (Limited Liability Company)
Corporation

▼▼

to do this would be a violation of the law, and it's easy to get caught these days when sales tax agents are showing up at craft fairs across the country.

Even if rounding off the price and including the tax within that figure turns out to be legal in your state, it will definitely complicate your bookkeeping. For example, if you normally sell an item for $5 or some other round figure, you must have a firm retail price on which to calculate sales tax to begin with. Adding tax to a round figure makes it uneven. Then you must either raise or lower the price, and if you lower it, what you're really doing is paying the sales tax for your customer out of your profits. This is no way to do business.

I suggest that you set your retail prices based on the pricing formulas given in this book, calculate the sales tax accordingly, and give your customers change if they pay in cash. You will be perceived as a professional when you operate this way, whereas crafters who insist always on "cash only" sales are sending signals to buyers that they don't intend to report this income to tax authorities.

▲▲

As a hobby seller, you automatically become a sole proprietor when you start selling what you make. Although most professional crafters remain sole proprietors throughout the life of their business, some do form craft partnerships or corporations when their business begins to generate serious money, or if it happens to involve other members of their family. You don't need a lawyer to start a sole proprietorship, but it would be folly to enter into a partnership, LLC, or corporation, without legal guidance. Here is a brief look at the main advantages and disadvantages of each type of legal business structure.

Sole Proprietorship

No legal formalities are involved in starting or ending a sole proprietorship. You're your own boss here, and the business starts when you say it does and ends automatically when you stop running it. As discussed earlier, income is reported annually on a Schedule C form and taxed at the personal level. The sole proprietor is fully liable for all business debts and actions. In the event of a lawsuit, personal assets are not protected.

Partnership

There are two kinds of partnerships: general and limited.

A *general partnership* is easy to start, with no federal requirements involved. Income is taxed at the personal level and the partnership ends as soon as either partner withdraws from the business. Liability is unlimited. The most financially dangerous thing about a partnership is that the debts incurred by one partner must be assumed by all other partners. Before signing a partnership agreement, make sure the tax obligations of your partner are current.

In a *limited partnership*, the business is run by general partners and financed by silent (limited) partners who have no liability beyond an investment of money in the business. This kind of partnership is more complicated to establish, has special tax withholding regulations, and requires the filing of a legal contract with the state.

> ***Avoid this pitfall:*** Partnerships between friends often end the friendship when disagreements over business policies occur. Don't form a partnership with anyone without planning in advance how the partnership will eventually be dissolved, and spell out all the details in a written agreement. What will happen if either partner dies, wants out of the business, or wants to buy out the other partner? Also ask your attorney about the advisability of having partnership insurance, to protect against the complications that would arise if one of the partners becomes ill, incapacitated, or dies. For an additional perspective on the pros and cons of partnerships, read the book *The Perils of Partners* (see page 291 for inforamtion).

The Limited Legal Protection of a Corporation

Business novices often think that by incorporating their business they can protect their personal assets in the event of a lawsuit. This is true if you have employees who do something wrong and cause your business to be sued. As the business owner, however, if you personally do something wrong and are sued as a result, you might in some cases be held legally responsible, and the "corporation door" will offer no legal protection for your personal assets.

Or, as CPA Bernard Kamoroff explains in *Small Time Operator*, "A corporation will not shield you from personal liability that you normally should be responsible for, such as not having car insurance or acting with gross negligence. If you plan to incorporate solely or primarily with the intention of limiting your legal liability, I suggest you find out first exactly how limited the liability really is for your particular venture. Hire a knowledgeable lawyer to give you a written opinion." (See section 7, Insurance Tips.)

LLC (Limited Liability Company)

This legal form of business reportedly combines the best attributes of other small-business forms while offering a better tax advantage than a limited partnership. It also affords personal liability protection similar to that of a corporation. To date, few craft businesses appear to be using this business form.

Corporation

A corporation is the most complicated and expensive legal form of business and not recommended for any business whose earnings are less than $25,000 a year. If and when your business reaches this point, you should study some books on this topic to fully understand the pros and cons of a corporation. Also consult an accountant or attorney for guidance on the type of corporation you should select—a "C" (general corporation) or an "S" (subchapter S corporation). One book that offers good perspective on this topic is *INC Yourself—How to Profit by Setting Up Your Own Corporation* (see page 291 for information).

The main disadvantage of incorporation for the small-business owner is that profits are taxed twice: first as corporate income and again when they are distributed to the owner-shareholders as dividends. For this reason, many small businesses elect to incorporate as subchapter S corporations, which allows profits to be taxed at owners' regular individual rates. (See sidebar, The Limited Legal Protection of a Corporation, on page 227.)

4. Local and State Laws and Regulations

This section will acquaint you with laws and regulations that affect the average art or crafts business based at home. If you've unknowingly broken one of these laws, don't panic. It may not be as bad as you think. It is often possible to get back on the straight and narrow merely by filling out a required form or by paying a small fee of some kind. What's important is that you take steps now to comply with the laws that pertain to your particular business. Often, the fear of being caught when you're breaking a law is much worse than doing whatever needs to be done to set the matter straight. In the end, it's usually what you don't know that is most likely to cause legal or financial problems, so never hesitate to ask questions about things you don't understand.

Even when you think you know the answers, it can pay to "act dumb." It is said that Napoleon used to attend meetings and pretend to know nothing about a topic, asking many probing questions. By feigning ignorance, he was able to draw valuable information and insight out of everyone around him. This strategy is often used by today's small-business owners, too.

Business Name Registration

If you're a sole proprietor doing business under any name other than your own full name, you are required by law to register it on both the local and state level. In this case, you are said to be using an "assumed," "fictitious," or "trade" name. Registration enables authorities to connect an assumed name to an individual who can be held responsible for the actions of a business. If you're doing business under your own name, such as Kay Jones, you don't have to register your business name on either the local or state level. If your name is part of a longer name, however (for example, Kay Jones Designs), you should check to see if your county or state requires registration.

Local Registration

To register your name, contact your city or county clerk, who will explain what you need to do to officially register your business on

Picking a Good Business Name

If you haven't done it already, think up a great name for your new business. You want something that will be memorable—catchy, but not too cute. Many crafters select a simple name that is attached to their first name, such as "Mary's Quilts" or "Tom's Woodcrafts." This is fine for a hobby business, but if your goal is to build a full-time business at home, you may wish to choose a more professional-sounding name that omits your personal name. If a name sounds like a hobby business, you may have difficulty getting wholesale suppliers to take you seriously. A more professional name may also enable you to get higher prices for your products. For example, the above names might be changed to "Quilted Treasures" or "Wooden Wonders."

Don't print business cards or stationery until you find out if someone else is already using the name you've chosen. To find out if the name has already been registered, you

the local level. At the same time, ask if you need any special municipal or county licenses or permits to operate within the law. (See the next section, Licenses and Permits.) This office can also tell you how and where to write to register your name at the state level. If you've been operating under an assumed name for a while and are worried because you didn't register the name earlier, just register it now, as if the business were new.

Registration involves filling out a simple form and paying a small fee, usually around $10 to $25. At the time you register, you will get details about a classified ad you must run in a general-circulation newspaper in your county. This will notify the public at large that you are now operating a business under an assumed name. (If you don't want your neighbors to know what you're doing, simply run the ad in a newspaper somewhere else in the county.) After publication of this ad, you will receive a Fictitious Name Statement that you must send to the county clerk, who in turn will file it with your registration form to make your business completely legit-

▼▼▼

can perform a trademark search through a search company or hire an attorney who specializes in trademark law to conduct the search for you. And if you are planning to eventually set up a Web site, you might want to do a search to see if that domain name is still available on the Internet. Go to www.networksolutions.com to do this search. Business names have to be registered on the Internet, too, and they can be "parked" for a fee until you're ready to design your Web site.

It's great if your business name and Web site name can be the same, but this is not always possible. A crafter told me recently she had to come up with 25 names before she found a domain name that hadn't already been taken. (Web entrepreneurs are grabbing every good name they can find. Imagine my surprise when I did a search and found that two different individuals had set up Web sites using the titles of my two best-known books, *Creative Cash* and *Homemade Money*.)

▲▲

imate. This name statement or certificate may also be referred to as your DBA ("doing business as") form. In some areas, you cannot open a business checking account if you don't have this form to show your bank.

> ***Avoid this pitfall:*** Failure to register your business name may result in your losing it—after you've spent a considerable amount of money on business cards, stationery, advertising, and so on. If someone sees your name, likes it, and finds on checking that it hasn't been registered, they can simply register the name and force you to stop using it.

State Registration

Once you've registered locally, contact your secretary of state to register your business name with the state. This will prevent its use by a corporate entity. At the same time, find out if you must obtain any kind of state license. Generally, home-based crafts businesses will not need a license from the state, but there are always exceptions. An artist who built an open-to-the-public art studio on his property reported that the fine in his state for operating this kind of business without a license was $50 a day. In short, it always pays to ask questions to make sure you're operating legally and safely.

Federal Registration

The only way to protect a name on the federal level is with a trademark, discussed in section 9.

Licenses and Permits

A "license" is a certificate granted by a municipal or county agency that gives you permission to engage in a business occupation. A "permit" is similar, except that it is granted by local authorities. Until recently, few crafts businesses had to have a license or permit of any kind, but a growing number of communities now have new laws on their books that require home-based business owners to obtain a "home occupation permit." Annual fees for such permits may range from $15 to $200 a year. For details about the law in your particular community or county, call your city or county clerk (depending on whether you live within or outside city limits).

Use of Personal Phone for Business

Although every business writer stresses the importance of having a business telephone number, craftspeople generally ignore this advice and do business on their home telephone. Although it's okay to use a home phone to make outgoing business calls, you cannot advertise a home telephone number as your business phone number without being in violation of local telephone regulations. That means you cannot legally put your home telephone number on a business card or business stationery or advertise it on your Web site.

That said, let me also state that most craftspeople totally ignore this law and do it anyway. (I don't know what the penalty for breaking this law is in your state; you'll have to call your telephone company for that information and decide if this is something you want to do.) Some phone companies might give you a slap on the wrist and tell you to stop, while others might start charging you business line telephone rates if they discover you are advertising your personal phone number.

The primary reason to have a separate phone line for your business is that it enables you to freely advertise your telephone number to solicit new business and invite credit card sales, custom order inquiries, and the like. Further, you can deduct 100% of the costs of a business telephone line on your Schedule C tax form, while deductions for the business use of a home phone are severely limited. (Discuss this with your accountant.)

If you plan to connect to the Internet or install a fax machine, you will definitely need a second line to handle the load, but most crafters simply add an additional personal line instead of a business line. Once on the Internet, you may have even less need for a business phone than before because you can simply invite contact from buyers by advertising your e-mail address. (Always include your e-mail and Internet addresses on your business cards and stationery.)

If your primary selling methods are going to be consignment shops, craft fairs, or craft malls, a business phone number would be necessary only if you are inviting orders by phone. If you present a holiday boutique or open house once or twice a year, there should be no problem with putting your home phone number on promotional flyers because you are, in fact, inviting people to your home and not your business (similar to running a classified ad for a garage sale).

If and when you decide a separate line for your business is necessary, you may find it is not as costly as you think. Telephone companies today are very aware of the number of people who are working at home, and they have come up with a variety of affordable packages and second-line options, any one of which might be perfect for your crafts-business needs. Give your telephone company a call and see what's available.

Zoning Regulations

Before you start any kind of home-based business, check your home's zoning regulations. You can find a copy at your library or at city hall. Find out what zone you're in and then read the information under "Home Occupations." Be sure to read the fine print and note the penalty for violating a zoning ordinance. In most cases, someone who is caught violating zoning laws will be asked to cease and desist and a penalty is incurred only if this order is ignored. In other cases, however, willful violation could incur a hefty fine.

Zoning laws differ from one community to another, with some of them being terribly outdated (actually written back in horse-and-buggy days). In some communities, zoning officials simply "look the other way" where zoning violations are concerned because it's easier to do this than change the law. In other places, however, zoning regulations have recently been revised in light of the growing number of individuals working at home, and these changes have not always been to the benefit of home-based workers or self-employed individuals. Often there are restrictions as to (1) the amount of space in one's home a business may occupy (impossible to enforce, in my opinion), (2) the number of people (customers, students) who can come to your home each day, (3) the use of non-family employees, and so on. If you find you cannot advertise your home as a place of business, this problem can be easily solved by renting a P.O. box or using a commercial mailbox service as your business address.

Although I'm not suggesting that you violate your zoning law, I will tell you that many individuals who have found zoning to be a problem do ignore this law, particularly when they have a quiet business that is unlikely to create problems in their community.

Zoning officials don't go around checking for people who are violating the law; rather, they tend to act on complaints they have received about a certain activity that is creating problems for others. Thus, the best way to avoid zoning problems is to keep a low profile by not broadcasting your home-based business to neighbors. More important, never annoy them with activities that emit fumes or odors, create parking problems, or make noise of any kind.

Although neighbors may grudgingly put up with a noisy hobby activity (such as sawing in the garage), they are not likely to tolerate the same noise or disturbance if they know it's related to a home-based business. Likewise, they won't mind if you have a garage sale every year, but if people are coming to your home every year to buy from your home shop, open house, home parties, or holiday boutiques, you could be asking for trouble if the zoning laws don't favor this kind of activity.

> *Avoid this pitfall:* If you're planning to hold a holiday boutique or home party, check with zoning officials first. (If they don't know what a holiday boutique is, tell them it's a temporary sales event, like a garage sale.) Generally, the main concerns will be that you do not post illegal signs, tie up traffic, or otherwise annoy your neighbors. In some areas, however, zoning regulations strictly prohibit (1) traffic into one's home for any commercial reason; (2) the exchange of money in a home for business reasons; or (3) the transfer of merchandise within the home (affecting party plan sellers, in particular). Some sellers have found the solution to all three of these problems as simple as letting people place orders for merchandise that will be delivered later, with payment collected at time of delivery.

5. General Business and Financial Information

This section offers introductory guidelines on essential business basics for beginners. Once your business is up and running, however, you need to read other crafts-business books to get detailed information on the following topics and many others related to the successful growth and development of a home-based art or crafts business.

Making a Simple Business Plan

As baseball star Yogi Berra once said, "If you don't know where you are going, you might not get there." That's why you need a plan.

Like a road map, a business plan helps you get from here to there. It doesn't have to be fancy, but it does have to be in written form. A good business plan will save you time and money while helping you stay focused and on track to meet your goals. The kind of business plan a craftsperson makes will naturally be less complicated than the business plan of a major manufacturing company, but the elements are basically the same and should include:

- *History*—how and why you started your business
- *Business description*—what you do, what products you make, why they are special
- *Management information*—your business background or experience and the legal form your business will take
- *Manufacturing and production*—how and where products will be produced and who will make them; how and where supplies and materials will be obtained, and their estimated costs; labor costs (yours or other helpers); and overhead costs involved in the making of products
- *Financial plan*—estimated sales and expense figures for 1 year
- *Market research findings*—a description of your market (fairs, shops, mail order, Internet, and so on), your customers, and your competition
- *Marketing plan*—how you are going to sell your products and the anticipated cost of your marketing (commissions, advertising, craft fair displays, and so on)

If this all seems a bit much for a small crafts business, start managing your time by using a daily calendar/planner and start a

▼▼▼

Get a Safety Deposit Box

The longer you are in business, the more important it will be to safeguard your most valuable business records. When you work at home, there is always the possibility of fire or damage from some natural disaster, be it a tornado, earthquake, hurricane, or flood. You will worry less if you keep your most valuable business papers, records, computer disks, and so forth off-premises, along with other items that would be difficult or impossible to replace. Some particulars I have always kept in my business safety deposit box include master software disks and computer back-up disks; original copies of my designs and patterns, business contracts, copyrights, insurance policies, and a photographic record of all items insured on our homeowner's policy. Remember: Insurance is worthless if you cannot prove what you owned in the first place.

▲▲▲

notebook you can fill with your creative and marketing ideas, plans, and business goals. In it, write a simple mission statement that answers the following questions:

- What is my primary mission or goal in starting a business?
- What is my financial goal for this year?
- What am I going to do to get the sales I need this year to meet my financial goal?

The most important thing is that you start putting your dreams, goals, and business plans on paper so you can review them regularly. It's always easier to see where you're going if you know where you've been.

When You Need an Attorney

Many business beginners think they have to hire a lawyer the minute they start a business, but that would be a terrible waste of money if you're just starting a simple art or crafts business at home, operating as a sole proprietor. Sure, a lawyer will be delighted to hold your hand and give you the same advice I'm giving you here (while charging you $150 an hour or more for his or her time). With this book in hand, you can easily take care of all the "legal details" of a small-business start-up. The day may come, however, when you do need legal counsel, such as when you:

Form a Partnership or Corporation

As stated earlier, an attorney's guidance is necessary in the formation of a partnership. Although many people have incorporated without a lawyer using a good how-to book on the topic, I wouldn't recommend doing this because there are so many details involved, not to mention different types of corporate entities.

Defend an Infringement of a Copyright or Trademark

You don't need an attorney to get a simple copyright, but if someone infringes on one of your copyrights, you will probably need legal help to stop the infringer from profiting from your creativity. You can file your own trademark application (if you are exceedingly careful about following instructions), but it would be difficult to protect your trademark without legal help if someone tries to steal it. In both cases, you would need an attorney who specializes in copyright, patent, and trademark law. (If you ever need a good attorney who understands the plight of artists and crafters, contact me by e-mail at barbara@crafter.com and I'll refer you to the attorney who has been helpful to me in protecting my common-law trademark to *Homemade Money*, my home-business classic. The sixth edition of this book includes the details of my trademark infringement story.)

Negotiate a Contract

Many craft hobbyists of my acquaintance have gone on to write books and sell their original designs to manufacturers, suddenly finding themselves with a contract in hand that contains a lot of confusing legal jargon. When hiring an attorney to check any kind of contract, make sure he or she has experience in the particular field involved. For example, a lawyer specializing in real estate isn't going to know a thing about the inner workings of a book publishing company and how the omission or inclusion of a particular clause or phrase might impact the author's royalties or make it difficult to get publishing rights back when the book goes out of print. Although I have no experience in the licensing industry, I presume the same thing holds true here. What I do know for sure is that the problem with most contracts is not so much what's *in* them, as what *isn't*. Thus you need to be sure the attorney you hire for specialized contract work has done this kind of work for other clients.

Hire Independent Contractors

If you ever grow your business to the point where you need to hire workers and are wondering whether you have to hire employees or can use independent contractors instead, I suggest you seek counsel from an attorney who specializes in labor law. This topic is very complex and beyond the scope of this beginner's guide, but I do want you to know that the IRS has been on a campaign for the past several years to abolish independent contractors altogether. Many small businesses have suffered great financial loss in back taxes and penalties because they followed the advice of an accountant or regular attorney who didn't fully understand the technicalities of this matter.

If and when you do need a lawyer for general business purposes, ask friends for a reference, and check with your bank, too, because bank representatives will probably know most of the attorneys with private practices in your area. Note that membership in some small-business organizations will also give you access to affordable prepaid legal services. If you ever need serious legal help but have no funds to pay for it, contact the Volunteer Lawyers for the Arts.

Why You Need a Business Checking Account

Many business beginners use their personal checking account to conduct the transactions of their business, *but you must not do this* because the IRS does not allow commingling of business and personal income. If you are operating as a business, reporting income on a Schedule C form and taking deductions accordingly, the lack of a separate checking account for your business would surely result in an IRS ruling that your endeavor was a hobby and not a business. That, in turn, would cost you all the deductions previously taken on earlier tax returns and you'd end up with a very large tax bill. Don't you agree that the cost of a separate checking account is a small price to pay to protect all your tax deductions?

You do not necessarily need one of the more expensive business checking accounts; you just need a *separate account* through which you run all business income and expenditures. Your business name does not have to be on these checks so long as only your name (not your spouse's) is listed as account holder. You can save money on your checking account by first calling several banks and savings and loan institutions and comparing the charges they set for imprinted checks, deposits, checks written, bounced checks, and other services. Before you open your account, be sure to ask if the bank can set you up to take credit cards (merchant account) at some point in the future.

> *Avoid this pitfall:* Some banks charge extra for each out-of-state check that is deposited, an expense that is prohibitively expensive for active mail-order businesses. For that reason, I have always maintained a business checking account in a savings and loan association, which has no service charges of any kind (except for bad checks). S&L's also pay interest on the amount in a checking account, whereas a bank may not. The main disadvantage of doing your business checking through an S&L is that they do not offer credit card services or give business loans. At the

point where I found I needed the latter two services for my publishing business, I had to open a second account with a local bank.

Accepting Credit Cards

Most of us today take credit cards for granted and expect to be able to use them for most everything we buy. It's nice to be able to offer credit card services to your craft fair customers, but it is costly and thus not recommended for beginning craft sellers. If you get into selling at craft fairs on a regular basis, however, at some point you may find you are losing sales because you don't have "merchant status" (the ability to accept credit cards as payment).

Some craftspeople have reported a considerable jump in sales once they started taking credit cards. That's because some people who buy with plastic may buy two or three items instead of one, or may be willing to pay a higher price for something if they can charge it. Thus, the higher your prices, the more likely you are to lose sales if you can't accept credit cards. As one jewelry maker told me, "I always seem to get the customers who have run out of cash and left their checkbook at home. But even when they have a check, I feel uncomfortable taking a check for $100 or more."

This section discusses the various routes you can travel to get merchant status. You will have to do considerable research to find out which method is best for you. All will be costly, and you must have sufficient sales, or the expectation of increased sales, to consider taking credit cards in the first place. Understand, too, that taking credit cards in person (called face-to-face transactions where you have the card in front of you) is different from accepting credit cards by phone, by mail, or through a Web site (called non–face-to-face transactions). Each method of selling is treated differently by bankcard providers.

> ***Avoid this pitfall:*** If you are relatively new at selling, and uncertain about whether you will be taking credit cards for a long time, do not sign a leasing arrangement for credit card processing equipment. Instead, leave yourself an escape route by opting for a rental agreement you can get out of with a month's notice, such as that offered by some banks and organizations discussed below.

Merchant Status from Your Bank

When you're ready to accept credit cards, start with the bank where you have your business checking account. Where you bank, and where you live, has everything to do with whether you can get merchant status from your bank. Home-business owners in small towns often have less trouble than do those in large cities. One crafter told me Bank of America gave her merchant status with no problem, but some banks simply refuse to deal with anyone who doesn't operate out of a storefront. Most banks now insist that credit card sales be transmitted electronically, but a few still offer manual printers and allow merchants to send in their sales slips by mail. You will be given details about this at the time you apply for merchant status. All banks will require proof that you have a running business and will want to see your financial statements.

Merchant Status Through a Crafts Organization

If you are refused by your bank because your business is home based or just too new, getting bankcard services through a crafts or home-business organization is the next best way to go. Because such organizations have a large membership, they have some negotiating power with the credit card companies and often get special deals for their members. As a member of such an organization, the chances are about 95% that you will automatically be accepted into its bankcard program, even if you are a brand-new business owner.

One organization I can recommend to beginning sellers is the National Craft Association. Managing Director Barbara Arena tells me that 60% of all new NCA members now take the

MasterCard/VISA services offered by her organization. "Crafters who are unsure about whether they want to take credit cards over a long period of time have the option of renting equipment," says Barbara. "This enables them to get out of the program with a month's notice. NCA members can operate on a software basis through their personal computer (taking their laptop computer to shows and calling in sales on their cell phone) or use a swipe machine. Under NCA's program, crafters can also accept credit card sales on their Internet site."

For more information from NCA and other organizations offering merchant services, see Trade and Professional Associations, Societies and Guilds on page 316.

Merchant Status from Credit Card Companies

If you've been in business for a while, you may find you can get merchant status directly from American Express or Novus Services, Inc., the umbrella company that handles the Discover, Bravo, and Private Issue credit cards. American Express says that in some cases it can grant merchant status immediately on receipt of some key information given on the phone. As for Novus, many crafters have told me how easy it was to get merchant status from this company. Novus says it needs only your social security number and information to check your credit rating. If Novus accepts you, it can also get you set up to take VISA and MasterCard as well, if you meet the special acceptance qualifications of these two credit card companies. (Usually, they require you to be in business for at least 2 years.)

Merchant Status from an Independent Service Organization Provider (ISO)

ISOs act as agents for banks that authorize credit cards, promoting their services by direct mail, through magazine advertising, telemarketing, and on the Internet. Most of these bankcard providers are operating under a network marketing program (one agent representing one agent representing another, and so on). They are everywhere on the Internet, sending unsolicited e-mail messages to Web site owners. In addition to offering the merchant account service itself, many are also trying to get other Web site owners to promote the same service in exchange for some kind of referral fee. I do not recommend that you get merchant status through an ISO because I've heard too many horror stories about them. If you want to explore this option on the Internet, however, use your browser's search button and type "credit cards + merchant" to get a list of such sellers.

In general, ISOs may offer low discount rates but will sock it to you with inflated equipment costs, a high application fee, and extra fees for installation, programming, and site inspection. You will also have to sign an unbreakable 3- or 4-year lease for the electronic equipment.

> **Avoid this pitfall:** Some people on the Internet may offer to process your credit card sales through their individual merchant account, but this is illegal as it violates credit card company rules. And if you were to offer to do this for someone else, your account would be terminated. In short, if you do not ship the goods, you can't process the sale.

As you can see, you must really do your homework where bankcard services are concerned. In checking out the services offered by any of the providers noted here, ask plenty of questions. Make up a chart that lets you compare what each one charges for application and service fees, monthly charges, equipment costs, software, discount rates, and transaction fees.

Transaction fees can range from $0.20 to $0.80 per ticket, with discount rates running anywhere from 1.67 to 5%. Higher rates are usually attached to non–face-to-face credit card transactions, paper transaction systems, or a low volume of sales. Any rate higher than

5% should be a danger signal because you could be dealing with an unscrupulous seller or some kind of illegal third-party processing program.

I'm told that a good credit card processor today may cost around $800, yet some card service providers are charging two or three times that amount in their leasing arrangements. I once got a quote from a major ISO and found it would have cost me $40 a month to lease the terminal—$1,920 over a period of 4 years—or I could buy it for just $1,000. In checking with my bank, I learned I could get the same equipment and the software to run it for just $350!

In summary, if you're a nervous beginner, the safest way to break into taking credit cards is to work with a bank or organization that offers equipment on a month-by-month rental arrangement. Once you've had some experience in taking credit card payments, you can review your situation and decide whether you want to move into a leasing arrangement or buy equipment outright.

6. Minimizing the Financial Risks of Selling

This book contains an informative chapter on how and where to sell your crafts, but I thought it would be helpful for you to have added perspective on the business management end of selling through various outlets, and some things you can do to protect yourself from financial loss and legal hassles.

You must accept the fact that all businesses occasionally suffer financial losses of one kind or another. That's simply the nature of business. Selling automatically carries a certain degree of risk in that we can never be absolutely sure that we're going to be paid for anything until we actually have payment in hand. Checks may bounce, wholesale buyers may refuse to pay their invoices, and consignment shops can close unexpectedly without returning merchandise to crafters. In the past few years, a surprising number of craft mall owners have stolen out of town in the middle of the night, taking with them all the money due their vendors, and sometimes the vendors' merchandise as well. (This topic is beyond the scope of this book, but if you'd like more information on it, see my *Creative Cash* book and back issues of my *Craftsbiz Chat* newsletter on the Internet at www.crafter.com/brabec.)

Now, I don't want you to feel uneasy about selling or be suspicious of every buyer who comes your way, because that would take all the fun out of selling. But I *do* want you to know that bad things sometimes happen to good craftspeople who have not done their homework (by reading this book, you are doing *your* homework). If you will follow the cautionary guidelines discussed in this section, you can avoid some common selling pitfalls and minimize your financial risk to the point where it will be negligible.

Selling to Consignment Shops

Never consign more merchandise to one shop than you can afford to lose, and do not send new items to a shop until you see that payments are being made regularly according to your written consignment agreement. It should cover the topics of:

- Insurance (see Insurance Tips, section 7)
- Pricing (make sure the shop cannot raise or lower your retail price without your permission)
- Sales commission (40% is standard; don't work with shop owners who ask for more than this. It makes more sense to wholesale products at 50% and get payment in 30 days)
- Payment dates
- Display of merchandise

- Return of unsold merchandise (some shops have a clause stating that if unsold merchandise is not claimed within 30 to 60 days after a notice has been sent, the shop can dispose of it any way it wishes)

Above all, make sure your agreement includes the name and phone number of the shop's owner (not just the manager). If a shop fails and you decide to take legal action, you want to be sure your lawyer can track down the owner. (See sidebar, State Consignment Laws, below.)

Selling to Craft Malls

Shortly after the craft mall concept was introduced to the crafts community in 1988 by Rufus Coomer, entrepreneurs who understood the profit potential of such a business began to open malls all over the country. But there were no guidebooks and everyone was flying by the seat of his or her pants, making up operating rules along the way. Many mall owners, inexperienced in retailing, have

State Consignment Laws

Technically, consigned goods remain the property of the seller until they are sold. When a shop goes out of business, however, consigned merchandise may be seized by creditors in spite of what your consignment agreement may state. You may have some legal protection here, however, if you live in a state that has a consignment law designed to protect artists and craftspeople in such instances. Such laws exist in the states of CA, CO, CT, IL, IA, KY, MA, NH, NM, NY, OR, TX, WA, and WI. Call your secretary of state to confirm this or, if your state isn't listed here, ask whether this law is now on the books. Be sure to get full details about the kind of protection afforded by this law because some states have different definitions for what constitutes "art" or "crafts."

since gone out of business, often leaving crafters holding the bag. The risks of selling through such well-known chain stores as Coomer's or American Craft Malls are minimal, and many independently owned malls have also established excellent reputations in the industry. What you need to be especially concerned about here are new malls opened by individuals who have no track record in this industry.

I'm not telling you *not* to set up a booth in a new mall in your area—it might prove to be a terrific outlet for you—but I am cautioning you to keep a sharp eye on the mall and how it's being operated. Warning signs of a mall in trouble include:

- **Less than 75% occupancy**
- **Little or no ongoing advertising**
- **Not many shoppers**
- **Crafters pulling out (usually a sign of too few sales)**
- **Poor accounting of sales**
- **Late payments**

If a mall is in trouble, it stands to reason that the logical time for it to close is right after the biggest selling season of the year, namely Christmas. Interestingly, this is when most of the shady mall owners have stolen out of town with crafters' Christmas sales in their pockets. As stated in my *Creative Cash* book:

> If it's nearing Christmastime, and you're getting uncomfortable vibes about the financial condition of a mall you're in, it might be smart to remove the bulk of your merchandise— especially expensive items—just before it closes for the holidays. You can always restock after the first of the year if everything looks rosy.

Avoiding Bad Checks

At a craft fair or other event where you're selling directly to the public, if the buyer doesn't have cash and you don't accept credit cards, your only option is to accept a check. Few crafters have bad check problems for sales held in the home (holiday boutique, open house, party plan, and such), but bad checks at craft fairs are always possible. Here are several things you can do to avoid accepting a bad check:

- Always ask to see a driver's license and look carefully at the picture on it. Write the license number on the check.

- If the sale is for a large amount, you can ask to see a credit card for added identification, but writing down the number will do no good because you cannot legally cover a bad check with a customer's credit card. (The customer has a legal right to refuse to let you copy the number as well.)

- Look closely at the check itself. Is there a name and address printed on it? If not, ask the customer to write in this information by hand, along with his or her phone number.

- Look at the sides of the check. If at least one side is not perforated, it could be a phony check.

- Look at the check number in the upper right-hand corner. Most banks who issue personalized checks begin the numbering system with 101 when a customer reorders new checks. The Small Business Administration says to be more cautious with low sequence numbers because there seems to be a higher number of these checks that are returned.

- Check the routing number in the lower left-hand corner and note the ink. If it looks shiny, wet your finger and see if the ink rubs off. That's a sure sign of a phony check because good checks are printed with magnetic ink that does not reflect light.

Collecting on a Bad Check

No matter how careful you are, sooner or later, you will get stuck with a bad check. It may bounce for one of three reasons:

Nonsufficient funds (NSF)
Account closed
No account (evidence of fraud)

I've accepted tens of thousands of checks from mail-order buyers through the years and have rarely had a bad check I couldn't collect with a simple phone call asking the party to honor his or her obligation to me. People often move and close out accounts before all checks have cleared, or they add or subtract wrong, causing their account to be overdrawn. Typically, they are embarrassed to have caused a problem like this.

When the problem is more difficult than this, your bank can help. Check to learn its policy regarding bounced checks. Some automatically put checks through a second time. If a check bounces at this point, you may ask the bank to collect the check for you. The check needs to be substantial, however, because the bank fee may be $15 or more if they are successful in collecting the money.

If you have accepted a check for a substantial amount of money and believe there is evidence of fraud, you may wish to do one of the following:

- Notify your district attorney's office
- Contact your sheriff or police department (because it is a crime to write a bad check)
- Try to collect through small claims court

For more detailed information on all of these topics, see *The Crafts Business Answer Book & Resource Guide* (see page 290 for information).

7. Insurance Tips

As soon as you start even the smallest business at home, you need to give special attention to insurance. This section offers an introductory overview of insurance concerns of primary interest to crafts-business owners.

Homeowner's or Renter's Insurance

Anything in the home being used to generate income is considered to be business-related and thus exempt from coverage on a personal policy. Thus your homeowner's or renter's insurance policy will not cover business equipment, office furniture, supplies, or inventory of finished goods unless you obtain a special rider. Such a rider, called a "Business Pursuits Endorsement" by some companies, is inexpensive and offers considerable protection. Your insurance agent will be happy to give you details.

As your business grows and you have an ever-larger inventory of supplies, materials, tools, and finished merchandise, you may find it necessary to buy a special in-home business policy that offers broader protection. Such policies may be purchased directly from insurance companies or through craft and home-business organizations that offer special insurance programs to their members.

Avoid this pitfall: If you have an expensive computer system, costly tools, equipment, or office furnishings, the coverage

Insuring Your Art or Crafts Collection

The replacement cost insurance you may have on your personal household possessions does not extend to "fine art," which includes such things as paintings, antiques, pictures, tapestries, statuary, and other articles that cannot be replaced with new articles. If you have a large collection of art, crafts, memorabilia, or collector's items, and its value is more than $1,500, you may wish to have your collection appraised so it can be protected with a separate all-risk endorsement to your homeowner's policy called a "fine arts floater."

afforded by a simple business rider to your homeowner's policy may be insufficient for your needs. Although you may have replacement-value insurance on all your personal possessions, anything used for business purposes would be exempt from such coverage. In other words, the value of everything covered by the rider would be figured on a depreciable basis instead of what it would cost to replace it. (See also sidebar, Insuring Your Art or Crafts Collection, on page 251.)

Liability Insurance

There are two kinds of liability insurance. *Product* liability insurance protects you against lawsuits by consumers who have been injured while using one of your products. *Personal* liability insurance protects you against claims made by individuals who have suffered bodily injury while on your premises (either your home or the place where you are doing business, such as in your booth at a craft fair).

Your homeowner's or renter's insurance policy will include some personal liability protection, but if someone were to suffer bodily injury while on your premises for *business* reasons, that coverage might not apply. Your need for personal liability insurance will be greater if you plan to regularly present home parties, holiday boutiques, or open house sales in your home where many people might be coming and going throughout the year. If you sell at craft fairs, you would also be liable for damages if someone were to fall and be injured in your booth or if something in your booth falls and injures another person. For this reason, some craft fair promoters now require all vendors to have personal liability insurance.

As for product liability insurance, whether you need it depends largely on the type of products you make for sale, how careful you are to make sure those products are safe, and how and where you sell them. Examples of some crafts that have caused injury to consumers and resulted in court claims in the past are stuffed toys with wire or pins that children have swallowed; items made of yarn or fiber that burned rapidly; handmade furniture that collapsed when someone put an ordinary amount of weight on it; jewelry with sharp points or other features that cut the wearer, and so on. Clearly, the best way to avoid injury to consumers is to make certain your products have no health hazards and are safe to use. (See discussion of Consumer Safety Laws in section 8.)

Few artists and craftspeople who sell on a part-time basis feel they can afford product liability insurance, but many full-time craft professionals, particularly those who sell their work wholesale, find it a necessary expense. In fact, many wholesale buyers refuse to buy from suppliers that do not carry product liability insurance.

I believe the least expensive way to obtain both personal and product liability insurance is with one of the comprehensive in-home or crafts-business policies offered by a crafts- or home-business organization. Such policies generally offer $1 million of both personal and product liability coverage. (See A "Things to Do" Checklist with Related Resources on page 280 and the Resources section for some organizations you can contact for more information. Also check with your insurance agent about the benefits of an umbrella policy for extra liability insurance.)

Insurance on Crafts Merchandise

As a seller of art or crafts merchandise, you are responsible for insuring your own products against loss. If you plan to sell at craft fairs, in craft malls, rent-a-space shops, or consignment shops, you may want to buy an insurance policy that protects your merchandise both at home or away. Note that while craft shops and malls generally have fire insurance covering the building and its fixtures, this coverage cannot be extended to merchandise offered for sale because it is not the property of the shop owner. (Exception: Shops and malls in shopping centers are mandated by law to buy fire insurance on their contents whether they own the merchandise or not.)

This kind of insurance is usually part of the home- or crafts-business insurance policies mentioned earlier.

Auto Insurance

Be sure to talk to the agent who handles your car insurance and explain that you may occasionally use your car for business purposes. Normally, a policy issued for a car that's used only for pleasure or driving to and from work may not provide complete coverage for an accident that occurs during business use of the car, particularly if the insured is to blame for the accident. For example, if you were delivering a load of crafts to a shop or on your way to a craft fair and had an accident, would your business destination and the "commercial merchandise" in your car negate your coverage in any way? Where insurance is concerned, the more questions you ask, the better you'll feel about the policies you have.

8. Important Regulations Affecting Artists and Craftspeople

Government agencies have a number of regulations that artists and craftspeople must know about. Generally, they relate to consumer safety, the labeling of certain products, and trade practices. Following are regulations of primary interest to readers of books in Prima's FOR FUN & PROFIT series. If you find a law or regulation related to your particular art or craft interest, be sure to request additional information from the government agency named there.

Consumer Safety Laws

All product sellers must pay attention to the Consumer Product Safety Act, which protects the public against unreasonable risks of injury associated with consumer products. The Consumer Product

Safety Commission (CPSC) is particularly active in the area of toys and consumer goods designed for children. All sellers of handmade products must be doubly careful about the materials they use for children's products because consumer lawsuits are common where products for children are concerned. To avoid this problem, simply comply with the consumer safety laws applicable to your specific art or craft.

Toy Safety Concerns

To meet CPSC's guidelines for safety, make sure any toys you make for sale are:

- Too large to be swallowed
- Not apt to break easily or leave jagged edges
- Free of sharp edges or points
- Not put together with easily exposed pins, wires, or nails
- Nontoxic, nonflammable, and nonpoisonous

The Use of Paints, Varnishes, and Other Finishes

Since all paint sold for household use must meet the Consumer Product Safety Act's requirement for minimum amounts of lead, these paints are deemed to be safe for use on products made for children, such as toys and furniture. Always check, however, to make sure the label bears a nontoxic notation. Specialty paints must carry a warning on the label about lead count, but "artist's paints" are curiously exempt from CPS's lead-in-paint ban and are not required to bear a warning label of any kind. Thus you should *never* use such paints on products intended for use by children unless the label specifically states they are *nontoxic* (lead-free). Acrylics and other water-based paints, of course, are nontoxic and completely safe for use on toys and other products made for children. If you plan to use a finishing coat, make sure it is nontoxic as well.

Fabric Flammability Concerns

The Flammable Fabrics Act is applicable only to those who sell products made of fabric, particularly products for children. It prohibits the movement in interstate commerce of articles of wearing apparel and fabrics that are so highly flammable as to be dangerous when worn by individuals, and for other purposes. Most fabrics comply with this act, but if you plan to sell children's clothes or toys, you may wish to take an extra step to be doubly sure the fabric you are using is safe. This is particularly important if you plan to wholesale your products. What you should do is ask your fabric supplier for a *guarantee of compliance with the Flammability Act*. This guarantee is generally passed along to the buyer by a statement on the invoice that reads "continuing guarantee under the Flammable Fabrics Act." If you do not find such a statement on your invoice, you should ask the fabric manufacturer, wholesaler, or distributor to furnish you with their "statement of compliance" with the flammability standards. The CPSC can also tell you if a particular manufacturer has filed a continuing guarantee under the Flammable Fabrics Act.

Labels Required by Law

The following information applies only to crafters who use textiles, fabrics, fibers, or yarn products to make wearing apparel, decorative accessories, household furnishings, soft toys, or any product made of wool.

Different government agencies require the attachment of certain tags or labels to products sold in the consumer marketplace, whether manufactured in quantity or handmade for limited sale. You don't have to be too concerned about these laws if you sell only at local fairs, church bazaars, and home boutiques. As soon as you get out into the general consumer marketplace, however—doing large craft fairs, selling through consignment shops, craft malls, or wholesaling to shops—it would be wise to comply with all the federal labeling laws. Actually, these laws are quite easy to comply with because the required labels are readily available at inexpensive prices, and you can even make your own if you wish. Here is what the federal government wants you to tell your buyers on a tag or label:

- *What's in a product, and who has made it.* The Textile Fiber Products Identification Act (monitored both by the Bureau of Consumer Protection and the Federal Trade Commission) requires that a special label or hangtag be attached to all textile wearing apparel and household furnishings, with the exception of wall hangings. "Textiles" include products made of any fiber, yarn, or fabric, including garments and decorative accessories, quilts, pillows, placemats, stuffed toys, rugs, and so on. The tag or label must include (1) the name of the manufacturer and (2) the generic names and percentages of all fibers in the product in amounts of 5% or more, listed in order of predominance by weight.

- *How to take care of products.* Care Labeling Laws are part of the Textile Fiber Products Identification Act, details about which are available from the FTC. If you make wearing apparel or household furnishings of any kind using textiles, suede, or leather, you must attach a permanent label that explains how to take care of the item. This label must indicate whether the item is to be dry-cleaned or washed. If it is washable, you must indicate whether in hot or cold water, whether bleach may or may not be used, and the temperature at which it may be ironed.

- *Details about products made of wool.* If a product contains wool, the FTC requires additional identification under a separate law known as the Wool Products Labeling Act of 1939. FTC rules require that the labels of all wool or textile products clearly indicate when imported ingredients are used. Thus, the label for a skirt knitted in the United States from wool yarn imported from England would read, "Made in the USA from imported products" or similar wordage.

If the wool yarn was spun in the United States, a product made from that yarn would simply need a tag or label stating it was "Made in the USA" or "Crafted in USA" or some similarly clear terminology.

The Bedding and Upholstered Furniture Law

This is a peculiar state labeling law that affects sellers of items that have a concealed filling. It requires the purchase of a license, and products must have a tag that bears the manufacturer's registry number.

A Proper Copyright Notice

Although a copyright notice is not required by law, you are encouraged to put a copyright notice on every original thing you create. Adding the copyright notice does not obligate you to formally register your copyright, but it does serve to warn others that your work is legally protected and makes it difficult for anyone to claim they have "accidentally stolen" your work. (Those who actually do violate a copyright because they don't understand the law are called "innocent infringers" by the Copyright Office.)

A proper copyright notice includes three things:

1. The word *copyright,* its abbreviation, *copr.,* or the copyright symbol, ©

2. The year of first publication of the work (when it was first shown or sold to the public)

3. The name of the copyright owner. Example: © 2000 by Barbara Brabec. (When the words *All Rights Reserved* are added to the copyright notation, it means that copyright protection has been extended to include all of the Western Hemisphere.)

The copyright notice should be positioned in a place where it can easily be seen. It can be stamped, cast, engraved, painted, printed, wood-burned, or simply written by hand in permanent ink. In the case of fiber crafts, you can attach an inexpensive label with the copyright notice and your business name and logo (or any other information you wish to put on the label).

Bedding laws have long been a thorn in the side of crafters because they make no distinction between the large manufacturing company that makes mattresses and pillows, and the individual craft producer who sells only handmade items. "Concealed filling" items include not just bedding and upholstery, but handmade pillows and quilts. In some states, dolls, teddy bears, and stuffed soft sculpture items are also required to have a tag.

Fortunately, only 29 states now have this law on the books, and even if your state is one of them, the law may be arbitrarily enforced. (One exception is the state of Pennsylvania, which is reportedly sending officials to craft shows to inspect merchandise to see if it is properly labeled.) The only penalty that appears to be connected with a violation of this law in any state is removal of merchandise from store shelves or craft fair exhibits. That being the case, many crafters choose to ignore this law until they are challenged. If you learn you must comply with this law, you will be required to obtain a state license that will cost between $25 and $100, and you will have to order special "bedding stamps" that can be attached to your products. For more information on this complex topic, see *The Crafts Business Answer Book & Resource Guide*.

FTC Rule for Mail-Order Sellers

Even the smallest home-based business needs to be familiar with Federal Trade Commission (FTC) rules and regulations. A variety of free booklets are available to business owners on topics related to advertising, mail-order marketing, and product labeling (as discussed earlier). In particular, crafters who sell by mail need to pay attention to the FTC's Thirty-Day Mail-Order Rule, which states that one must ship customer orders within 30 days of receiving payment for the order. This rule is strictly enforced, with severe financial penalties for each violation.

Unless you specifically state in your advertising literature how long delivery will take, customers will expect to receive the product within 30 days after you get their order. If you cannot meet this shipping date, you must notify the customer accordingly, enclosing a postage-paid reply card or envelope, and giving them the option to cancel the order if they wish. Now you know why so many catalog sellers state, "Allow 6 weeks for delivery." This lets them off the hook in case there are unforeseen delays in getting the order delivered.

9. Protecting Your Intellectual Property

"Intellectual property," says Attorney Stephen Elias in his book, *Patent, Copyright & Trademark,* "is a product of the human intellect that has commercial value."

This section offers a brief overview of how to protect your intellectual property through patents and trademarks, with a longer discussion of copyright law, which is of the greatest concern to individuals who sell what they make. Because it is easy to get patents, trademarks, and copyrights mixed up, let me briefly define them for you:

- A *patent* is a grant issued by the government that gives an inventor the right to exclude all others from making, using, or selling an invention within the United States and its territories and possessions.

- A *trademark* is used by a manufacturer or merchant to identify his or her goods and distinguish them from those manufactured or sold by others.

- A *copyright* protects the rights of creators of intellectual property in five main categories (described in this section).

Perspective on Patents

A patent may be granted to anyone who invents or discovers a new and useful process, machine, manufacture, or composition of matter, or any new and useful improvement thereof. Any new, original, and ornamental design for an article of manufacture can also be patented. The problem with patents is that they can cost as much as $5,000 or more to obtain, and, once you've got one, they still require periodic maintenance through the U.S. Patent and Trademark Office. To contact this office, you can use the following Web sites: www.uspto.com or www.lcweb.loc.gov.

Ironically, a patent doesn't even give one the right to sell a product. It merely excludes anyone else from making, using, or selling your invention. Many business novices who have gone to the trouble to patent a product end up wasting a lot of time and money because a patent is useless if it isn't backed with the right manufacturing, distribution, and advertising programs. As inventor Jeremy Gorman states in *Homemade Money*, "Ninety-seven percent of the U.S. patents issued never earn enough money to pay the patenting fee. They just go on a plaque on the wall or in a desk drawer to impress the grandchildren 50 years later."

What a Trademark Protects

Trademarks were established to prevent one company from trading on the good name and reputation of another. The primary function of a trademark is to indicate origin, but in some cases it also serves as a guarantee of quality.

You cannot adopt any trademark that is so similar to another that it is likely to confuse buyers, nor can you trademark generic or descriptive names in the public domain. If, however, you come up with a particular word, name, symbol, or device to identify and distinguish your products from others, you may protect that mark by trademark provided another company is not already using a similar mark. Brand names, trade names, slogans, and phrases may also qualify for trademark protection.

Many individual crafters have successfully registered their own trademarks using a how-to book on the topic, but some would say never to try this without the help of a trademark attorney. It depends on how much you love detail and how well you can follow directions. Any mistake on the application form could cause it to be rejected, and you would lose the application fee in the process. If this is something you're interested in, and you have designed a mark you want to protect, you should first do a trademark search to see if someone else is already using it. Trademark searches can be done using library directories, an online computer service (check with your library), through private trademark search firms, or directly on the Internet through the Patent and Trademark Office's online search service (see A "Things to Do" Checklist with Related Resources on page 280). All of these searches together could still be inconclusive, however, because many companies have a stash of trademarks in reserve waiting for just the right product. These "nonpublished" trademarks are in a special file that only an attorney or trademark search service could find for you.

Selling How-To Projects to Magazines

If you want to sell an article, poem, or how-to project to a magazine, you need not copyright the material first because copyright protection exists from the moment you create that work. Your primary consideration here is whether you will sell "all rights" or only "first rights" to the magazine.

The sale of first rights means you are giving a publication permission to print your article, poem, or how-to project once, for a specific sum of money. After publication, you then have the right to resell that material or profit from it in other ways. Although it is always desirable to sell only "first rights," some magazines do not offer this choice.

If you sell all rights, you will automatically lose ownership of the copyright to your material and you can no longer profit from that work. Professional designers often refuse to work this way because they know they can realize greater profits by publishing their own pattern packets or design leaflets and wholesaling them to shops.

Like copyrights, trademarks have their own symbol, which looks like this: ®. This symbol can be used only after the trademark has been formally registered through the U.S. Patent and Trademark Office. Business owners often use the superscript initials ™ with a mark to indicate they've claimed a logo or some other mark, but this offers no legal protection. While this does not guarantee trademark protection, it does give notice to the public that you are claiming this name as your trademark. However, after you've used a mark for some time, you do gain a certain amount of common-law protection for that mark. I have, in fact, gained common-law protection for the name of my *Homemade Money* book and successfully defended it against use by another individual in my field because this title has become so closely associated with my name in the home-business community.

Whether you ever formally register a trademark or not will have much to do with your long-range business plans, how you feel about protecting your creativity, and what it would do to your business if someone stole your mark and registered it in his or her own name. Once you've designed a trademark you feel is worth protecting, get additional information from the Patent and Trademark Office and read a book or two on the topic to decide whether this is something you wish to pursue. (See A "Things to Do" Checklist with Related Resources on page 280.)

What Copyrights Protect

As a serious student of the copyright law, I've pored through the hard-to-interpret copyright manual, read dozens of related articles and books, and discussed this subject at length with designers, writers, teachers, editors, and publishers. I must emphasize, however, that I am no expert on this topic, and the following information does not constitute legal advice. It is merely offered as a general guide to a very complex legal topic you may wish to research further on your own at some point. In a book of this nature, addressed to hobbyists and beginning crafts-business owners, a discussion of copyrights must be limited to three basic topics:

- What copyrights do and do not protect
- How to register a copyright and protect your legal rights
- How to avoid infringing on the rights of other copyright holders

One of the first things you should do now is send for the free booklets offered by the Copyright Office (see A "Things to Do" Checklist with Related Resources on page 280). Various free circulars explain copyright basics, the forms involved in registering a copyright, and how to submit a copyright application and register a

Protecting Your Copyrights

If someone ever copies one of your copyrighted works, and you have registered that work with the Copyright Office, you should defend it as far as you are financially able to do so. If you think you're dealing with an innocent infringer—another crafter, perhaps, who has probably not profited much (if at all) from your work—a strongly worded letter on your business stationery (with a copy to an attorney, if you have one) might do the trick. Simply inform the copyright infringer that you are the legal owner of the work and the only one who has the right to profit from it. Tell the infringer that he or she must immediately cease using your copyrighted work, and ask for a confirmation by return mail.

If you think you have lost some money or incurred other damages, consult with a copyright attorney before contacting the infringer to see how you can best protect your rights and recoup any financial losses you may have suffered. This is particularly important if the infringer appears to be a successful business or corporation. Although you may have no intention of ever going to court on this matter, the copyright infringer won't know that, and one letter from a competent attorney might immediately resolve the matter at very little cost to you.

copyright. They also discuss what you cannot copyright. Rather than duplicate all the free information you can get from the Copyright Office with a letter or phone call, I will only briefly touch on these topics and focus instead on addressing some of the particular copyright questions crafters have asked me in the past.

Things You Can Copyright

Some people mistakenly believe that copyright protection extends only to printed works, but that is not true. The purpose of the copyright law is to protect any creator from anyone who would use the creator's work for his or her own profit. Under current copyright law, claims are now registered in seven classes, five of which pertain to crafts:

1. *Serials* (Form SE)—periodicals, newspapers, magazines, bulletins, newsletters, annuals, journals, and proceedings of societies.
2. *Text* (Form TX)—books, directories, and other written works, including the how-to instructions for a crafts project. (You could copyright a letter to your mother if you wanted to— or your best display ad copy, or any other written words that represent income potential.)
3. *Visual Arts* (Form VA)—pictorial, graphic, or sculptural works, including fine, graphic, and applied art; photographs, charts; technical drawings; diagrams; and models. (Also included in this category are "works of artistic craftsmanship insofar as their form but not their mechanical or utilitarian aspects are concerned.")
4. *Performing Arts* (Form PA)—musical works and accompanying words, dramatic works, pantomimes, choreographic works, motion pictures, and other audiovisual works.
5. *Sound Recordings* (Form SR)—musical, spoken, or other sounds, including any audio- or videotapes you might create.

Things You Cannot Copyright

You can't copyright ideas or procedures for doing, making, or building things, but the *expression* of an idea fixed in a tangible medium may be copyrightable—such as a book explaining a new system or technique. Brand names, trade names, slogans, and phrases cannot be copyrighted, either, although they might be entitled to protection under trademark laws.

The design on a craft object can be copyrighted, but only if it can be identified separately from the object itself. Objects themselves (a decorated coffee mug, a box, a tote bag) cannot be copyrighted.

Copyright Registration Tips

First, understand that you do not have to formally copyright anything because copyright protection exists from the moment a work is created, whether you add a copyright notice or not.

So why file at all? The answer is simple: If you don't file the form and pay the fee (currently $30), you'll never be able to take anyone to court for stealing your work. Therefore, in each instance where copyright protection is considered, you need to decide how important your work is to you in terms of dollars and cents, and ask yourself whether you value it enough to pay to protect it. Would you actually be willing to pay court costs to defend your copyright, should someone steal it from you? If you never intend to go to court, there's little use in officially registering a copyright; but because it costs you nothing to add a copyright notice to your work, you are foolish not to do this. (See sidebar, Protecting Your Copyrights, on page 264.)

If you do decide to file a copyright application, contact the Copyright Office and request the appropriate forms. When you file the copyright application form (which is easy to complete), you must include with it two copies of the work. Ordinarily, two actual copies of copyrighted items must be deposited, but certain items are exempt from deposit requirements, including all three-dimensional sculptural works and any works published only as reproduced in or on jewelry, dolls, toys, games, plaques, floor coverings, textile and other fabrics, packaging materials, or any useful article. In these cases, two photographs or drawings of the item are sufficient.

Note that the Copyright Office does not compare deposit copies to determine whether works submitted for registration are similar to any material already copyrighted. It is the sender's responsibility to determine the originality of what's being copyrighted. (See discussion of "original" in the next section, under Respecting the Copyrights of Others.)

Mandatory Deposit Requirements

Although you do not have to officially register a copyright claim, it *is* mandatory to deposit two copies of all "published works" for the collections of the Library of Congress within 3 months after publication. Failure to make the deposit may subject the copyright owner to fines and other monetary liabilities, but it does not affect copyright protection. No special form is required for this mandatory deposit.

Note that the term *published works* pertains not just to the publication of printed matter, but to the public display of any item. Thus you "publish" your originally designed craftwork when you first show it at a craft fair, in a shop, on your Web site, or any other public place.

Respecting the Copyrights of Others

Just as there are several things you must do to protect your "intellectual creations," there are several things you must not do if you wish to avoid legal problems with other copyright holders.

Copyright infringement occurs whenever anyone violates the exclusive rights covered by copyright. If and when a copyright case goes to court, the copyright holder who has been infringed on must

Changing Things

Many crafters have mistakenly been led to believe that they can copy the work of others if they simply change this or that so their creation doesn't look exactly like the one they have copied. But many copyright court cases have hinged on someone taking "a substantial part" of someone else's design and claiming it as their own. If your "original creation" bears even the slightest resemblance to the product you've copied—and you are caught selling it in the commercial marketplace—there could be legal problems.

Crafters often combine the parts of two or three patterns in an attempt to come up with their own original patterns, but often this only compounds the possible copyright problems. Let's imagine you're making a doll. You might take the head from one pattern, the arms and legs from another, and the unique facial features from another. You may think you have developed an original creation (and perhaps an original pattern

prove that his or her work is the original creation and that the two works are so similar that the alleged infringer must have copied it. This is not always an easy matter, for *original* is a difficult word to define. Even the Copyright Office has trouble here, which is why so many cases that go to court end up setting precedents.

In any copyright case, there will be discussions about "substantial similarity," instances where two people actually have created the same thing simultaneously, loss of profits, or damage to one's business or reputation. If you were found guilty of copyright infringement, at the very least you would probably be ordered to pay to the original creator all profits derived from the sale of the copyrighted work to date. You would also have to agree to refund any orders you might receive for the work in the future. In some copyright cases where the original creator has experienced considerable financial loss, penalties for copyright infringement have been as high as $100,000. As you can see, this is not a matter to take lightly.

you might sell), but you haven't. Because the original designer of any of the features you've copied might recognize her work in your "original creation" or published pattern, the designer could come after you for infringing on "a substantial part" of his or her design. In this case, all you've done is multiply your possibilities for a legal confrontation with three copyright holders.

"But I can't create my own original designs and patterns!" you moan. Many who have said this in the past were mistaken. With time and practice, most crafters are able to develop products that are original in design, and I believe you can do this, too. Meanwhile, check out Dover Publications' *Pictorial Archive* series of books (see A "Things to Do" Checklist with Related Resources). Here you will find thousands of copyright-free designs and motifs you can use on your craft work or in needlework projects. And don't forget the wealth of design material in museums and old books that have fallen into the public domain. (See sidebar, What's in the Public Domain? on page 272.)

This is a complex topic beyond the scope of this book, but any book on copyright law will provide additional information if you should ever need it. What's important here is that you fully understand the importance of being careful to respect the legal rights of others. As a crafts-business owner, you could possibly infringe on someone else's designs when you (1) quote someone in an article, periodical, or book you've written; (2) photocopy copyrighted materials; or (3) share information on the Internet. Following is a brief discussion of these topics.

1. **Be careful when quoting from a published source.** If you're writing an article or book and wish to quote someone's words from any published source (book, magazine, Internet, and so on), you should always obtain written permission first. Granted, minor quotations from published sources are okay when they fall under the Copyright Office's Fair Use Doctrine, but unless you completely understand this doctrine, you should protect yourself by

obtaining permission before you quote anyone in one of your own written works. It is not necessarily the quantity of the quote, but the value of the quoted material to the copyright owner.

In particular, never *ever* use a published poem in one of your written works without written permission. To the poet, this is a "whole work," much the same as a book is a whole work to an author. Although the use of one or two lines of a poem, or a paragraph from a book, may be considered "fair use," many publishers now require written permission even for this short reproduction of a copyrighted work.

2. **Photocopying can be dangerous.** Teachers often photocopy large sections of a book (sometimes whole books) for distribution to their students, but this is a flagrant violation of the copyright law. Some publishers may grant photocopying of part of a work if it is to be used only once as a teaching aid, but written permission must always be obtained first.

   It is also a violation of the copyright law to photocopy patterns for sale or trade because such use denies the creator the profit from a copy that might have been sold.

3. **Don't share copyrighted information on the Internet.** People everywhere are lifting material from *Reader's Digest* and other copyrighted publications and "sharing" them on the Internet through e-mail messages, bulletin boards, and the like. *This is a very dangerous thing to do.* "But I didn't see a copyright notice," you might say, or "It indicated the author was anonymous." What you must remember is that *everything* gains copyright protection the moment it is created, whether a copyright notice is attached to it or not. Many "anonymous" items on the Internet are actually copyrighted poems and articles put there by someone who not only

violated the copyright law but compounded the matter by failing to give credit to the original creator.

If you were to pick up one of those "anonymous" pieces of information and put it in an article or book of your own, the original copyright owner, upon seeing his or her work in your publication, would have good grounds for a lawsuit. Remember, pleading ignorance of the law is never a good excuse.

Clearly there is no financial gain to be realized by violating the rights of a copyright holder when it means that any day you might be contacted by a lawyer and threatened with a lawsuit. As stated in my *Crafts Business Answer Book & Resource Guide:*

> The best way to avoid copyright infringement problems is to follow the "Golden Rule" proposed by a United States Supreme Court justice: "Take not from others to such an extent and in such a manner that you would be resentful if they so took from you."

Using Commercial Patterns and Designs

Beginning crafters who lack design skills commonly make products for sale using commercial patterns, designs in books, or how-to instructions for projects found in magazines. The problem here is that all of these things are published for the general consumer market and offered for *personal use* only. Because they are all protected by copyright, that means only the copyright holder has the right to profit from their use.

That said, let me ease your mind by saying that the sale of products made from copyrighted patterns, designs, and magazine how-to projects is probably not going to cause any problems *as long as sales are limited, and they yield a profit only to you, the crafter.* That means no sales through shops of any kind where a sales commission or profit is received by a third party, and absolutely no wholesaling of such products.

It's not that designers and publishers are concerned about your sale of a few craft or needlework items to friends and local buyers; what they are fighting to protect with the legality of copyrights is their right to sell their own designs or finished products in the commercial marketplace. You may find that some patterns, designs, or projects state "no mass-production." You are not mass-producing if you make a dozen handcrafted items for sale at a craft fair or holiday boutique, but you would definitely be considered a mass-producer if you made dozens, or hundreds, for sale in shops.

Consignment sales fall into a kind of gray area that requires some common-sense judgment on your part. This is neither wholesaling nor selling direct to consumers. One publisher might con-

What's in the Public Domain?

For all works created after January 1, 1978, the copyright lasts for the life of the author or creator plus 50 years after his or her death. For works created before 1978, there are different terms, which you can obtain from any book in your library on copyright law.

Once material falls into the public domain, it can never be copyrighted again. As a general rule, anything with a copyright date more than 75 years ago is probably in the public domain, but you can never be sure without doing a thorough search. Some characters in old books—such as Beatrix Potter's *Peter Rabbit*—are now protected under the trademark law as business logos. For more information on this, ask the Copyright Office to send you its circular "How to Investigate the Copyright Status of a Work."

Early American craft and needlework patterns of all kinds are in the public domain because they were created before the copyright law was a reality. Such old patterns may

sider such sales a violation of a copyright while another might not. Whenever specific guidelines for the use of a pattern, design, or how-to project are not given, the only way to know for sure if you are operating on safe legal ground is to write to the publisher and get written permission on where you can sell reproductions of the item in question.

Now let's take a closer look at the individual types of patterns, designs, and how-to projects you might consider using once you enter the crafts marketplace.

Craft, Toy, and Garment Patterns

Today, the consumer has access to thousands of sewing patterns plus toy, craft, needlework, and woodworking patterns of every kind and description found in books, magazines, and design or project leaflets. Whether you can use such patterns for commercial use

show up in books and magazines that are copyrighted, but the copyright in this case extends only to the book or magazine itself and the way in which a pattern has been presented to readers, along with the way in which the how-to-make instructions have been written. The actual patterns themselves cannot be copyrighted by anyone at this point.

Quilts offer an interesting example. If a contemporary quilt designer takes a traditional quilt pattern and does something unusual with it in terms of material or colors, this new creation would qualify for a copyright, with the protection being given to the quilt as a work of art, not to the traditional pattern itself, which is still in the public domain. Thus you could take that same traditional quilt pattern and do something else with it for publication, but you could not publish the contemporary designer's copyrighted version of that same pattern.

depends largely on who has published the pattern and owns the copyright, and what the copyright holder's policy happens to be for how buyers may use those patterns.

To avoid copyright problems when using patterns of any kind, the first thing you need to do is look for some kind of notice on the pattern packet or publication containing the pattern. In checking some patterns, I found that those sold by *Woman's Day* state specifically that reproductions of the designs may not be sold, bartered, or traded. *Good Housekeeping,* on the other hand, gives permission to use their patterns for "income-producing activities." When in doubt, ask!

Whereas the general rule for selling reproductions made from commercial patterns is "no wholesaling and no sales to shops," items made from the average garment pattern (such as an apron, vest, shirt, or simple dress) purchased in the local fabric store *may* be an exception. My research suggests that selling such items in your local consignment shop or craft mall isn't likely to be much of a problem because the sewing pattern companies aren't on the lookout for copyright violators the way individual craft designers and major corporations are. (And most people who sew end up changing those patterns and using different decorations to such a degree that pattern companies might not recognize those patterns even if they were looking for them.)

On the other hand, commercial garment patterns that have been designed by name designers should never be used without permission. In most cases, you would have to obtain a licensing agreement for the commercial use of such patterns.

> ***Avoid this pitfall:*** In addition to problems in using copyrighted patterns, anyone who uses fabric to make a product for the marketplace has yet another concern: designer *fabrics*. Always look at the selvage of a patterned fabric. If you see a copyright notice with a designer's name and the phrase "for individual consumption only" (or similar wordage), *do not use this fabric to make any item for*

sale without first obtaining written permission from the fabric manufacturer. In many instances, designer fabrics can be used commercially only when a license has been obtained for this purpose.

Be especially careful about selling reproductions of toys and dolls made from commercial patterns or design books. Many are likely to be for popular copyrighted characters being sold in the commercial marketplace. In such cases, the pattern company will have a special licensing arrangement with the toy or doll manufacturer to sell the pattern, and reproductions for sale by individual crafters will be strictly prohibited.

Take a Raggedy Ann doll, for example. The fact that you've purchased a pattern to make such a doll does not give you the right to sell a finished likeness of that doll any more than your purchase of a piece of artwork gives you the right to re-create it for sale in some other form, such as notepaper or calendars. Only the original creator has such rights. You have simply purchased the *physical property* for private use.

> ***Avoid this pitfall:*** Don't *ever* make and sell *any* replica in any material of a famous copyrighted character anywhere, such as the Walt Disney or Warner Brothers characters, Snoopy, or the Sesame Street gang. It's true that a lot of crafters are doing this, but they are inviting serious legal trouble if they ever get caught. Disney is particularly aggressive in defending its copyrights.

How-To Projects in Magazines and Books

Each magazine and book publisher has its own policy about the use of its art, craft, or needlework projects. How those projects may be used depends on who owns the copyright to the published projects. In some instances, craft and needlework designers sell their original designs outright to publishers of books, leaflets, or magazines. Other designers authorize only a one-time use of their projects, which gives

Online Help

Today, one of the best ways to network and learn about business is to get on the Internet. The many online resources included in A "Things to Do" Checklist in the next section will give you a jump-start and lead to many exciting discoveries.

For continuing help and advice from Barbara Brabec, be sure to visit her Web sites at www.Barbara Brabec and www.ideaforest.com. Here you will find a wealth of information to help you profit from your crafts, including newsletters, feature articles, special tips, and recommended books.

them the right to republish or sell their designs to another market or license them to a manufacturer. If guidelines about selling finished products do not appear somewhere in the magazine or on the copyright page of a book, you should always write and get permission to make such items for sale. In your letter, explain how many items you would like to make, and where you plan to sell them, as that could make a big difference in the reply you receive.

In case you missed the special note on the copyright page of this book, you *can* make and sell all of the projects featured in this and any other book in Prima's For Fun & Profit series.

As a columnist for *Crafts Magazine,* I can also tell you that its readers have the right to use its patterns and projects for money-making purposes, but only to the extent that sales are limited to places where the crafter is the only one who profits from their use. That means selling directly to individuals, with no sales in shops of any kind where a third party would also realize some profit from a sale. Actually, this is a good rule-of-thumb guideline to use if you plan to sell only a few items of any project or pattern published in any magazine, book, or leaflet.

In summary, products that aren't original in design will sell, but their market is limited, and they will never be able to command the kind of prices that original-design items enjoy. Generally speaking, the more original the product line, the greater one's chances for building a profitable crafts business.

As your business grows, questions about copyrights will arise, and you will have to do a little research to get the answers you need. Your library should have several books on this topic and there is a wealth of information on the Internet. (Just use your search button and type "copyright information.") If you have a technical copyright question, remember that you can always call the Copyright Office and speak to someone who can answer it and send you additional information. Note, however, that regulations prohibit the Copyright Office from giving legal advice or opinions concerning the rights of persons in connection with cases of alleged copyright infringement.

10. To Keep Growing, Keep Learning

Everything we do, every action we take, affects our life in one way or another. Reading a book is a simple act, indeed, but trust me when I say that your reading this particular book *could ultimately change your life.* I know this to be true because thousands of men and women have written to me over the years to tell me how their lives changed after they read one or another of my books and decided to start a crafts business. My life has changed, too, as a result of reading books by other authors.

Many years ago, the purchase of a book titled *You Can Whittle and Carve* unleashed a flood of creativity in me that has yet to cease. That simple book helped me to discover unknown craft talents, which in turn led me to start my first crafts business at home. That experience prepared me for the message I would find a decade later in the book *On Writing Well* by William Zinsser. This author changed my life by giving me the courage to try my hand at writing professionally. Dozens of books later, I had learned a lot about the art and craft of writing well and making a living in the process.

Now you know why I believe reading should be given top priority in your life. Generally speaking, the more serious you become about anything you're interested in, the more reading you will need to do. This will take time, but the benefits will be enormous. If a crafts business is your current passion, this book contains much of the information you need to know to get started. To keep growing, read some of the wonderful books recommended in the Resources section. (If you don't find the books you need in your local library, ask your librarian to obtain them for you through the inter-library loan program.) Join one or more of the organizations recommended. Subscribe to a few periodicals or magazines, and "grow your business" through networking with others who share your interests.

Motivational Tips

As you start your new business or expand a money making hobby already begun, consider the following suggestions:

- *Start an "Achievement Log."* Day by day, our small achievements may seem insignificant, but viewed in total after several weeks or months, they give us important perspective. Reread your achievement log periodically in the future, especially on days when you feel down in the dumps. Make entries at least once a week, noting such things as new customers or accounts acquired, publicity you've gotten, a new product you've designed, the brochure or catalog you've just completed, positive feedback received from others, new friendships, and financial gains.

- *Live your dream.* The mind is a curious thing—it can be trained to think success is possible or to think that success is only for other people. Most of our fears never come true, so allowing our minds to dwell on what may or may not happen cripples us, preventing us from moving ahead, from having confidence, and from living out our dreams. Instead of "facing fear," focus on the result you want. This may automatically eliminate the fear.

■ *Think positively.* As Murphy has proven time and again, what can go wrong will, and usually at the worst possible moment. It matters little whether the thing that has gone wrong was caused by circumstances beyond our control or by a mistake in judgment. What does matter is how we deal with the problem at hand. A positive attitude and the ability to remain flexible at all times are two of the most important ingredients for success in any endeavor.

■ *Don't be afraid to fail.* We often learn more from failure than from success. When you make a mistake, chalk it up to experience and consider it a good lesson well learned. The more you learn, the more self-confident you will become.

■ *Temper your "dreams of riches" with thoughts of reality.* Remember that "success" can also mean being in control of your own life, making new friends, or discovering a new world of possibilities.

Until now you may have lacked the courage to get your craft ideas off the ground, but now that you've seen how other people have accomplished their goals, I hope you feel more confident and adventurous and are ready to capitalize on your creativity. By following the sound advice in this book, you can stop dreaming about all the things you want to do and start making plans to do them!

I'm not trying to make home-business owners out of everyone who reads this book, but my goal is definitely to give you a shove in that direction if you're teetering on the edge, wanting something more than just a profitable hobby. It's wonderful to have a satisfying hobby, and even better to have one that pays for itself; but the nicest thing of all is a real home business that lets you fully utilize your creative talents and abilities while also adding to the family income.

"The things I want to know are in books," Abraham Lincoln once said. "My best friend is the person who'll get me a book I ain't read." You now hold in your hands a book that has taught you many things you wanted to know. To make it a *life-changing book,* all you have to do is act on the information you've been given.

I wish you a joyful journey and a potful of profits!

A "Things to Do" Checklist with Related Resources

INSTRUCTIONS: Read through this entire section, noting the different things you need to do to get your crafts business "up and running." Use the checklist as a plan, checking off each task as it is completed and obtaining any recommended resources. Where indicated, note the date an action was taken so you have a reminder about any follow-up action that should be taken.

Business Start-Up Checklist

☐ Call city hall or county clerk

    ☐ to register fictitious business name
    ☐ to see if you need a business license or permit
    ☐ to check on local zoning laws
    (info also available in your library)
    *Follow up:*_____

☐ Call state capitol

    ☐ secretary of state: to register your business name;
    ask about a license
    ☐ Department of Revenue: to apply for sales tax number
    *Follow up:*_____

☐ Call your local telephone company about

    ☐ cost of a separate phone line for business
    ☐ cost of an additional personal line for Internet access

☐ any special options for home-based businesses

*Follow up:*_____

☐ Call your insurance agent(s) to discuss

☐ business rider on house insurance
(or need for separate in-home insurance policy)
☐ benefits of an umbrella policy for extra liability insurance
☐ using your car for business
(how this may affect your insurance)

*Follow up:*_____

☐ Call several banks or S&L's in your area to

☐ compare cost of a business checking account
☐ get price of a safety deposit box for valuable business records

*Follow up:*_____

☐ Visit office and computer supply stores to check on

☐ manual bookkeeping systems, such as the
Dome Simplified Monthly
☐ accounting software
☐ standard invoices and other helpful business forms

*Follow up:*_____

☐ Call National Association of Enrolled Agents at (800) 424-4339

☐ to get a referral to a tax professional in your area
☐ to get answers to any tax questions you may have (no charge)

*Follow up:*_____

☐ Contact government agencies for information relative to your business.

(See Government Agencies checklist.)

☐ Request free brochures from organizations

(See Craft and Home-Business Organizations.)

☐ Obtain sample issues or subscribe to selected publications
(See Recommended Crafts-Business Periodicals.)

☐ Obtain other information of possible help to your business
(See Other Services and Suppliers.)

☐ Get acquainted with the business information available to you in
your library.
(See list of Recommended Business Books and Helpful Library
Directories.)

Government Agencies

☐ Consumer Product Safety Commission (CPSC), Washington, DC
20207. (800) 638-2772. Information Services: (301) 504-0000. Web
site: www.cpsc.gov. (Includes a "Talk to Us" e-mail address
where you can get answers to specific questions.) If you make
toys or other products for children, garments (especially children's wear), or use any kind of paint, varnish, lacquer, or shel-
lac on your products, obtain the following free booklets:

☐ *The Consumer Product Safety Act of 1972*
☐ *The Flammable Fabrics Act*

Date Contacted:_____Information Received:_____

*Follow up:*_____

☐ Copyright Office, Register of Copyrights, Library of Congress,
Washington, DC 20559. To hear recorded messages on the Copyright Office's automated message system (general information,
registration procedures, copyright search info, and so on), call
(202) 707-3000. You can also get the same information online at
www.loc.gov/copyright.

To get free copyright forms, a complete list of all publications
available, or to speak personally to someone who will answer
your special questions, call (202) 797-9100. In particular, ask for:

☐ Circular R1, *The Nuts and Bolts of Copyright*
☐ Circular R2 (a list of publications available)

Date Contacted:_____Information Received:_____

*Follow up:*_____

☐ Department of Labor. If you should ever hire an employee
or independent contractor, contact your local Labor Department, Wage & Hour Division, for guidance on what you must
do to be completely legal. (Check your phone book under
"U.S. Government.")

Date Contacted:_____Information Received:_____

*Follow up:*_____

☐ Federal Trade Commission (FTC), 6th Street and Pennsylvania
Avenue, NW, Washington, DC 20580. Web site: www.ftc.gov. Request
any of the following booklets relative to your craft or business:

☐ *Textile Fiber Products Identification Act*
☐ *Wool Products Labeling Act of 1939*
☐ *Care Labeling of Textile Wearing Apparel*
☐ *The Hand Knitting Yarn Industry* (booklet)
☐ *Truth-in-Advertising Rules*
☐ *Thirty-Day Mail-Order Rule*

Date Contacted:_____Information Received:_____

Follow up: _____

☐ Internal Revenue Service (IRS). Check the Internet at
www.irs.gov to read the following information online or
call your local IRS office or (800) 829-1040 to get the following booklets and other free tax information:

☐ *Tax Guide for Small Business*—#334
☐ *Business Use of Your Home*—#587
☐ *Tax Information for Direct Sellers*

Date Contacted:_____Information Received:_____

*Follow up:*_____

☐ Patent and Trademark Office (PTO), Washington, DC 20231. Web site: www.uspto.gov.

For patent and trademark information 24 hours a day, call (800) 786-9199 [in northern Virginia, call (703) 308-9000] to hear various messages about patents and trademarks or to order the following booklets:

☐ *Basic Facts about Patents*
☐ *Basic Facts about Trademarks*

To search the PTO's online database of all registered trademarks, go to www.uspto.gov/tmdb/index.html.

Date Contacted:_____Information Received:_____

*Follow up:*_____

☐ Social Security Hotline. (800) 772-1213. By calling this number, you can hear automated messages, order information booklets, or speak directly to someone who can answer specific questions.

Date Contacted:_____Information Received:_____

*Follow up:*_____

☐ U.S. Small Business Administration (SBA). (800) U-ASK-SBA. Call this number to hear a variety of prerecorded messages on starting and financing a business. Weekdays, you can speak personally to an SBA adviser to get answers to specific questions and request such free business publications as:

☐ *Starting Your Business* —#CO-0028
☐ *Resource Directory for Small Business Management*—#CO-0042
    (a list of low-cost publications available from the SBA)

The SBA's mission is to help people get into business and stay there. One-on-one counseling, training, and workshops are available through 950 small-business development centers across the country. Help is also available from local district offices of the SBA in the form of free business counseling and training from SCORE volunteers. The SBA office in Washington has a special Women's Business Enterprise section that provides free information on loans, tax deductions, and other financial matters. District offices offer special training programs in management, marketing, and accounting.

A wealth of business information is also available online at www.sba.gov and www.business.gov (the U.S. Business Adviser site). To learn whether there is an SBA office near you, look under U.S. Government in your telephone directory, or call the SBA's toll-free number.

Date Contacted:_____Information Received:_____

*Follow up:*_____

☐ SCORE (Service Corps of Retired Executives). (800) 634-0245. There are more than 12,400 SCORE members who volunteer their time and expertise to small-business owners. Many crafts businesses have received valuable in-depth counseling and training simply by calling the organization and asking how to connect with a SCORE volunteer in their area.

In addition, the organization offers e-mail counseling via the Internet at www.score.org. You simply enter the specific expertise required and retrieve a list of e-mail counselors who represent the best match by industry and topic. Questions can then be sent by e-mail to the counselor of your choice for response.

Date Contacted:_____Information Received:_____

*Follow up:*_____

Craft and Home-Business Organizations

In addition to the regular benefits of membership in an organization related to your art or craft (fellowship, networking, educational conferences or workshops, marketing opportunities, and so on), membership may also bring special business services, such as insurance programs, merchant card services, and discounts on supplies and materials. Each of the following organizations will send you membership information on request.

☐ The American Association of Home-Based Businesses, P.O. Box 10023, Rockville, MD 20849. (800) 447-9710. Web site: www.aahbb.org. This organization has chapters throughout the country. Members have access to merchant card services, discounted business products and services, prepaid legal services, and more.

Date Contacted:_____Information Received:_____

*Follow up:*_____

☐ American Crafts Council, 72 Spring Street, New York, NY 10012. (800)-724-0859. Web site: www.craftcouncil.org. Membership in this organization will give you access to a property and casualty insurance policy that will cost between $250 and $500 a year, depending on your city, state, and the value of items being insured in your art or crafts studio. The policy includes insurance for a craftsperson's work in the studio, in transit, or at a show; $1 million coverage for bodily injury and property damage in studio or away; and $1 million worth of product liability insurance. This policy is from American Phoenix Corporation; staff members will answer your specific questions when you call (800) 274-6364, ext. 337.

Date Contacted:_____Information Received:_____

*Follow up:*_____

☐ Arts & Crafts Business Solutions, 2804 Bishop Gate Drive, Raleigh, NC 27613. (800) 873-1192. This company, known in the industry as the Arts Group, offers a bankcard service specifically for and tailored to the needs of the arts and crafts marketplace. Several differently priced packages are available, and complete information is available on request.

Date Contacted:_____Information Received:_____

*Follow up:*_____

☐ Home Business Institute, Inc., P.O. Box 301, White Plains, NY 10605-0301. (888) DIAL-HBI; Fax: (914) 946-6694. Web site: www.hbiweb.com. Membership benefits include insurance programs (medical insurance and in-home business policy that includes some liability insurance); savings on telephone services, office supplies, and merchant account enrollment; and free advertising services.

Date Contacted:_____Information Received:_____

*Follow up:*_____

☐ National Craft Association (NCA), 1945 E. Ridge Road, Suite 5178, Rochester, NY 14622-2647. (800) 715-9594. Web site: www.craftassoc.com. Members of NCA have access to a comprehensive package of services, including merchant account services; discounts on business services and products; a prepaid legal program; a check-guarantee merchant program; checks by fax, phone, or e-mail; and insurance programs. Of special interest to this book's readers is the "Crafters Business Insurance" policy (through RLI Insurance Co.) that includes coverage for business property; art/craft merchandise or inventory at home, in transit, or at a show; theft away from premises; up to $1 million in both personal and product liability insurance; loss of business income; and more. Members have the option to select the exact benefits they need. Premiums range from $150 to $300, depending on location, value of average inventory, and the risks associated with one's art or craft.

Date Contacted:_____Information Received:_____

*Follow up:*_____

Recommended Crafts-Business Periodicals

Membership in an organization generally includes a subscription to a newsletter or magazine that will be helpful to your business. Here are additional craft periodicals you should sample or subscribe to:

☐ *The Crafts Report—The Business Journal for the Crafts Industry,* Box 1992, Wilmington, DE 19899. (800) 777-7098. On the Internet at www.craftsreport.com. A monthly magazine covering all areas of crafts-business management and marketing, including special-interest columns and show listings.

☐ *Craft Supply Magazine—The Industry Journal for the Professional Crafter,* Krause Publications, Inc., 700 E. State Street, Iowa, WI 54990-0001. (800) 258-0929. Web site: www.krause.com. A monthly magazine that includes crafts-business and marketing articles and wholesale supply sources.

☐ *Home Business Report,* 2949 Ash Street, Abbotsford, BC, V2S 4G5 Canada. (604) 857-1788; Fax: (604) 854-3087. Canada's premier home-business magazine, relative to both general and craft-related businesses.

☐ *SAC Newsmonthly,* 414 Avenue B, P.O. Box 159, Bogalusa, LA 70429-0159. (800) TAKE-SAC; Fax: (504) 732-3744. A monthly national show guide that also includes business articles for professional crafters.

☐ *Sunshine Artist Magazine,* 2600 Temple Drive, Winter Park, FL 32789. (800) 597-2573; Fax: (407) 539-1499. Web site: www. sunshineartist.com. America's premier show and festival guide. Each monthly issue contains business and marketing articles of interest to both artists and craftspeople.

Other Services and Suppliers

Contact any of the following companies that offer information or services of interest to you.

☐ American Express. For merchant account information, call the Merchant Establishment Services Department at (800) 445-AMEX.

Date Contacted:_____Information Received:_____

*Follow up:*_____

☐ Dover Publications, 31 E. 2nd Street, Mineola, NY 11501. Your source for thousands of copyright-free designs and motifs you can use in your craftwork or needlecraft projects. Request a free catalog of books in the *Pictorial Archive* series.

Date Contacted:_____Information Received:_____

*Follow up:*_____

☐ Novus Services, Inc. For merchant account information, call (800) 347-6673.

Date Contacted:_____Information Received:_____

*Follow up:*_____

☐ Volunteer Lawyers for the Arts (VLA), 1 E. 53rd Street, New York, NY 10022. Legal hotline: (212) 319-2910. If you ever need an attorney, and cannot afford one, contact this nonprofit organization, which has chapters all over the country. In addition to providing legal aid for performing and visual artists and craftspeople (individually or in groups), the VLA also provides a range of educational services, including issuing publications concerning taxes, accounting, and insurance.

Date Contacted:_____Information Received:_____

*Follow up:*_____

☐ Widby Enterprises USA, 4321 Crestfield Road, Knoxville, TN 37921-3104. (888) 522-2458. Web site: www.widbylabel.com. Standard and custom-designed labels that meet federal labeling requirements.

Date Contacted:_____Information Received:_____

*Follow up:*_____

Recommended Business Books

When you have specific business questions not answered in this beginner's guide, check your library for the following books. Any not on library shelves can be obtained through the library's inter-library loan program.

☐ *Business and Legal Forms for Crafts* by Tad Crawford (Allworth Press)

☐ *Business Forms and Contracts (in Plain English) for Crafts People* by Leonard D. DuBoff (Interweave Press)

☐ *Crafting as a Business* by Wendy Rosen (Chilton)

☐ *The Crafts Business Answer Book & Resource Guide: Answers to Hundreds of Troublesome Questions about Starting, Marketing & Managing a Homebased Business Efficiently, Legally & Profitably* by Barbara Brabec (M. Evans & Co.)

☐ *Creative Cash: How to Profit from Your Special Artistry, Creativity, Hand Skills, and Related Know-How* by Barbara Brabec (Prima Publishing)

☐ *422 Tax Deductions for Businesses & Self-Employed Individuals* by Bernard Kamoroff (Bell Springs Publishing)

☐ *Homemade Money: How to Select, Start, Manage, Market, and Multiply the Profits of a Business at Home* by Barbara Brabec (Betterway Books)

☐ *How to Register Your Own Trademark with Forms,* 2nd ed., by Mark Warda (Sourcebooks)

☐ *INC Yourself: How to Profit by Setting Up Your Own Corporation,* by Judith H. McQuown (HarperBusiness)

☐ *Make It Profitable! How to Make Your Art, Craft, Design, Writing or Publishing Business More Efficient, More Satisfying, and More Profitable* by Barbara Brabec (M. Evans & Co.)

☐ *Patent, Copyright & Trademark: A Desk Reference to Intellectual Property Law* by Stephen Elias (Nolo Press)

☐ *The Perils of Partners* by Irwin Gray (Smith-Johnson Publisher)

☐ *Small Time Operator: How to Start Your Own Business, Keep Your Books, Pay Your Taxes & Stay Out of Trouble* by Bernard Kamoroff (Bell Springs Publishing)

☐ *Trademark: How to Name a Business & Product* by Kate McGrath and Stephen Elias (Nolo Press)

Helpful Library Directories

☐ *Books in Print* and *Guide to Forthcoming Books* (how to find out which books are still in print, and which books will soon be published)

☐ *Encyclopedia of Associations* (useful in locating an organization dedicated to your art or craft)

☐ *National Trade and Professional Associations of the U.S.* (more than 7,000 associations listed alphabetically and geographically)

☐ *The Standard Periodical Directory* (annual guide to U.S. and Canadian periodicals)

☐ *Thomas Register of American Manufacturers* (helpful when you're looking for raw material suppliers or the owners of brand names and trademarks)

☐ *Trademark Register of the U.S.* (contains every trademark currently registered with the U.S. Patent and Trademark Office)

Glossary

▼▼▼

Acrylic molds: Seamless molds made of a transparent resin, which can be handled when filled with hot wax without danger to your hands. They are clear, which is a great aid for embedding objects in candles in just the right place.

Aggressive (warm) colors: Reds, oranges, and yellows.

Aniline: A colorless derivative of benzene used in many candlemaking dyes.

Aromatherapy: The branch of herbal medicine that utilizes the therapeutic properties of essential oils. Aromatherapy candles are meant to deliver the power of essential oils as the scent is emitted from the burning candle and is gently inhaled. Traditionally, aromatherapy candles are candles scented with fragrant oils from herbs, flowers, and other plants. The term "aromatherapy" has been loosely used in candle labeling to describe a candle scented with any type of fragrance that may stimulate aromatic recollections that arouse positive feelings.

Bayberry wax: Obtained by boiling the berries of bayberry shrubs. It is sage green, has a woodsy-sweet scent, and smells better with age. It is rather brittle and expensive due to the fact that it takes 15 pounds of berries to produce one pound of wax. Bayberry wax is even more expensive than beeswax and has a melting point of 118 degrees Fahrenheit.

Beaded candles: Containers of small beads of wax or sandlike granules of wax considered as candles, although the wax is not melted to pour it into the container. Candlemaking of this type is popular and widely available because you only have to fill a container with a positioned wick with the wax; heat is not required in the candlemaking process to melt wax.

Beeswax candles: Beeswax is a natural, yellowish, waxy substance secreted by honeybees to build their honeycomb. Candles primarily made of beeswax are smokeless and have a faint to strong smell of honey.

Birthday candles: A children's favorite, these are small candles placed on a birthday cake for "making a wish" and blowing them out in one blow to make the wish come true. Birthday candles used to be just tiny tapers. Now you can find all kinds of novelty candles suitable for birthday cakes.

Block candles: "Block" and "pillar" are the traditional terms for any symmetrically shaped molded candle, although there are many symmetrical candles that are neither "block" nor "pillar" in shape. Today, you'll find star pillars, square obliques, octagon spirals, diamond tapers—the possibilities are endless! Typically, these are wide candles usually referred to by their diameter followed by their height (that is, a 4 × 6 candle is 4 inches in diameter and 6 inches tall).

Cake candles: Shaped like small round cakes and decorated on the exterior with wax whipped to look like frosty cake icing. These candles are usually colored and scented to simulate yummy food cakes without the fat! Also called country candles.

Candelabra: A large branched candlestick.

Candelilla wax: A wax extracted from a shrub native to the U.S. Southwest and Mexico. It can be used to make a candle harder without increasing the melting point of the wax.

Candle: A mass of solid fuel formed around a wick that gives light when burned. As the wick burns, the heat of the flame melts the surrounding fuel, which is transported via capillary action to the flame, which then consumes the fuel and burns it off.

Candle decorating: Involves the many types of surface techniques applied to a finished candle to render a particular appearance for display purposes. Decorating a candle involves effort *after* the candle is made, so candle decorating techniques are not considered a candlemaking method.

Candle glaze: Various finishes that can be applied to candles by brushing, overdipping, or spraying. These glazes give a candle a shiny, lustrous surface and a protective coating.

Candlemas Day: A Catholic church feast on February 2, commemorating the purification of the Virgin Mary. Candles for sacred uses are blessed on this day.

Candlewood: A resinous wood used for kindling or torches.

Capillary action: Occurs when liquid molecules are more attracted to the surface they travel along than to each other. In a wick, the wax molecules move along the tiny fibers that form the wick.

Carnauba wax: A hard wax extracted from a Brazilian palm tree, which can be used to raise a candle's melting point. Waxes extracted from other South American palms, such as ouricury wax, possess properties similar to carnauba wax.

Chandelier: A lighting fixture hung from a ceiling with branches for candles or other lights.

Chandler: A maker or seller of candles.

Chandlery: A candle warehouse or storeroom, or a chandler's business or merchandise.

Chunk candles: Molded candles consisting of wax poured over small cut-up blocks of wax that are usually colored to produce variegated, structurally decorated candles.

Church candles: Traditionally round pillar candles of different sizes used in religious rituals and made with a high concentration of beeswax. Church-type candles are popular in the home as well because of their simple, natural look and smokeless quality.

Clear additives: See translucent additives.

Clear hot melt glue stick: Common items in craft stores to use as additives, especially if you cannot find any other hardening additives. Glue sticks are similar to luster additives in character and make a strong candle with vivid colors. Recommended usage is one part to ten parts wax.

Complementary colors: Opposite colors, such as orange and blue, red and green, and yellow and violet. Mixing complementary colors together always produces a brown color. To darken a color, mix it with a little of its complementary color (for example: 1¼ parts orange + 1 part blue = darker blue).

Container/canister candles: Candles poured into containers and intended for burning in those containers. There are countless containers suitable for candles, and container candlemaking is a popular project for beginner candlemakers because making these candles does not require a special mold. The most popular containers are made of glass, ceramics, and metal. Canister candles are container candles with lids to cover the candle when not in use. Highly scented candles are often poured into canisters to preserve the scent between burnings.

Container waxes: Super-soft wax blends specifically suited for filling a container with as little shrinkage as possible. Some retailers sell "one-pour" container blends that have no shrinkage and do not require additional pourings under certain conditions. Container blends can hold more fragrance if formulated with a higher oil content.

Core wicks: A square braid wick with a wire or paper core that supports the wick so that it stands straight. Core wicking comes in three varieties: zinc, paper, and cotton. It is possible to obtain lead core wicks, but these types should not be used for candlemaking due to lead toxicity issues.

Country candles: See cake candles.

Cut and curl candles: Also called "dip and carve" candles, these are molded core pillar candles, often in a star shape, dipped repeatedly into different colors of wax that is then cut and partly peeled away to show the colorful layers underneath. When lit, the flame burns the core candle down and illuminates the carved candle from within. Like hurricane candles, cut and curl candles can be refilled or illuminated by tea lights placed inside the cavity.

Dinner candles: Traditionally common taper candles, but today, votive candles, tea lights, and many other candles are used at dinnertime. Dinner candles are usually unscented so as not to interfere with the aromas of dinner.

Dip and carve candles: See cut and curl candles.

Dipping: Dipping a wick in molten wax several times until the desired thickness of the candle is reached.

Dipping rings or frames: Dipping contraptions that allow you to make multiple hand-dipped taper pairs connected together at the wick.

Direct-heat method: Placing the melting pot directly on the heat source, or melting the wax directly in a concealed element heater. This method works even if you don't need heat higher than 212 degrees Fahrenheit (the temperature of boiling water), but you must make sure that you do not overheat your wax.

Double-boiler method: An arrangement of two vessels, one of which fits above and partly inside the other. Wax is melted in the upper vessel by the water boiling in the lower one. With this arrangement, you will be able to melt wax up to the temperature of boiling water, 212 degrees Fahrenheit (100 degrees Celsius).

Essential oil: Obtained by the distillation of a plant extraction. The oil has the characteristic scent of the plant from which it was extracted.

Flash point: The lowest temperature at which a volatile solid or the vapor of a liquid (such as melted wax) will flash (ignite) when heated.

Flat braid wicks: Old-fashioned cotton wicks good for tapers, nonsymmetrical candles, and novelty candles. They tend to fold over to aid in burning and sometimes drown themselves out without the proper trimming. Flat braid wicks are identified by the total number of threads making up the wick. For example, a 15-ply wick ("ply" specifies the number of threads) consists of three strands, each containing five threads, for a total of 15 threads.

Flexible molds: Molds made of materials such as rubber or PVC (polyvinyl chloride). These molds come in a variety of novelty shapes and are best for objects that have finely detailed surfaces.

Floating candles: Although most candles can float, floating candles are made in special shapes that minimize water contact with the wick so the candle can stay aflame while floating.

Fragrance oil: Artificial fragrance usually delivered within a petroleum-based solvent. It is not a traditional aromatherapy oil.

Garden/outdoor candles: Candles utilized for outdoor purposes. Originally, the only kinds of garden/outdoor candles were container candles (called patio or lantern candles), but today garden candles include other types of candles such as candle flares (torches) and citronella candles.

Gel: Candle fuel composed of about 5% gellant (patented gel resin) and 95% mineral oil. Different manufacturers provide different grades and types of gel. Penreco holds a patent on this technology and is the manufacturer of Versagel, which only comes premixed in three different blends that vary in thickness and fragrance retention. All are very clear gels with a thick, rubbery feel in their solid form.

Gel candles: Not made of wax, these candles use gel for fuel. Gel candles are usually produced as container candles in clear or see-through glass. Due to the gel's ability to contain a higher concentration of scent oil than wax candles, highly scented gel containers have become widely popular as a medium for strong home fragrance.

Glass molds: Professional tempered-glass molds are cylindrical in shape and have pointed tops. They are fragile and much care must be taken to make them last.

Grungy candles: See primitive candles.

Holiday/seasonal candles: All the kinds of candles used to celebrate a holiday or certain time of year.

Hurricane candles: Not really candles, these consist of a wide wax shell, usually embedded with objects, that surrounds a votive or a tea light, similar to a hurricane lamp. Hurricane candles can also be wide with a hard exterior wax shell; a votive or tea light can be placed inside once the inner wax has burned away.

Ice candles: An early favorite kitchen craft made by placing a core candle in a mold and filling the mold with ice. Pouring the wax into the mold melts the ice and quickly hardens the wax, leaving interesting cavities within the molded shape of the candle.

Improvised molds: Any heat-tolerant item you can imagine that allows you to remove the candle from the candle mold or break the mold away from the candle (if it is of a disposable kind). The opening of the mold must be its largest part and, depending on the type of mold, you may need a mold release to help prevent the mold from sticking.

Insert plugs: A plug inserted in the mold prior to pouring instead of inserting a wick. Available in votive and tea light sizes, the insert plug produces a candle with a cavity at the top for placing a votive glass or tea light container, allowing the consumer to use the "candle" without burning it down or messing up any surface decorations.

Intensity: The brightness or dullness of a color.

Japan wax: A waxy fat obtained from the fruit of sumacs native to Japan and China. It is white, malleable, and sticky, and has a slight tallow odor. It can be used to make a candle harder without increasing the melting point of the wax.

Key color: Dominant color in a color scheme or mixture.

Layered/striped candles: Can be made in a variety of ways, but typically are made by pouring successive layers of color into a mold.

Luster additives: Similar to clear additives in function, but luster additives make the wax opaque instead of clear and produce good white candles. Both additives are man-made microcrystalline (highly refined) waxes that thicken wax and produce a small flame and less smoke. Different varieties of luster additives vary in their effect on color and opaqueness. Recommended usage is 1 to 2 teaspoons per pound of wax. The melting point is 200 to 215 degrees Fahrenheit.

Melting point (MP): The temperature at which the wax changes from a solid to a liquid.

Metal core inserts: Metal cylinders sized to fit various mold widths. The cylinder is placed inside the mold, and the cavity in between the mold wall and the cylinder can then be filled with objects and wax to form a hurricane shell.

Metal molds: The most widely used professional-quality molds today. With proper care, molds made of metal can last a lifetime. They come in a variety of symmetrical shapes and are capable of producing an unlimited number of candles. Most metal molds are slightly tapered to ensure easy removal of the candle from the mold.

Millefiori candles: See stained glass candles.

Mold handle: A sturdy wire apparatus that fits around a metal mold so you can safely transport it when the mold is filled with hot wax. A handle is especially useful when you need to place a mold in a water bath.

Mold releasing agent: A silicone spray made specifically for candlemaking, or a light, unflavored vegetable oil spray.

Molding: Making candles by molding involves melting and pouring wax into a particular shape or container to form a candle. The candle is removed from the container when the wax is hard.

Mottling wax: A paraffin blend with additives that render a marble-like, bubbly, or frothy look to the wax, depending on the manufacturer's definition of "mottling." It is sold in different blends suitable for container candles or molded candles.

Neutral grey: Black + white.

Novelty candles: Variable, asymmetrical candles that, in many cases, give the appearance of being something other than a candle, such as a frog or female bust. Novelty candles can be decorated on the surface of the candle to look like a particular object or cast from a mold to replicate an object. Novelty candles can be made by any or a combination of the three basic candlemaking methods (rolling, dipping, and molding).

Oil candles: More accurately termed an oil *lamp*, an oil candle is a container with a wick for burning oil or alcohol, usually in a tube-shaped glass.

Overdipping a candle: Dipping a candle in a different wax or color to achieve a particular appearance. You can overdip candles to seal the surface and any surface decorations by dipping the candle into wax as you would finish a taper. Use the same color as the candle for the overdip or experiment with different colors, additives, and wax for interesting effects.

Palmatine: A palm oil derivative similar to stearin; patented as a wax alternative.

Paraffin: A petroleum by-product. It comes in different grades classified by its melting point (MP), the temperature at which the wax changes from a solid to a liquid. Paraffin suitable for candlemaking is further classified into low MP, medium MP, and high MP grades. Paraffin is white, waxy, odorless, and tasteless. It is solid at room temperature, but when melted into its liquid state, its chemical composition can be modified by means of additives that render a particular effect (such as color and scent) when combined with the wax.

Peg candles: Pillar candles specially shaped at the bottom of the candle to fit smaller taper holders. Peg candles are utilized when longer burning is needed than the burning attained from conventional tapers.

Pillar candles: See block candles.

Pillar/votive wax: A wax blend usually of paraffin mixed with stearic acid to increase hardness and vybar to increase its ability to hold fragrance. The common melting point for this blend is 145 degrees Fahrenheit.

Plastic floater molds: Can come in one or two pieces, depending on the floater candle shape. If the candle is a small floater, you can find two to six molds on a single sheet. A single mold sheet will have one exposed side of the mold for pouring which is also the top of the floater.

Plastic molds: Come in a variety of novelty shapes and are manufactured by vacuum-forming plastic around an object to form the mold. Due to the irregularity of novelty shapes, plastic molds come in

two pieces and, depending on the manufacturer, are held together by a groove that locks the two halves together or by clamps that are fitted along the sides of the mold. The mold is placed in a special stand to keep it upright for pouring.

Polycarbonate molds: Easy to use—not to be confused with acrylic molds! With their clear walls and symmetrical shapes, they resemble acrylic molds, but are actually made of a rigid plastic. They cannot withstand the high pouring temperatures acrylic molds can.

Primary colors: Red, yellow, and blue. These colors cannot be produced by blending other colors.

Primed wick: A wick dipped in wax to improve the burning quality of the wick and prevent air bubbles from sticking to the wick during pouring.

Primitive candles: Made like cake candles, decorated on the exterior with wax whipped to look like frosty cake icing, but can be any shape and are usually rolled in herbs or natural substances to give them a grungy appearance.

Receding (cool) colors: Greens, blues, and violets.

Rolling: Making candles by rolling involves rolling a sheet of wax around a wick until the desired thickness of the candle is reached.

Buffing waxes: A great way to highlight candle details on novelty candles. The wax buff is applied in small amounts, using your finger, but smudging your finger first on a piece of paper to remove excess wax.

Sand candles: Candles poured into sand molds. Sand molds are formed by making an impression in wet sand. When wax is poured in the sand mold, a hard crust of wax and sand forms the candle surface.

Scented candles: Available in an endless variety of aromas and by far the most popular type of candle. Votives, floaters, and containers are the most popular kinds of scented candles. Scented candles serve a variety of purposes, such as eliminating odors and filling an area with fragrance.

Secondary colors: Two primary colors mixed together resulting in orange (yellow + red), green (yellow + blue), and violet (red + blue).

Shade: Color + black.

Shrinkage: The phenomenon of a hole or cavity that occurs after pouring a candle around the wick when the wax molecules cool from their heated, excited state and settle down to a more compact solid. Wax with shrinkage requires extra effort when pouring a candle, and candlemakers usually look for a wax with as little shrinkage as possible.

Soot: A black substance consisting chiefly of carbon particles formed by the incomplete combustion of burning matter. It is the environmental hazard arising from the use of petroleum-based candles (those made from paraffin and gel).

Soy wax: A plant-derived natural wax made of a blend of botanical oils in a soy-bean base. Soy wax has very little shrinkage and is available in container, pillar/votive, and novelty blends. A great alternative to paraffin, soy wax is an economical, all-natural, quality wax.

Spermaceti: A wax crystallized from the oil of the sperm whale.

Square braid wicks: Woven tighter than flat braid wicks, these wicks stand upright and burn evenly. Although mainly used for symmetrical candles, this kind of wick is a good, general all-purpose cotton wick. It comes in numbered sizes from #1 to #6. The lower the number, the smaller the wick.

Squeeze pen: A simple device, similar to a dropper, for painting and drawing with melted wax.

Stained glass/millefiori candles: Candles that have an outer coating of colored wax in a complex pattern of color that resembles millefiori, a type of stained glass. As the candle burns down, the flame illuminates the colored surface. An advanced technique, stained glass candles are most often made by commercial candle manufacturers.

Stearic acid: A white, crystalline substance found in most animal and vegetable fats and used to make candles harder and prevent them from losing their shape in hot weather. Stearic acid does not raise the melting point of wax, but does make a candle harder and stronger and therefore longer burning. It makes colors pastel and creamy, and gives wax a soapy feel. It can also make colors fade quicker, so a color fade inhibitor additive is recommended with its use. The ratio for using stearic acid ranges from 2 to 9 tablespoons per pound of wax. If you're conscious about using animal by-products in your candles, make sure the stearic acid you buy is of the vegetable kind, derived from palm oil instead of animal fats. The melting point of stearic acid is 160 degrees Fahrenheit.

Stearin: A substance with a minor difference in its chemical makeup from stearic acid that is not evident in candlemaking. The word and substance is often used interchangeably with stearic acid.

Tallow: An almost colorless and tasteless solid fat extracted from the natural fat of cattle, sheep, and pigs. A soft wax, it is best used for container candlemaking, if used at all. Depending on the tallow source, tallow can be smoky and stinky. Tallow candles are still used to make authentic, period-style candles.

Taper candles: Typically long, slender candles made to fit in a holder. Tapers can be poured, dipped, or rolled, and may not always taper (tapers increase in breadth and thickness toward the bottom of the candle).

Tea light candles: Small utility candles, usually ¾ inch tall and contained in a metal cup. In the past, tea lights were mainly used to heat potpourri and foods, but many decorative candleholders and lanterns today are designed particularly for tea lights because of their popularity as easily disposable and inexpensive candlelight.

Tertiary (intermediate) colors: One primary color and one secondary color mixed together (yellow-green, blue-green, blue-violet, red-violet, red-orange, and yellow-orange).

Tint: Color + white.

Tone: Color + gray.

Translucent or clear additives: Won't make your wax see-through or clear, but definitely aids in making candles such as hurricanes glow while they burn. This additive is also good for highlighting embedded objects in your candles. Due to its high melting point, it also makes your wax harder and longer burning. Colors become more vivid and the wax glossy. Recommended usage is 1 teaspoon per pound of wax. This additive's melting point is 215 degrees Fahrenheit.

Treasure candles: Typically block candles embedded with small objects such as charms, trinkets, or lucky stones. These "buried treasures" are revealed as the candle burns down, presenting a memento of the candle (or the gift giver).

Twisted/braided candles: Typically tapers twisted and flattened into spiral shapes or wound or braided around other tapers while the candles are warm and pliable.

Ultraviolet (UV) light absorbers: A color fading inhibitor additive used to prevent fading in candles. This substance is highly concentrated and only ½ teaspoon is needed for 10 pounds of wax.

Unity candles: Used during a wedding ceremony to symbolize the union of marriage between the couple. Typically, two taper candles, representing the couple as individuals, are used to light a large pillar candle (the unity candle) as a visible symbol of their commitment to each other. Unity candles are often ornate, heirloom quality, and expensive.

Utility candles: Used to provide light or heat, or to light other candles or lamps. Utility candles are usually unscented, small, and white, and are commonly found as votives, tea lights, and emergency pillar candles in grocery stores.

Value: The lightness or darkness of a color.

Votive candles: Although the term "votive" is used to describe any candle serving as a vigil light, the term "votive" most often refers to pillar candles 2 inches × 2 inches and smaller. Like tea lights, votives have become popular sources of everyday home candlelight because of their versatile size and ability to unobtrusively provide scent and light in small areas.

Vybar: An additive that enhances color and increases the ability of wax to hold more oil, enabling the candle to contain more scent. It comes in two varieties, one for containers (MP 130 degrees Fahrenheit) and another for molded candles (MP 160 degrees Fahrenheit). Recommended usage is 1 to 2 teaspoons per pound of wax when adding fragrance or essential oils.

Wax beads: Granulated wax particles larger than wax sand, at least 1 millimeter in diameter. Used for refilling poured candles that have burned hollow (allowing them to be reused) or filling containers to be used as candles.

Wax melter palette: A heatable tray with small containers to hold different colors or blends of wax for wax painting.

Wax sand: Finely granulated wax used for refilling poured candles that have burned hollow (allowing them to be reused) or filling containers to be used as candles.

Wax sand candles: See beaded candles.

Wick: There are five types of wicking produced specifically for candlemaking: square braid, flat braid, zinc core, paper core, and cotton core. Each comes in different plies ("ply" means the number of threads) of small, medium, large, and extra large, but the sizes vary by manufacturer. Wicks can also be bought primed (pre-dipped in wax) or unprimed.

Wick clips: Small, square, or round metal tabs with a hole in the center used to support and hold the wick in place in container candles, votives, and tea lights.

Wick rod: A device to position the wick within the mold: This can be any rod, such as a pencil, skewer, or knitting needle.

Wick screw: A small Phillips or flathead screw to hold the wick in place and plug the wick entrance to the mold. Some merchants provide rubber plugs instead.

Wick sealer: A soft, pliable, gumlike substance used to cover the wick screw and prevent leakage. Wick sealer is reusable, but you need to replace it periodically. White poster putty (an adhesive used to hang things on a wall without nails or tacks) works well as a wick sealer.

Resources

▼▼▼

Recommended Books

The following books are great sources of inspiration and candlemaking information. In these books you'll discover the many different techniques people have developed from their own candlemaking efforts. I've also included books that contain aromatherapy recipes and ideas, and useful books on the business of arts and crafts.

Candlemaking

Beeswax Crafts by David Constable and Polly Pinder (Search Press, 1997).

Beginner's Guide to Candlemaking by David Constable (A. Schwartz, 1998).

Book of Candlemaking: Creating Scent, Beauty and Light by Chris Larkin (Sterling, 1999).

Book of Candles by Miranda Innes (DK Publishing Merchandise, 1991).

The Candle Book by Pamela Allardice (Lothian, 1997).

Candlecraft by Paul Marko and Debbie Davis (Book Sales, 1999).

Candle Creations by Simon Lycett (Contemporary Books, 1999).

The Candlemaker's Companion: A Complete Guide to Rolling, Pouring, Dipping, and

Decorating Your Own Candles by Betty Oppenheimer (Storey Books, 1997).

Creative Designs and Techniques by David Constable (Search Press Limited, 1993).

Candle Making: Funstation by David Constable (Silver Dolphin, 1998).

Candle Making in a Weekend: Inspirational Ideas and Practical Projects by Sue Spear (North Light Books, 1999).

Candle-Making Is Fun by Valerie Meyer (BHB International, 2000).

Candles: Elements of the Table, Vol. 1 by Deborah Jones (Harper Collins, 1996).

Candles (Home Decorating Workbooks) by Paula Pryke (Watson-Guptill, 1998).

Candles: Over 20 Projects for Making and Displaying Candles (Inspirations series) by Diana Civil and Marion Elliot (Lorenz Books, 1998).

Celebrations of Light by Nancy Luenn (Simon & Schuster, 1998).

The Complete Candlemaker: Techniques, Projects, and Inspirations by Norma J. Coney (Lark Books, 1997).

Country Living Handmade Candles: Recipes for Crafting Candles at Home by Jane Blake and Emily Paulsen (Hearst Books, 1998).

Creative Candles: The Crafty Hands Collection by Chantal Truber (Aurum Press, 1995).

Creative Candles: Over 40 Inspiring Projects for Making and Decorating Candles for Every Occasion by Sue Spear (Book Sales, 1996).

Easy Festive Candles by Valerie Meyer (Van Schaik, 2000).

Easy-To-Make Candles by Gary V. Guy (Dover, 1980).

Fragrant Candles: A Practical Guide to Making Candles for the Home and Garden by Rhondda Cleary (Sterling, 1999).

Making Candles: Kids Can Do It by Judy Sadler (Kids Can Press, 1998).

Naturally Creative Candles: Discover the Craft of Candle Making and Decorating Using Nature's Bounty by Letty Oates (Chilton Book Co, 1997).

The New Candle Book: Inspirational Ideas for Displaying, Using and Making Candles by Gloria Nicol (Lorenz Books, 1995).

Traditional Candlemaking: Simple Methods of Manufacture by Deborah Millington (Intermediate Technology, 1992).

Craft-Related Topics

The Artist's Guide to New Markets by Peggy Hadden (Allworth Press, 1998).

Art Marketing 101: A Handbook for the Fine Artist by Constance Smith (ArtNetwork, 1997).

Business and Legal Forms for Crafts by Tad Crawford (Allworth Press, 1998).

The Craft Business Answer Book and Resource Guide by Barbara Brabec (M. Evans, 1998).

The Crafter's Guide to Pricing Your Work by Dan Ramsey (Betterway Books, 1997).

Crafting as a Business by Wendy Rosen (Chilton, 1998).

Crafting for Dollars: How to Establish and Profit from a Career in Crafts by Sylvia Landman (Prima, 1996).

The Craft Supply Source Book by Margaret Boyd (Betterway Books, 1999).

Crafts Market Place: Where and How to Sell Your Crafts by Angie Manolis (Betterway Books, 1997).

Creative Cash: How to Profit from Your Special Artistry, Creativity, and Related Know-How, 6th Ed. by Barbara Brabec (Prima, 1998).

Handmade for Profit: Hundreds of Secrets to Success in Selling Arts and Crafts by Barbara Brabec (M. Evans, 1996).

How to Show and Sell Your Crafts by Kathryn Caputo (Betterway Books, 1997).

How to Survive and Prosper as an Artist, 4th Edition by Caroll Michaels (Owl Books/H. Holt, 1997).

Marketing Your Arts and Crafts by Janice West (Summit, 1994).

Selling What You Make: Profit from Your Handcrafts by James Seitz, Ph.D. (Tab Books, 1992).

Selling Your Crafts by Susan Joy Sager (Allworth Press, 1998).

Aromatherapy

The Aromatherapy Book by Jeanne Rose (North Atlantic Books, 1992).

The Complete Illustrated Guide to Aromatherapy by Julia Lawless (Element Books, 1997).

500 Formulas for Aromatherapy by Carol and David Schiller (Sterling, 1994).

New Perspectives: Aromatherapy by Christine Wildwood (Element Books, 2000).

Magical Aromatherapy by Scott Cunningham (Llewellyn, 1989).

Today's Herbal Health by Louise Tenney (Woodland Books, 2000).

Craft Business Periodicals

American Craft
American Craft Council
72 Spring Street
New York, NY 10012
Phone: (212) 274-0630
E-mail: membership@craftcouncil.org
Web site: www.craftcouncil.org

American Style
The Rosen Group
3000 Chestnut Avenue, Suite 304
Baltimore MD 21211
Phone: (410) 889-3093
E-mail: lesli@rosengrp.com
Web site: www.AmericanStyle.com
Covers the American art scene and arts and crafts events.

Choices for Craftsmen and Artists
P.O. Box 484
Rhinebeck, NY 12572
Phone: (914) 876-2996
E-mail: www.choices.cc

Includes feature articles and show listings for the Northeast (New York, New Jersey, Vermont, Pennsylvania, Massachusetts, and Connecticut).

The Crafts Report
P.O. Box 1992
Wilmington, DE 19899
Phone: (800) 777-7098
Fax: (302) 656-4894
Web site: www.craftsreport.com
Monthly magazine for craft professionals in all fields of endeavor.

Craftrends/Show Business
P.O. Box 1790
Peoria, IL 61656
Phone: (309) 682-6626
Web site: www.craftrends.com
Trade magazine catering to the creative leisure industry.

Recommended Web Sites

General

www.about.com (Great resource for virtually everything)

www.botweb.com (Best of the Web)

www. thomasregister.com (The Thomas Register of American Manufacturers); lists all types of manufacturers from every industry.

General Candlemaking

www.angelfire.com/ca/SSaSSSy/candle.html (The Melting Pot, a comprehensive candlemaking site)

ansel.his.duq.edu/~doughert/CANDLE.HTM (Candlemaking 101)

www.beemaid.com/wax/candles.html (Western Wax Works)

www.candle.moulder.com (Patty's Candles, candlemaking tips)

candleandsoap.miningco.com (The Mining Company Candle & Soapmaking Page)

www.candlecauldron.com (The Complete Candlemaker's Resource on the Web)

www.candlelady.com/candlemak.html; candle@candlelady.com (Candlemaking Tips)

www.candlemaking.cjb.net (The Essential Survival Guide to Candlemaking)

www.candlestoo.com; sales@candlestoo.com (Candles Too! A full service candlemaking and candle supply company)

www.candlesupply.com (Candle Projects)

www.earthguild.com (The Candlemaking Riff)

www.fastforums.com/candlemaking/index1.html (The Candle Making Forum)

www.geocities.com/Heartland/Pointe/9841/index.html (Bob's Candlemaking Page)

www.geocities.com/Heartland/Valley/3208/index.html (Candlemaking Tips and Ideas)

www.geocities.com/SoHo/Lofts/2403/Candles.html (Serena Sublime's Candle Page—For the love of candles):

www.geocities.com/SoHo/Square/1775/index.html (Cathy's Candles—Tips for the Art of Candlemaking)

www.hobbylobby.com (Hobby Lobby Presents Crackle Candles)

www.jinet.com/bellbookcandle (Candlemaking & Candle Carving by Andy Hastings)

www.makestuff.com (The Art of Candlemaking)

http://tcanet.arts.state.tx.us/crafts/candles.htm (Texas Cultural Arts Network: Crafts—Candles and Flat Glass)

http://tqjunior.thinkquest.org/4017/candlemaking.html (Candlemaking—Colonial Style) http://users.wantree.com.au/~campbell/prod.htm (Sharon's Candlemaking Page, compiled from 20 years as a candle-making hobbyist, with tips from other candlemakers)

www.vashti.net/WaxedOut (Waxed Out Candles—Candlemaking How-To)

History of Candlemaking

www.candlexpress.com/historyF.html (History of Candlemaking)

www.nca.org (History of Candlemaking)

Candlemaking Supplies

(see also sites listed in the Art and Craft Suppliers/Product Resources section)

www.candlemakers.co.uk (Candle Makers Supplies)

www.thedarkgift.com (Candlemaking Supply Kits)

Scents

(see also sites listed in the Art and Craft Suppliers/Product Resources section)

www.aff4aromas.com (Aromatic Fragrances and Flavors International)

www.essencefactory.com (The Essence Factory, Aromatherapy for everyone)

www.essentialoils.org (Essential Oil University, the most comprehensive site on essential oils)

Crafts Business-Related Sites

www.artandcraftshows.net (Art and Craft Show Net, database of over 2,000 events)

www.artcraftmall.com; crafters @artcraftmall.com (The Arts and Crafts Internet Mall)

http://artsandcrafts.about.com/hobbies/artsandcrafts/ (About.com, a guide to craft business resources on the Internet)

www.aztexonline.com (Aztex Wax and Candle Store)

www.bonus.com (SuperSite for Kids)

www.crafter.com (a site designed to help professional crafters in their arts and crafts businesses)

www.crafterscatalogs.com (Crafters Catalog—A Virtual Craft Show)

www.craftmarketer.com/ (craft articles and tips on how to succeed for craft people and artists)

www.craftscenter.org (The Crafts Center, a unique clearinghouse of information about and for low-income artisans)

www.craftsfaironline.com/Business.html (The Craft Fair Online's Crafter's Business Resources)

www.craftsreport.com (The Crafts Report Online)

www.creativethought.com (offers a variety of information and services to creative businesses)

www.dity.com (Do It Yourself—The Supreme "Do it Yourself Directory")

www.ecraftsmall.com (eCraftsmall—
for locating craft supplies; tips for setting
up shop)

www.festivalnet.com;
Info@festivalnet.com (Festival Network
Online)

www.makestuff.com (For crafters, hobbyists, entrepreneurs, and people who just
like to make stuff)

www.reigate.demon.co.uk/index.htm
(Reigate Division of Surrey Beekeepers
Association, Beekeepers in action)

http://welcome.to/professional-crafters
(The Professional Crafter's Mailing List)

Art and Craft Suppliers/Product Resources

General Candlemaking

Alabaster Candle Supply
P.O. Box 1662
Alabaster, AL 35007
Phone (toll free): (877) 621-2325
E-mail: Info@AlabasterCandleSupply.com
Web site: www.alabastercandlesupply.com

The Barker Company
15106 10th Avenue Southwest
Seattle, WA 98166
Phone: (800) 543-0601
Fax: (206) 244-7334
Web site: www.barkerco.com

Bitter Creek Candle Supply, Inc.
Route 4, Box 184
Ashland, WI 54806
Phone (toll free): (877) MELT-WAX
(635-8929)
Fax: (715) 278-3904
Web site: www.candlesupply.com

Bobby's Craft Boutique, Inc.
120 Hillside Avenue
Williston Park, NY 11596

Phone: (516) 877-2499
Web site: www.craftcave.com

The Cajun Candle Factory
P.O. Box 784
Kaplan, Louisiana 70548
Phone: (800) 667-6424
Web site: www.cajuncandles.com

The Candlemaker
P.O. Box 474
5626 Broad Street
Greendale, WI 53129
Phone (toll free): (888) 251-4618
Web site: www.thecandlemaker.com

The Candle Factory
4411 South IH 35
Georgetown, TX 78628
Phone: (800) 955-6973
Fax: (512) 863-9597
Web site: www.thecandlefactory.com

The Candle Shop
6237 West National Avenue
West Allis, WI 53214
Phone: (414) 607-6542

Fax: (414) 607-6543
E-mail: thecandleshop@yahoo.com
Web site: www.the-candle-shop.com

The Candelwic Company
8244 Easton Road
Ottsville, PA 18942
Phone: (610) 847-2076
Fax: (610) 847-2069
Web site: www.candlewic.com

Connie's Candles
1499D State Route 522
Wheelersburg, OH 45694,
Phone (toll free): (877) 574-1224
Fax: (740) 574-0414
E-mail: info@conniescandles.com
Web site: www.conniescandles.com

The Craft King
P.O. Box 90637
Lakeland, FL 33811
Phone (toll free): (800) 769-9494
Web site: www.weshop.com/craftking

Candlechem Company, Inc.
56 Intervale Street
Brockton, MA 02302
Phone: (508) 586-1880
Fax: (508) 586-1784
E-mail: candlechem@mediaone.net
Web site: www.alcasoft.com
/candlechem/index.html

Dharma Trading Company
P.O. Box 150916
San Rafael, CA 94915
Phone: (800) 542-5227
Fax: (415) 456-8747
E-mail: catalog@dharmatrading.com
Web site: www.dharmatrading.com

Dreams Come True Crafts and Gifts
1614 East 95th Street
Brooklyn, NY 11236
Web site: www.dctcrafts.com.

Earth Guild
33 Haywood Street
Asheville, NC 28801
Phone: (800) 327-8448
Fax: (828) 255-8593
E-mail: inform@earthguild.com
Web site: www.earthguild.com

General Wax & Candle Co. Factory Outlet
Store
6863 Beck Avenue
North Hollywood, CA 91605
Phone: (800) 929-7867
Fax: (818) 764-3878
E-mail: Sales@genwax.com
Web site: www.genwax.com

Lumina Candles & Art
P.O. Box 340
Cedar Creek, TX 78612
Phone: (512) 321-2737
E-mail: lumina@borsheimarts.com
Web site: www.borsheimarts.com
/lumina.htm

Lynden House International Inc.
5527-137 Avenue
Edmonton, Alberta, T5L 3L4
Canada
Phone: (780) 448-1994
Fax: (780) 448-0086
Web site: www.lyndenhouse.net.

The Maine Candle Connection
764 Bucksport Road
Ellsworth, ME 04605
Phone: (877) DOWNEAST (369-6327)

Fax: (207) 667-2424
E-mail:
karen@mainecandleconnection.com
Web site: www.downeastscents.com

McGiffins Hobbies & Crafts
1200 South Washington
Grand Forks, ND 58201
Phone: (701) 772-5311
Fax: (701) 772-5380
E-mail: sales@makeitmcgiffins.com
Web site: www.makeitmcgiffins.com

Missy's Candles, Inc.
366 U.S. Route 35
Ray, OH 45672
US Orders: (888) MISSYS1
International Orders: (740) 884-4516
Fax: (740) 884-4513/4017
E-mail:
missyscandles@candlemaking.com
Web site: www.candlemaking.com

Pemaquid Lights Candle Co.
P.O. Box 221
Round Pond, Maine 04564
1370 Bristol Road
Bristol, Maine 04539
Phone: (207) 563-8650
Fax: (888) 563-8650
Web site: www.pemaquidlights.com

Pourette Manufacturing
P.O. Box 70469
Seattle, WA 98107
Phone (toll free): (800) 888-9425
Fax: (206) 789-3640
E-mail: pourette@aol.com
Web site: www.pourette.com

Rocky Mountain Candle Co.
915 N. Lincoln Avenue (Hwy. 287)
Loveland, CO 80537

Phone (toll free): (888) 695-5914
Fax: (970) 278-9446
E-mail: www.rockymountaincandle.com/

Rustic Candle Company
5625 Post Road
East Greenwich, RI 02818
Phone: (401) 886-5497
E-mail: Rusticandl@aol.com
Web site: www.angelfire.com

Sissie's Candles
13955 Murphy Road, Suite 404
Stafford, Texas 77477
Phone (toll free): (800) 854-5678
Web site: www.sissiescandles.com.

The Soap Saloon
5710 Auburn Boulevard, #6
Sacramento, CA. 95841
Phone: (916) 334-4894
Fax: (916) 334-4897
Web site: www.soapsaloon.com

Sun Coast Soaps and Supplies
12415 Haley Street
Sun Valley, CA 91352
Phone: (818) 252-1452
Fax: (818) 252-1034
Web site: www.suncoastsoaps.com

Walnut Hill Enterprises, Inc.
P.O. Box 599
Bristol, PA 19007
Orders: (800) NEED-WAX
Fax: (215) 785-6594
E-mail: info@walnuthillco.com
Web site: www.walnuthillco.com

Wax Creations, Bee Cee Wicks and Wax,
Hodgson Bee Supplies
3072 Beta Avenue

Burnaby, British Columbia V5G 4K4
Canada
Phone: (604) 294-1232
Fax: (604) 294-1231
E-mail: candles@wicksandwax.com
Web site: www.wicksandwax.com

The Wax House
236 Arch Avenue
Waynesboro, VA 22980
Phone: (888) WAX-971
Fax (toll free): (877) WAX-9711
Web site: www.waxhouse.com

Wick 'n' Clip, Inc.
1513 Lincoln Avenue,
Holbrook, NY 11741
Phone: (631) 471-WICK
Fax: (631) 471-5034
E-mail: info@wicknclip.com
Web site: www.wicknclip.com

Wick's End
100 Grove Street
Worcester, MA 01605
Phone: (888) WICKS-END
Fax: (508) 753-9923
E-mail: CustomerService@wicksend.com
Web site: www.wicksend.com

Wix-n-Wax Candle Supply
220 Lockerplant
Gladewater, TX 75647
Phone: (903) 845-6404
Fax: (903) 844-9909
E-mail: info@wixnwax.com;
sales@wixnwax.com
Web site: www.wixnwax.com

Yaley Enterprises
7664 Avianca Drive
Redding, CA 96002

Phone (toll free): (877) 365-5212
Fax: (530) 365-6483
E-mail: info@yaley.com
Web site: www.yaley.com

Wax

Chevron Products Company/
Global Lubricants Division
Wax Business Unit, 40
West 786 Aberdeen Lane
St. Charles, IL 60175
Phone: (630) 584-5611
E-mail: sold@chevron.com
Web site: www.cheveron.com

C. J. Robinson Specialty Waxes and Oils
522 New Gulph Road
Haverford, PA 19041
Phone: (610) 896-5022
Fax: (610) 896-5031
E-mail: wxes@cjrobinson.com
Web site: www.cjrobinson.com

The International Group, Inc.
85 Old Eagle School Road
P.O. Box 383
Wayne, PA 19087
Phone: (800) 852-6537
Fax: (610) 254-8548
Web site: www.igiwax.com

Moore & Munger, Inc.
Two Corporate Drive, Suite 434
Shelton, CT 06484
Phone: (800) 423-7071
E-mail: bonniea@mooremunger.com
Web site: www.mooremunger.com

Paraffin

Astor Specialty Chemicals/Honeywell
1425 Oakbrook Drive, Suite 600
Norcross, GA 30049
Phone: (770) 448-8083
E-mail: astorlite@honeywell.com

Dussek Campbell, Inc.
3650 Touhy Avenue
Skokie, IL 60076
Phone: (847) 679-6300
Web site: www.dussekwax.com

Exxon/Mobil Corporation, Special
Products Business
3225 Gallows Road, Room 7C2131
Fairfax, VA 22037
Phone: (800) 662-4525

Industrial Raw Materials Corp.
645 Madison Avenue
New York, NY 10022
Phone: (800) 346-3729
E-mail: IRMWAX@aol.com

Penreco
P.O. Box 4274
Houston, TX 77210
Phone (in Texas): (800) 458-5845
Phone (in Pennsylvania): (800) 245-3952
E-mail: info@penreco.com

Petrofin Corporation
666 Fifth Avenue, 21st Floor
New York, NY 10103
Phone: (212) 247-9100
E-mail: petrofin@worldnet.att.net

Reed Wax
167 Pleasant Street
Reading, MA 01867
Phone: (800) 336-5877

Wenesco, Inc.
3990 West Barry Avenue
Chicago, IL 60618
Phone: (800) 233-4430
Fax: (773) 286-9940
Web site: www.wenesco.com

Beeswax

Beemaid Honey
Box 3909
70 Alberta
Spruce Grove, Alberta T7X 3B170
Canada
Phone (toll free): (800) 213-6131
Fax: (780)-962-1653
E-mail: honey@beemaid.com
Web site: www.beemaid.com

Glorybee Foods, Inc.
120 North Seneca Road
Eugene, OR 97402
Phone: (800) 456-7923

Honey Wax & Candle Flex Molds
A Division of Mann Lake, Ltd.
501 South First Street
Hackensack, MN 56452
Phone: (800) 880-7694
Fax: (218) 675-6156
E-mail: honeywax@mannlakeltd.com
Web site: www.mannlakeltd.com

Silver City Apiaries
P.O. Box 141
West Peterborough, NH 03468
Phone: (800) 439-1012
Fax (toll free): (800) 439-1012

Soy Wax

Heartland Candleworks
2920 Industrial Park Road
Iowa City, IA 52240
Phone: (877) 848-8680
E-mail: candleworks@austin.rr.com
Web site: www.candleworks.org

Natures Gifts, Inc. (Ecowax)
200 E. 37th Street, Suite 2
Boise, ID 83714
Phone: (208) 426-0516
E-mail: ecowax@cs.com
Web site: www.ngiwax.com

Wicks

Atkins & Pearce
One Braid Way
Covington, KY 41017-9702
Phone: (606) 356-2001

Stimpson Company, Inc.
900 Sylvan Avenue
Bayport, NY 11705-1097
Phone: (516) 472-2000
E-mail: ginger_farrell@stimpsonco.com

Wicks Unlimited, Inc.
22355 Route 48, Unit #18
Cutchogue, NY 11935
Phone: (516) 734-7332
E-mail: sales@wicksunlimited.com

Scents

Aroma Tech, Inc.
130 Industrial Parkway
Somerville, NJ 08876
Phone: (800) 542-7662

E-mail: mail@aromatec.com
Web site: www.aromatec.com

Atlantic Spice Company
2 Shore Road
P.O. Box 205
North Truro, MA 02652
Phone: (800) 316-7965
Fax: (508) 487-2550
Web site: www.atlanticspice.com

Aura Cacia
P.O. Box 399
Weaverville, CA 96093
Phone: (800) 926-6100

Avena Botanicals
20 Mill Street
Rockland, ME 04841
Phone: (207) 594-0694

Belle-Aire Fragrances, Inc.
1600 Baskin Road
Mundelein, IL 60060
Phone: (800) 373-4709
Fax: (847) 816-7695
Web site: www.belle-aire.com

Camden-Grey Essential Oils
8567 Coral Way #178
Miami, FL 33155
Phone (toll free): (877) 232-7662

Candle Cents
129 Industrial Park Drive, Building #5,
Suite F
Hollister, MO 65616
Phone (toll free): (888) 336-3915
Fax: (417) 336-4955
E-mail: candlecents@branson.net
Web site: www.candlecents.com

Common Scents
1016 Tiffin Avenue
Findlay, OH 45840
Phone (toll free): (888) 832-1021
Web site: www.commonscents.org

Creative Fragrances Manufacturing
10890 Alder Circle
Dallas, TX 75238
Phone: (241) 341-3666

The Essential Oil Company
1719 Southeast Umatilla Street
Portland, OR 97202
Phone: (800) 729-5912
Fax: (503) 872-8767
E-mail: office@essentialoil.com
Web site: www.essentialoil.com

Exotic Fragrances Inc., Intl.
1645 Lexington Avenue
Department W
New York, NY 10029
Phone: (212) 410-0600
Fax (toll free): (800) 777-7593
E-mail: info@exoticfragrances.com
Web site: www.exoticfragrances.com

French Color & Chemical Company
488 Grand Avenue
Englewood, NJ 07631
Phone: (800) 762-9098
E-mail: sales@frenchcolor.com

The Good Scents Company
1977 East Montana Avenue
Oak Creek, WI 53154
Phone: (414) 764-2659
Fax: (414) 764-6035
E-mail: goodscnt@execpc.com

Lavender Lane/Hard-to-Find Herbalware
7337 #1 Roseville Road
Sacramento, CA 95842
Phone (toll free): (888) 593-4400
Fax: (916) 339-0842
E-mail:
healthychoices@lavenderlane.com
Web site: www.lavenderlane.com

Nature's Gift Aromatherapy Products
1040 Cheyenne Boulevard
Madison, TN 37115
Phone: (615) 612-4270
Fax: (615) 860-9171
E-mail: orderdesk@naturesgift.com
Web site: www.naturesgift.com

Royal Aromatics
903 Mattison Avenue
Asbury Park, NJ 07712
Phone: (732) 502-9666
Fax: (732) 502-9095
E-mail: info@RoyalAromatics.com

Uncommon Scents, Inc.
380 West First Avenue
Eugene, OR 97401
Phone: (800) 426-4336
Fax (toll free): (888) 343-8196
E-mail: store@uncommonscents.com
Web site: www.uncommonscents.com

Molds

North Valley Candle Molds
6928 Danyeur Road
Redding, CA 96002
Phone: (530) 247-0447
Fax: (530) 247-0147
Web site: www.moldman.com

Smooth-On Flexible Mold Material
2000 Saint John Street
Easton, PA 18042
Phone: (800) 762-0744
Fax: (610) 252-6200
E-mail: smoothon@smooth-on.com

Equipment

Candle Equipment and Sales, Inc.
4128-½ California Avenue SW #201
Seattle, WA 98116
Phone: (206) 932-9576
E-mail: info@waxmelters.com
Web site: www.waxmelters.com

Trade and Professional Associations, Societies, and Guilds

Arts and Creative Materials Institute
100 Boylston Street, Suite 1050
Boston, MA 02116
Phone: (617) 426-6400

Craft Alliance
6640 Delmar Boulevard
St. Louis, MO 63130
Phone: (314) 725-1177

National Candle Association
1030 15th Street, Suite 870
Washington, DC 20005
Phone: (202) 393-2210
Web site: www.candles.org

National Craft Association
1945 East Ridge Road, Suite 5178
Rochester, NY 14622-2467
Phone: (800) 715-9594
Fax: (716) 785-3231
Web site: www.craftassoc.com

The Society of Arts and Crafts
101 Arch Street
Boston, MA 02110
Phone: (617) 345-0033

Society of Craft Designers
P.O. Box 3388
Zanesville, OH 43702-3388
Phone: (740) 452-4541

Business Associations

American Association of Home Based
Businesses
P.O. Box 10023
Rockville, MD 20849
Phone: (800) 447-9710
Fax: (301) 963-7042
E-mail: aahbb@crosslink.net
Web site: www.aahbb.org

Association of Crafts and Creative
Industries (ACCI)
P.O. Box 3388
Zanesville, OH 43702-3388
Phone (toll free): (888) 360-2224
Fax: (740) 452-2552
Web site: www.creative-industries.com/
Sponsors a large, well-publicized annual
trade show.

National Mail Order Association
2807 Polk Street
Minneapolis, MN 55418-2954
Phone: (612) 788-1673
Web site: www.nmoa.org
Offers information on how to start a
mail-order business and utilize effective
marketing techniques. Members receive
the *Mail Order Digest* newsletter.

Aromatherapy Organizations

American Alliance of Aromatherapy
P.O. Box 750428
Petaluma, CA 94975
Phone: (707) 778-6762
Fax: (707) 769-0868

American Aromatherapy Association
P.O. Box 3679
South Pasadena, CA 91031
Phone: (818) 457-1742

Atlantic Institute of Aromatherapy
16018 Saddlestring Drive
Tampa, FL 33612
Phone: (813) 265-2222
Web site: www.atlanticinstitute.com

National Association for Holistic
Aromatherapy
P.O. Box 17622
Boulder, CO 80308
Phone: (888) 275-6242
Web site: www.naha.org

Arts and Crafts Show Information

ABC Art & Craft Directory
P.O. Box 5388
Marysville, TN 37802-5388
Phone: (800) 678-3566
Fax: (423) 681-4733

Arts & Crafts Show Business
P.O. Box 26624
Jacksonville, FL 32226-0624
Phone: (904) 757-3913
Web site:
www.artscraftsshowbusiness.com
Lists festivals, fairs, and trade shows
in the Southeast (Florida, the Carolinas,
and Georgia).

Bizarre Bazaar
P.O. Box 8330
Richmond, VA 23226
Phone: (804) 673-7015

Fax: (804) 673-7017
Juried shows for Christmas and spring.

Cloud Productions
P.O. Box 586
Findlay, OH 45839
Phone: (419) 436-1457
Promoters of shows in Indiana and Ohio.

The Craft and Art Show Calendar
P.O. Box 424
Devault, PA 19432
Phone: (610) 640-2787
Information on top-ranked shows in
several eastern and northeastern states.

Crafters Showcase
10704 W. Oklahoma Avenue
Milwaukee, WI 53227
Phone: (414) 250-0400

Craftmaster News
P.O. Box 39429
Downey, CA 90239-0429
Phone: (562) 869-5882
Web site: www.craftmasternews.com
Lists shows on the West Coast.

Crafts America, LLC
P.O. Box 603
Greens Farms, CT 06436
Phone: (203) 254-0486
Fax: (203) 254-9672
E-mail: craftsamerica@hotmail.com
Web site: www.craftsamericashows.com

Hands On Guide
1835 South Centre City Parkway, #A434
Escondido, CA 92025-6544
Phone: (760) 338-0025
Lists better arts and crafts events in
12 western states.

Harvest Festival
601 North McDowell Boulevard
Petaluma, CA 94954
Phone: (800) 321-1213
Fax: (707) 763-5346
Web site: www.harvestfestival.com

Madison Street Festival, Inc.
137 Steele Drive
Madison, AL 35758
Phone: (256) 461-8181
Web site: www.madisonstreetfestival.com

National Art and Craft Festival
4845 Rumler Road
Chambersburg, PA 17201
Phone: (717) 369-4810
Fax: (717) 360-5001

The Network
P.O. Box 1248
Palatine, IL 60078
Phone: (312) 934-1511
Holds shows throughout the northern
Midwest.

The Ronay Guides
2090 Shadowlake Drive
Buckhead, GA 30625-2700
Phone: (800) 337-8329
Web site: www.events2000.com
Lists 1,500 shows, festivals, and fairs in
the Southeast (Georgia, Virginia, and
the Carolinas).

SAC Newsmonthly
P.O. Box 159
Bogalusa, LA 70429
Phone: (800) 825-3722
Fax: (504) 732-3744
Web site: www.sacnewsmonthly.com
Monthly newspaper for exhibitors at arts
and crafts shows nationwide.

Sunshine Artist Magazine
2600 Temple Drive
Winter Park, FL 32789
Phone: (800) 597-2573
Fax: (407) 539-1499
Web site: www.sunshineartist.com
The premier arts and crafts show publication. Provides descriptions of approximately 2,000 events and includes articles
and commentary on shows from particular artisans.

Business Contributors to
Candlemaking for Fun & Profit

The Candle Cauldron
Founder: Doneen St. John
E-mail: Crystal@candlecauldron.com
Web site: www.candlecauldron.com

Nature's Gifts, Inc. (Ecowax)
Owner: Dan Capp
208-200 East 37th Street, Suite 2
Boise, ID 83714
Phone: (208) 426-0516
Fax: (208) 342-8587
E-mail: ecowax@cs.com
Web site: www.ngiwax.com

Waxed Out Candles
Owners: Michelle Espino and Katie Maseri
Railroad Square
682 Industrial Drive
Tallahassee, FL 32310

Phone: (850) 222-7176
E-mail: WaxedOut@RailroadSquare.com
Web sites: www.waxedout.com;
www.RailroadSquare.com/WaxedOut/

Wick-It Craft Originals
Owner: Kim Beth-Poe
E-mail: poecasa@azstarnet.com

Wish Candles
Owner: Laura Leigh
154 Elena Drive
Tallahassee, FL 32310
Phone: (850) 421-6681
E-mail: wishcan@aol.com
Web site: www.wishcandles.com

Index